JAPANESE POLITICS
— AN INSIDE VIEW
Readings from Japan

Translated from the Japanese and

edited by **HIROSHI ITOH**

Cornell Paperbacks

CORNELL UNIVERSITY PRESS

Ithaca and London

First published 1973 by Cornell University Press.
Published in the United Kingdom by Cornell University Press Ltd., 2–4 Brook Street, London W1Y 1A.A.

First Printing Cornell Paperbacks 1973

International Standard Book Number 0–8014–9138–X
Library of Congress Catalog Card Number 72–12407

Printed in the United States of America by The Colonial Press, Inc.

Librarians: Library of Congress cataloging information appears on the last page of the book.

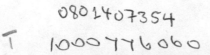

To Helen Harrington Schiff

Contents

PART IV. THE MAKING OF FOREIGN POLICY

Preface

The dearth of empirical studies on Japanese politics has been pointed out by many specialists. One observer, Yasumasa Kuroda, after surveying the research frontiers, concludes that the "future of the scientific study of politics is not bright in Japan," although "it is definitely on its way toward modernization." The present volume is compiled of nine representative samples chosen from among the limited number of empirical studies available in Japan. These selections, all taken from original works of Japanese scholars, deal with various aspects of policy-making in Japan through case studies or public-opinion polls. Many of them apply sound scientific methods and techniques to clearly defined research topics, with the result that their findings often render explicit many hitherto assumed or unknown facts about Japan's policy-making. Furthermore, several authors give their views of how political decision-making ought to be carried out.

The book consists of four parts. The first two parts are concerned with the major political forces which govern decision-making at the national level. A general discussion of the policy-making structure and process (Selection 1) is followed by a case study that reveals complex interactions among the various forces both within and without the Diet (Selections 2 and 3). Part II presents, through a study on voting behavior, the anatomy of the Liberal Democratic Party, which, for more than two decades, has provided the formal policy-making machinery with leadership and policy alternatives (Selections 4 and 5). In Selection 6 public-opinion polls on several issues are analyzed as they are relevant to a study of policy-making. The study of the structure and process of decision-making at a subnational level, the focus of Part III, has been slow to develop, and Selection 7 is one of the few empirical studies ever conducted on this subject. Finally, Part IV approaches the formulation of Japan's foreign policy through an examination of voting behavior at the United Nations (Selection 8) and public-opinion polls on national defense (Selection 9).

As editor and translator of this volume, I am indebted to Hibbert R. Roberts of Illinois State University, who took time from a busy schedule as Acting Chairman of the Department of Political Science to assist in selecting and organizing these materials as well as improving their translation. I also wish to express my appreciation to Lawrence W. Beer of the University of Colorado, whose valuable advice and suggestions significantly improved the final form of the manuscript. Thanks are also due Dixon Miyauchi of the State University College of New York at Plattsburgh, and John Eitenmiller, graduate student at Illinois State University, for their useful suggestions and assistance. My appreciation is also extended to the Japanese authors and publishers of the selections for their authorization of the English translation. I am very grateful to the staff of Cornell University Press, whose advice and suggestions greatly facilitated publication. It is also acknowledged that John M. Maki's report, "Survey of American Undergraduate and Graduate Teaching in the Field of Japanese Government and Politics," given at the 1969 meeting of the Association for Asian Studies, and Yasumasa Kuroda's article, "Recent Japanese Advances in Political Science" (*American Behavioral Scientist,* vol. 12, no. 3 [January–February 1969]), quoted above, provided immediate motivation for undertaking this compilation. Finally, the editor would like formally to express his gratitude to his wife, Nobu, who not only typed the manuscript but also assisted in research.

Throughout the book, the asterisked footnotes are the translator-editor's; the numbered notes at the end of the selections are the authors'.

HIROSHI ITOH

Plattsburgh, New York

Abbreviations

AA bloc	Afro-Asian bloc
DSP	Democratic Socialist Party (Nihon Minshu Shakaitō)
FPP	Fair Play Party (Kōmeitō)
GHQ,SCAP	General Headquarters of the Supreme Commander for the Allied Powers
JCP	Japan Communist Party (Nihon Kyōsantō)
JPLSME	Japanese Political League of Small and Medium-Sized Enterprises (Nihon Chūshōkigyō Seijirenmei)
JSP	Japan Socialist Party (Nihon Shakaitō)
LDP	Liberal Democratic Party (Jiyūminshutō)
NCLA	National Consumers Liaison Association (Zenkoku Shōhishadantai Renrakukai)
SDF	Self-Defense Force
SMEOL	Small and Medium-Sized Enterprises Organization Law (Chūshōkigyō Dantaisoshikihō)

PART I

POLICY-MAKING AT THE NATIONAL LEVEL

Editor's Introduction

In Selection 1, Shigeo Misawa employs a systems approach to construct a model of policy-making structures and processes in Japan. He shows the organic interrelations of the major political forces involved in decision-making. Indeed, his comprehensive model is basic to the other selections in the present volume. Selections 2 and 3 constitute a case study, one of the few empirical analyses ever carried out on legislative processes in Japan. Naoki Kobayashi describes in great detail the intensive and complex interactions of the various forces at work during the legislation of the Small and Medium-Sized Enterprises Organization Law (SMEOL). His research depended primarily on the following techniques: in-depth analysis of general reference works, Diet proceedings, publications of government agencies and interest groups, newspapers, and other available materials on the subject of small and medium-sized enterprises; interviews with those persons who were directly involved in the legislative process; and opinion polls administered to appropriate entrepreneurs in Tokyo.

In Selection 1, Misawa characterizes Japan's policy-making structure as a kind of unholy trinity of the Liberal Democratic Party (LDP), professional bureaucrats, and big business. A summary of the major political forces which participate in national policy-making in Japan follows.

The Diet. The 1947 Constitution made the Diet "the sole lawmaking organ of the State." The Diet is a bicameral body: the House of Representatives (lower house) and the House of Councillors (upper house). A speaker, normally a senior member of the majority party, and a vice-speaker, often chosen from among opposition parties, preside over deliberations in the 491-member House of Representatives. The full cooperation of the House speaker and the chairman of the House Steering Committee is very important for safe passage of a bill. The House operates in plenary session and committees. Functionally, standing committees play a more important deliberative role than plenary sessions, which usually endorse committee decisions. The committee hearings give the ruling party a chance to publicize its policy ideas and opposition parties a chance to attack them. Open committee hearings allow all sides to feel that they have received a fair hearing. But, by the very nature of the committee system, many of the members who are not in direct charge of a given bill often do not fully understand it and remain silent during deliberation of it; thus, the committee system tends to minimize meaningful discourse in decision-making. In addition, strict party discipline inhibits open criticism of the official party stand by rank-and-file members and obliges them to vote as a solid bloc both in committees and plenary sessions.

The House of Representatives is made to assume more legislative roles than the 252-member House of Councillors. The former may legislate a bill against the latter's opposition by passing it a second time with a majority of at least two-thirds of members present. In normal circumstances, though, any legislative differences between the two bodies can be handled by an interhouse conference committee. The House of Councillors was designed to check partisan politics in the House of Representatives, but, in practice, it has become equally partisan.

Negotiation and compromise are the normal modes of decision-making in the Diet. On the pragmatic issues with which the vast majority of bills are concerned, such as regional development, sanitation, and hygiene, negotiation and compromise have resulted in joint amendment by the ruling and opposition parties. The ruling party is oriented above all to practical considerations, whereas the members of the Japan Socialist Party, the major opposition, share some measure of common ideology but disagree radically on the formulation of practical policy alternatives. Hence, there is a dangerous lack of common ground between the two major parties in Japan. On such ideological issues as foreign relations, the Constitution, education, and domestic security, both sides become inflexible. On the one hand, there is little room in the political culture of the Japanese elite to accommodate the opposition. The ruling party becomes a "tyrannous majority in forcing through legislation or treaty ratification." The

Socialists, on the other hand, resort to filibustering and other violent, obstructionist tactics.

In practice, the Diet must rely on other political institutions and processes for policy ideas and support. A large number of policies are initiated and drafted by the bureaucracy; some bills originate with the cabinet or the policy boards of the parties. In any case, the Diet merely takes policies originating elsewhere and publicizes them; thus, it is often incapable of providing policy guidance and meaningful deliberation of public issues.

The Cabinet. The cabinet, the executive branch of government, consists of the prime minister (or premier), seventeen ministers, a chief cabinet secretary, and a director of the cabinet Legislative Bureau. The prime minister, under the parliamentary system of government, is selected from among the members of the Diet by resolution. In practice, the leader of the majority party or majority coalition in the House of Representatives is chosen, and he, in turn selects his cabinet members. (Following Premier Eisaku Satō's resignation in July 1972, Kakuei Tanaka made an alliance with influential faction leaders such as Takeo Miki, Masayoshi Ōhira, and Yasuhiro Nakasone, and defeated his opponent, Takeo Fukuda, a favorite son of outgoing Premier Satō. Thus he became a president of the LDP and prime minister.) Eleven of the cabinet members preside over ministries and the others normally hold such positions as the vice-premiership or the directorship of the Defense Agency or the Economic Planning Agency.

The gravity of policy-making has been shifted from the Diet to the cabinet. The authority of the cabinet extends to the formulation, or at least prior approval, of practically all major policies. The large staff of the office of the prime minister facilitates the exercise of the cabinet's leadership in decision-making. The cabinet traditionally makes decisions by discussing issues until some general consensus is reached. A cabinet member who seriously disagrees with this collectively made policy is expected to resign or face dismissal by the prime minister. The cabinet represents more general interests than the Diet, in which private bills initiated by its members tend to promote particular, more locally defined objectives. Intraparty and interfactional differences on policy or personnel matters within the ruling party oblige the prime minister to change cabinet members quite frequently, sometimes too frequently. This lack of cabinet stability, coupled with the constant influence of the professional bureaucracy, inhibits effective leadership of the cabinet in coordinating policy-making. Several counterbalancing factors, however, help to make up for what might be a highly unstable policy-making leadership. First, cabinet members are all recruited from among the ruling party. Second, the prime ministers stay in office twice as long, on the average, as cabinet members. Third, a continuity in policy-making structure and process is maintained by professional bureaucrats, headed by administrative vice-ministers, who are civil-service employees with many years of experience in the various ministries and agencies.

As the national leader, the prime minister, a visible, identifiable individual, represents general national interests; but he is also responsive to narrow, particular interests in the leadership of his party, the cabinet, and the bureaucracy. In practice, many Japanese prime ministers must maintain the delicate balance between factions in the ruling party and thus are incapable of exercising as strong a personal leadership as they might wish. While the Diet can make policy through bargaining and compromise, the premier is limited essentially to throwing the power and prestige of his office to one side or the other. Furthermore, his personal, as well as official, behavior strongly influences the effectiveness of his leadership.

The Bureaucracy. Although not elected to office, the professional bureaucrats assume an important role in policy-making; they provide a rich source of policy ideas and a great potential organizing force of support. The ruling party is not well prepared to deal with the complex problems of a rapidly developing country and must rely on the expertise and enterprise of the bureaucracy. Also, political questions have been so inextricably tied to administrative and technological problems that the two become inseparable in solving public issues. In Japan the higher echelon of bureaucracy has traditionally been involved in more than administrative questions. Furthermore, ex-bureaucrats increasingly have gained positions of influence in both the ruling party and the cabinet, partly because of their experience in particular aspects of government. Administrative vice-ministers meet regularly with the director of the cabinet Legislative Bureau, and this informal group is far better informed on policy and administrative matters than are average members of the cabinet.

Political Parties. Political policy-making in Japan has been conditioned to a considerable extent by a one-party dominance. As long as they maintain party unity, the Liberal Democrats are likely to continue to control the government and provide policy alternatives. The Satō administration has been credited with a stable economic growth and the second largest GNP in the noncommunist world, as well as with quieting student riots and the successful recovery of Japanese sovereignty over Okinawa. It has increased the strength of the LDP in the Diet after the 1969 general election (302 seats in the House of Representatives and 138 seats in the House of Councillors). The party is faction-fragmented and internally ununited, representing a loose coalition brought together for practical purposes of legislative and election advantages. Factions are formed on the basis of personal loyalty and advantages accorded by faction leaders rather than common principles or policies, with the result that much disagreement exists on major issues.

For purposes of most policy-making, the LDP is controlled almost solely by its faction leaders and other high members elected by the party congress. In this respect, the secretary-general, who directs the daily business of the party, and the chairman of the executive board and policy board occupy important positions in the party, because most major issues go through a protracted process of interfactional and intraparty negotiations, bargaining, and compromise. A party stand thus formulated is transmitted for legislative action through the LDP members in the Diet, in which strict party discipline almost always insures that rank-and-file members vote as a solid bloc. The ruling party maintains strong ties, both formal and informal, with the Diet and the cabinet, as well as keeping close contact with the other two members of the "unholy trinity": the bureaucracy and big business.

While essentially conservative causes are represented by the LDP, the progressive movement is highly fragmented among the Japan Socialist Party (JSP), the Democratic Socialist Party (DSP), the Fair Play Party (Kōmeitō) (FPP), and the Japan Communist Party (JCP). Although they have collectively managed to keep more than one-third of the seats in the House of Representatives, and thereby have prevented any attempts by the ruling party to adversely amend the Constitution (an amendment requires the concurrent votes of two-thirds or more of all the members of each house), the opposition parties have failed to form a united front. Indeed, the general elec-

tions in 1967 and 1969 hastened the tendency toward multiple opposition parties.

Although the JSP is still the single largest opposition party, its
strength drastically decreased when its lower house seats dropped
from 135 to 90 in the 1969 general election. The right and left wings
collided over the very nature of the party: the leftists' endorsement
of proletarian dictatorship was no more acceptable to the participants
in the April 1970 party convention than the rightists' rejection of
Marxism and Leninism. Only the sense of immediate crisis avoided
party disintegration with temporary support going to the present
rightist leadership.

The FPP, with 280,000 members as of August 1970, was created
in November 1964 as the political branch of a new Buddhist sect,
Sōkagakkai. After the 1969 general election, the FPP became the
second largest opposition party with 47 seats in the lower house and
24 seats in the upper house. Their increased strength in the Diet
often places the FPP in a pivotal position in which they can shift
their alliance between the two major parties. Toward the end of
1969, the FPP was severely criticized by other opposition parties in
the Diet for allegedly having obstructed the publication of books
critical of the Sōkagakkai. This incident, which revealed in a striking
manner the domination of the party by the Sōkagakkai, led to a general reorganization of the FPP including separation of politics and
religion, decentralization of decision-making by reducing the power
of party chairmen, and abolition of the party caucus, as well as the
institution of open election of party officials. The FPP now makes it
the party's goal to establish a welfare state and espouses a middle-
of-the-road stand.

The DSP separated from the JSP in 1960 to form a national party
working for democratic socialism. But since its inception, the right-
wing party has failed to capture enough popular votes and representa-
tion in the Diet to effectively challenge the two major parties. (It had
a 43,300 membership in July 1970, with 32 seats in the lower house
and 10 in the upper house.) The DSP not only has tried to expand
its own organization by open election of party chairmen, but also
began to talk openly about merger with the JSP by 1972, provided
that the latter renounces its status as a Marxist-oriented class party,
leading ultimately to a grand coalition of "democratic, progressive

parties" by 1975. As a step in that direction, the secretaries of the JSP, DSP, and FPP agreed to try for a united front starting with environmental issues.

For years the JCP has been openly at odds with its counterparts in both Communist China and the Soviet Union, whom the JCP accuses of domination and interference; denouncing Russian intervention in Eastern Europe and Mao's "people's war" strategy, the JCP allegedly has abandoned its time-honored subversive activities in favor of less violent tactics. Within the party, the JCP has tried recently to rejuvenate itself by giving younger party members important posts and by making most of its party convention activities known to the public. Its platform includes the "struggle against modern revisionism and dogmatic sectarianism." It also professes tolerance of opposition parties and advocates a coalition with democratic elements. These recent changes in party position have resulted in the expansion of the JCP. In the 1968 election for the upper house, the JCP received 3,577,000 popular votes, despite having only approximately 30,000 members (as of July 1970). It was the largest number of votes in the history of the party, and four seats were secured. In the 1969 election for the lower house, it increased its seats by 10, to total 14. Although the JCP has no official influence on the forming of either domestic or foreign policy, its growth deserves to be carefully watched.

A general election held on December 10, 1972 changed the power configuration in the House of Representatives as follows: the LDP, 282 seats; the JSP, 118; the JCP, 38; the FPP, 29; the DSP, 19, and 5 independents. On the one hand, the LDP led by Premier Tanaka suffered a substantial loss in house seats. It also failed to stop a slow but steady decline (from 47.6 percent in 1969 to 46.7 percent in 1972) in the conservatives' popular vote. On the other hand, the JSP and the JCP scored an unexpectedly large gain. Indeed, the JCP with its largest number of seats in the party's history leaped to the position of the second strongest opposition party next to the JSP. It also increased its popular vote from 6.8 percent in 1969 to 10.5 percent in 1972. The leftists' victory was in contrast to a decline of the moderate parties. The FPP suffered the first setback in its history, sliding down from the second to the third largest opposition party. Likewise, the DSP became weaker than before. The increased bipolarization of the power structure between the conservative LDP and the leftist JSP and JCP will almost certainly give the Tanaka administration some tough fighting.

Interest Groups. Pressure groups, representing organized concerns or causes, are less moderating and compromising than other political forces in policy-making. They can be a source of policy ideas, background information, and mobilization of support. They usually represent a narrower range of opinion and generate more intense, but more limited, support than political parties. They can, however, direct their resources toward developing a majority on a specific issue.

Interest groups, which became conspicuous in Japan after 1957, have definitely established a firm and expanding role in policy-making. They cover a wide area—business, labor, consumers, culture groups, religion, women—and range from local to national, rural to urban interests.

Business and organized labor are naturally the major interest groups. The Japan Federation of Employers' Associations (Nikkeiren), representing more than 20,000 of Japan's largest employers, is regarded as one of the most influential pressure groups. The Japanese Political League of Small and Medium-Sized Enterprises (Nihon Chūshōkigyō Seijirenmei) plays a similar role in representing the interests of a less moneyed segment of Japanese business. Through its successful activities, a Small and Medium-Sized Enterprises Organization Law (SMEOL) was enacted in 1957, and it has secured tax relief and improved credit services for its members. Although ties between business and the ruling party are extensive, they are also diffuse. The diversity of business interests and their uneven influence on the ruling party make vague and imprecise the details of their interrelationships, and the exact extent of business influence on the policy-making of the LDP is hard to determine.

The General Council of Trade Unions of Japan (Sōhyo), representing approximately 38 percent of the unionized Japanese workers, is the most influential of the labor interest groups. It has a close affiliation with the JSP and has taken left-wing socialist stands on many domestic and foreign policy issues. Its rival, the All Japan Labor Federation (Dōmei), is the second largest labor union. Their interests are more economic and less political than those of the

General Council of Trade Unions of Japan, and they identify themselves with the moderate socialism of the DSP.

Among other conspicuous interest groups are the Japan Teachers' Union (Nikkyōso) and the National Federation of Students' Self-Government Association (Zengakuren), who have used extreme and often violent tactics in their efforts to promote the interests of the leftist movement. But labor unions and left-wing affiliated interest groups normally have much greater difficulties in gaining access to policy-makers than do business and professional interest groups.

Inasmuch as the cabinet and the bureaucracy have been the foci of policy-making, they have become just as much the targets of interest-group activities as the Diet. Relations between the bureaucracy and their organized clientele, for example, between the Ministry of International Trade and Industry and business interest groups, are apt to be very close. Interest groups are also paying greater attention than before to the legislators in the Diet, and rank-and-file members have been serving as intermediaries between interest groups from their constituencies and higher bureaucrats in the effort to obtain subsidies and grants-in-aid.

Naoki Kobayashi, in Selection 3, describes in great detail the techniques of interest-group activities, their organizational strength and advantages, and internal characteristics such as size and cohesion, all of which bear upon the effectiveness of their activities in policy-making. Lobbying by pressure groups sometimes manifests itself in the form of outright bribery and the practice of providing positions for retired bureaucrats, who will then represent the interests of their new employer in negotiating with the ministry, bureau, or office which they formerly headed. Furthermore, as a long-range technique, many interest groups endorse and support candidates for national offices, either individually or collectively, with money or a bloc of votes, and expect, in return, preferential treatment once the candidates are in office.

An Outline of
the Policy-Making
Process in Japan*

SHIGEO MISAWA

The Policy-Making Structure

The term "policy-making structure" is not equivalent to the legal authority for policy-making; it includes the entire system under which decision-making power is distributed among major political forces which regularly participate in and exert explicit influences on the policy-making process.[1] It implies a complex mechanism by which public policies are made through the exercise of a noncentralized power, and furthermore, can be considered as only one facet of the policy-making process.

The original form of Japan's present policy-making structure was created in the fall of 1955, when several political parties were reorganized and the Liberal Democratic Party emerged (see Figure 1). Since that time, except for some minor changes in the distribution of power among and within the various political groupings, there has been no fundamental change in the overall policy-making structure.[2] The conservatives' merger into a single party has clearly determined the direction of Japanese politics in recent years. In this sense, Maurice Duverger's argument that the party system in modern nation-states constitutes the substratum of the governing structure can be applied to postwar Japan.[3]

The Liberal Democratic Party. The conservative parties merged and formed the Liberal Democratic Party (LDP) (Jiyūminshutō) in the fall of 1955. The founding of the LDP implied the emergence of a united front before the enemy, a growing Japan Socialist Party

---

* This selection is taken from "Seisaku kettei katei no gaikan" in *Nempō: Seijigaku* (The Annals of the Japanese Political Science Association) (Tokyo, 1967), pp. 5–33. Translated and reprinted with permission of the author.

(JSP) (Nihon Shakaitō). The merger was also in response to a firm demand, made by the most influential members of the Japanese financial community, for the establishment of a strong conservative government capable both of eradicating the unstable politics prevailing since the latter part of the Shigeru Yoshida administration (May 1946–December 1954) and of implementing solid economic policies.

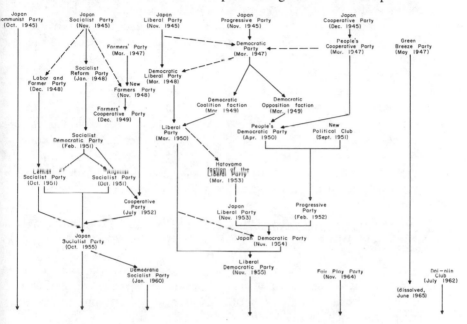

Figure 1. Postwar Japanese political parties. Solid line indicates direct descent or relationship. Broken line indicates indirect descent or relationship.

Since the formation of the LDP was motivated primarily by the conservatives' determination to retain the ruling power for themselves, the emergence of Japan's two major parties, the LDP and the JSP, did not result in a transfer of power from one party to another as in the British type of two-party system. As long as the conservative alliance did not weaken, the country would remain a one-party-dominant political system. Thus, the conservatives have achieved the original goal of effectively defending their position, but they have failed to stabilize politics, a second objective of the merger. The biggest problem in the successful creation of the LDP was the selection of a party president. The old German saying, "A good beginning is half the battle," is particularly relevant to the early days of this party. The need for a united front against the JSP obliged the new organization to adopt an awkward form of collective four-man leadership, thereby foreshadowing a dark future. In actuality, the LDP has been not so much a unified political party as a grand coalition of conservative factions such as the Ichirō Hatoyama faction of the Liberal Party, both the main and liberal factions of the Progressive Party, the Japan Liberal Party, and the Nobusuke Kishi, Taketora Ogata, and Shigeru Yoshida factions of the Liberal Party. Each administration after the third Hatoyama cabinet (November 1955–December 1956) was a coalition whose members were drawn from the most powerful conservative blocs of the former Liberal Party. This could be compared to a series of moves in which one conservative cabinet, when dissolved, is always replaced by another conservative one from the LDP. Since 1955 in Japan, a coalition of parties has emerged and persisted while assuming the appearance of a single political party, a rather peculiar situation in the history of party systems throughout the world.

It makes little difference if the LDP is called a political party or a coalition of parties. It is, of course, possible to conceive of it as a uniquely Japanese political party, but as long as the notion of "political party" cannot be given a single definition transcending time and space, it is merely a question of semantics whether the political forces composing the LDP should be considered factions within a party or parties within a coalition. An examination of successive LDP administrations raises salient issues which cannot be overlooked in a country espousing parliamentary politics. Various factions which participate in the formation of a coalition cabinet make their policies as well as their interfactional compromises public and hold themselves responsible to the people for their collective actions in the government. Therefore, if a cabinet is formed by various LDP factions, should not each faction face problems of collective responsibility to the people?

The fact is that interfactional compromises in coalition cabinets always have been made within the ruling party's private sanctuaries, beyond any supervision of the people, rather than in the public arena of the Diet. The ill effects of this mode of decision-making are many: compromises are apt to be unprincipled and without any clear direction, as exemplified by the selection of a party president in 1957; cabinet members who entertain views on important issues different from those of the prime minister remain in office; smaller factions within the ruling party do not feel themselves responsible to the people. When deciding such important matters as the Police Procedure Law, the United States–Japan Security Treaty, and a peace treaty with the Republic of Korea, the minority-faction LDP members in the Diet either abstained from voting or boycotted debates on these issues. They probably acted not so much from a sense of responsibility to the public as from their inclination to discredit the administration. Each faction, while hiding behind the party shield, feels released from the responsibility necessarily attached to a ruling party and thus frees itself to seek the most opportune moment to ascend to power.

The LDP appears to be destined to remain the single dominant party; it cannot be forced to collapse unless the JSP wins an election and is called upon to assume power. Desire to run the government and fear of the forces of international communism have been the major psychological factors that have held together the conservative coalition.

In modern politics a ruling party should assume the role, in a sense, of a motor driving two machines, the legislative and executive branches of government; in this context, the abnormal make-up of the LDP, particularly with its semipermanency, gravely affects each phase of the policy-making process. For example, the prime minister is placed in the position of trying to maintain a balance between the contending factions in the ruling party; as a result, he can neither exercise strong leadership nor choose members of his cabinet according to their ability. Because of instability within the LDP, the position of cabinet members always remains precarious, with their average tenure limited to one year, and under such circumstances, they cannot adequately perform their tasks. Thus, the deficiencies and cleavages existing within the LDP are projected on a larger scale throughout the entire formal policy-making structure.

The Diet. Since 1955, the decline in significance of the Diet within the policy-making structure has been accelerated. After the San Francisco Peace Treaty of September 1951 and the recovery of national independence in April 1952, Japan's policy-making structure began to function autonomously for the first time since World War II. The Diet continued, however, to play a secondary role and even after the removal of the restrictions of the Allied Occupation Forces the Diet failed to function as "the highest organ of state power."

The Diet never expected to monopolize the power to initiate bills as the "sole law-making organ of the state." It was fully aware of the world-wide tendency to shift legislative initiative into the executive branch of the government. This being the case, the Diet decided to delegate legislative power to the executive branch only as a last resort, in order to maintain the legislative function.[4] Since consent from the General Headquarters of the Supreme Commander for the Allied Powers (GHQ,SCAP) was no longer required to amend government-sponsored bills and budgets, the Diet could have had its will reflected in the deliberation of bills by exercising its power to investigate and interpellate the activities of the executive branch of government; it could have raised a strong voice concerning the formulation and implementation of policies by the LDP administration. But an important pamphlet on fundamental policy programs after the peace treaty, published by the ruling Liberal Party in October 1951, conspicuously omitted any reference to the Diet or a political party, thus indicating that Prime Minister Shigeru Yoshida had no intention of either changing the existing bureaucracy-centered ruling structure or placing the legislature at the center of policy-making. Yoshida's distrust of party men and his favoritism toward the bureaucracy were both well known. The longer his administration continued, the greater was his disregard of the Diet.

The prime minister, however, could not entirely ignore the Diet. Criticism against Yoshida's one-man rule grew both inside and outside his own party. As the depurged prewar conservative statesmen returned to politics en masse, challenging Yoshida's dictatorial position, and the power of the postwar statesmen increased, the prime minister's rule experienced a gradual decline. The Diet, meanwhile, energetically debated government-sponsored bills and criticized the government's overall performance, thereby substantially affecting policy-making. Especially after the sixteenth Diet session in May 1953, the ruling Liberal Party was no longer able to secure a majority in the House of Representatives, and opposition groups such as the Progressive Party, factions of the Liberal Party, and the Japan Liberal Party, at times even in collaboration with both left and right wings of the JSP, added major amendments to important government-sponsored bills.[5] Also, prior to the sixteenth session of the Diet, the

Green Breeze Party (Ryokufūkai), claiming to be a neutral force, succeeded in modifying major bills in cooperation with the Progressive Party in the House of Councillors where the Liberal Party was weak.[6] In the later part of the Yoshida administration, conservative factions often negotiated with and gained concessions from the Liberal Party by using as bait their cooperation for the passage of important bills and budgets.

As one end of a seesaw goes down when the other goes up, the influence of the Diet upon the policy-making process has decreased when the LDP has increased its seats in the Diet, and vice versa. The LDP, a ruling party with a larger majority than the former Liberal Party, has created the danger of reducing the Diet's power. Furthermore, the unification of the conservatives transformed the Diet from a buffer zone for negotiation and compromise into an arena for stiff confrontation between the LDP and JSP.

It must also be noted that even before the emergence of the LDP the Diet imposed upon itself rules which restricted its power. In the aftermath of the chaos which occurred during the debate over the proposed revision of the Police Procedure Law in the nineteenth session (November 1953 through June 1954), the Diet enacted three self-restricting laws. First, the Diet Law, as revised for the fifth time on January 24, 1955, changed the standing-committee system and restricted action on private bills. Second, the Joint Committee on Legal Statutes (Ryōinhōkiiinkai), which had fifteen members selected from both houses, was abolished.[7] It was responsible to both the Diet and cabinet for proposing new legislation and recommending the revision or abolition of existing laws and ordinances and was also charged with advising the chairmen of both houses concerning the revision of procedural rules governing the Diet. Had it exercised its authority, this committee could have performed the same function as the special committee set up in each session of the British House of Commons to review governmental ordinances, to examine the relationship between parliamentary supremacy and delegation of legislative power, and to recommend the revision or abolition of legal provisions of status lower than governmental ordinances. Third, the system of open debate, designed to afford Diet members the opportunity at least once every two weeks[8] to express their opinions and question the government, was abolished. It could have enabled the Diet to exercise control over the executive branch in a manner similar to the British Parliament's question time, which grants the representatives opportunities to freely criticize government policies. Both the Joint Committee of Legal Statutes and the open debate system were abolished on the ground which read, in part, as follows: "In view of the fact that open debate was last used, and then only once, at the seventh session of the Diet (December 1949 through May 1950), and that the Joint Committee on Legal Statutes has not been convened since the fourteenth session (August 7, 1952), and as these systems are not compatible with the parliamentary system in our country, it will be proper to abolish them." [9]

The inhibitive circumstances under the Occupation may well have resulted in unsympathetic views in the Diet toward these two practices, but even at the end of the Occupation they had been discontinued, instead of being actively in use. Their discontinuation seems particularly unfortunate in view of the fact that the main function of modern legislature tends to shift from legislation of public policies toward supervision of the executive. The bill to revise the Diet Law, which resulted in the abolition of the Joint Committee and open debate, was drafted by the Joint Subcommittee for Drafting the Revised Diet Law and was passed through both houses by omitting debate by the concerned committees. Therefore, there is no way of knowing the intent of its drafters except through examination of the brief proposal for the bill. In the midst of party outcries for the normalization of the Diet and the establishment of parliamentary politics in Japan, it seems rather strange that there should be no trace of debate in support of restoring these two practices, which seem so essential to the proper functioning of the Diet.

The 1955 merger of the conservatives also precipitated great changes in the structure of the House of Councillors. The Green Breeze Party held a peculiar kind of political force within the Diet. It gained a large number of seats in the House of Councillors from its very first session (and had 96 seats at its height), among which many were held by intellectuals and elders of the former bureaucracy. At the fourth general election on July 8, 1956, however, all Green Breeze Party candidates who ran from prefectural constituencies were defeated, thereby decreasing the party's seats in the House of Councillors from 45 to 29. In subsequent elections, many of its older members retired, and other candidates lost elections because of the organized votes for the LDP and JSP. Furthermore, cooption by the

LDP caused such a decrease in the party's membership that at the time of the seventh general election in July 1965, it was forced to dissolve. The so-called politicization of the House of Councillors seen in the elections after 1956 created controversies over the function and very existence of that house. Another feature of the 1956 election was the conspicuous presence of successful candidates from national constituencies, supported by nationwide professional interest groups, bureaucrats, and unions, and new problems arose when the House of Councillors began to assume the character of an agent representing these various interest groups.

The general decline in the power of the Diet, coupled with the loss in quality and sound judgment of the House of Councillors, weakened the ability of the Diet to oversee the government's policies. Even after the 1955 conservative merger, the Diet has undoubtedly filled an educational role in deliberating on bills and other policy matters. The criticism of national policies by opposition parties has aroused public opinion and has caused an opposition movement by the LDP's antimainstream factions. It was perhaps inevitable that the Diet's role in the overall policy-making process should have faded, partly because both houses have declined in quality and partly because the ruling party has maintained enough seats in the Diet with which to ensure the passage of its own bills.

The Bureaucracy. The increasingly close ties between the bureaucrats and the ruling party have become public knowledge. As part of the postwar Occupation policy to eliminate the harmful influence of a despotic bureaucracy, many leading bureaucrats were purged, local political systems were reformed, and the civil-service system as a whole experienced fundamental restructuring. These reforms, however, merely "skimmed the surface," and the supremacy of the bureaucrats within the policy-making structure has remained secure.[10]

During the Occupation, the cabinet conferred with and outlined its policies to the concerned ministries and then had them draft a bill for the cabinet, which would be put into effect after securing the approval of GHQ,SCAP. When the cabinet needed legislative action, it worked through the Policy Board (Seimuchōsakai) within the ruling party to obtain passage of bills in the Diet. As long as the Yoshida cabinet maintained an absolute majority in the Diet, policy-making functioned smoothly. Between the middle of the Occupation and the end of the Yoshida administration, however, a new trend started in which the leaders of each ministry wielded strong influence within the legislative process. Thus the unlimited discretionary power traditionally exercised by prewar bureaucrats was reasserted.

The principle of the modern administrative state that demands nonpartisanship and impartiality on the part of public officials has become largely illusory. As long as bureaucrats take the lead in each phase of initiating, deciding, and administering policies, and are called upon to act as mediators between conflicting interests, it is impossible for them to restrict their judgment only to facts as opposed to policy or to maintain impartiality. Herein lies the reason for the need to examine administrative responsibility as opposed to political responsibility. After 1955, Japan's political development as an administrative state undoubtedly negated the doctrine of bureaucratic impartiality.[11] The activities of interest groups, which became conspicuous after 1957, seem to reflect this tendency. Japanese tradition and the attributes of the modern administrative state have worked together to reinforce bureaucratic dominance.

The bureaucracy has strengthened its ties with the LDP since it has emerged as the semipermanent, conservative ruling party. The strength of such ties can be accounted for not by the formalistic explanation that bureaucratic impartiality has been lost because of the improbability of a shift in power to another party, but rather by realistic necessity. On the one hand, under the parliamentary cabinet system, the bureaucrats must not only secure the consent of the ruling party in making and administering policies, but must also rely upon it for authoritative resolution of conflicting interests among themselves; on the other hand, the LDP, which lacks the experience and ability to exercise policy-making leadership, must depend on the know-how of the bureaucracy. For the LDP coalition, the centralized bureaucracy is an essential prerequisite, freeing the party from the responsibilities of political leadership and enabling it to indulge in power struggles.

A further complication is that the LDP tends to get too deeply involved in the minor details of administrative proposals which should be left to the bureaucracy. Diet members and factions of the LDP try to influence bureaucrats in an attempt to gain privileges and subsidies for their constituents and interest groups, expecting in return votes and campaign funds; they thus turn the central bureaucracy into an agent for expanding party strength. The LDP, on the other hand, mobilizes the bureaucrats for party conferences on policy development, all in the name of party and government unity. Its high degree of command power is often compared to that of GHQ,SCAP. But does this show the real strength of the ruling party? No! The LDP intervenes in the bureaucratic and administrative processes mainly because of inadequate organization and lack of party discipline. The fact is that the party's election platforms as well as its overall policies usually are a mere rearrangement of a list of policy proposals submitted by the ministries, thus revealing the total dependence of the party on the organized bureaucracy. In spite of the institution of a liaison conference every Friday between the cabinet and the LDP, the party leaders are often seen to exert direct pressure upon cabinet members. For instance, Takechiyo Matsuda, the Minister of Education, was severely criticized by the members of the LDP's Executive Board in February 1960,[12] and the ministers of Agriculture and Finance are forced to be temporarily absent from their offices each year at the time when they must fix the price of rice in order to avoid various forms of pressure.[13] In cases like these, the cabinet must be said to have degenerated to a committee subordinate to the ruling party. Moreover, the significance of the bureaucracy as a source of candidates for the Diet cannot be overlooked as a factor contributing to the cohesiveness between the LDP and the bureaucracy.

Ex-bureaucrats obviously have abundant knowledge and experience in governmental structure and management and accordingly can expect an easier election victory than nonbureaucratic candidates, partly due to the prestige of the governmental agencies they formerly served. Inasmuch as they are extremely effective in expanding the party's power and governing capability, it is natural that the LDP should seek out these bureaucrats when it is recruiting new candidates for the Diet. It is also natural that bureaucrats, who can go no further than the rank of vice-minister, should aspire to go into politics in their desire to maintain after retirement a status consistent with their bureaucratic position and in search of further fame. Indeed Prime Minister Yoshida lured many of them into politics after the 1949 election. Following the return of purged prewar bureaucrats to the political arena, the strength of the ex-bureaucrats increased within the conservative parties, with 58 in the LDP and 14 in the Progressive Party as a result of the general election of 1953.[14] According to one calculation, 77 ex-bureaucrats (26 percent of the LDP members) were in the House of Representatives in November 1963, and 54 ex-bureaucrats (38 percent of the LDP members) were in the House of Councillors in January 1964.[15]

Ex-bureaucrats occupy a central position within the LDP and form the core of its policy-making body. They not only possess more administrative knowledge and experience than other party members, but they also seem to be more adept at locating the problem areas, grasping social demands, and formulating policies. Furthermore, because of their contacts with former subordinates in the bureaucracy, they can readily receive information, materials, and other forms of assistance helpful in working out policies. The prime ministers after

Table 1. Number and percentage of ex-bureaucrats among major cabinet members between the third Hatoyama cabinet (November 22, 1955–December 23, 1956) and the second Satō cabinet (June 3, 1965–July 31, 1966)

Cabinet position	Major cabinet members*	Ex-bureaucrats†	Percentage of ex-bureaucrats
Minister of Foreign Affairs	6	4	67
Minister of Finance	6	3	50
Minister of Justice	11	5	46
Minister of Education	9	5	56
Minister of Health and Welfare	12	7	58
Minister of Agriculture and Forestry	10	5	50
Minister of International Trade and Industry	11	5	46
Minister of Transportation	14‡	6	44
Minister of Postal Services	14	7	50
Minister of Labor	8	1	13
Minister of Construction	10	1	10
Minister of Local Self-Government	12	6	50
Director of Economic Planning Board	6	1	17
Total	129	56	43

* Those who remained in office from the preceding cabinet or held more than one cabinet post and acting ministers were excluded from this list.

† Those who occupied positions of section chief or higher at central administrative offices; mainly those who have passed the government's higher civil service examinations.

‡ Sensuke Fujieda, the minister of Transportation under the first Satō cabinet, was included in the figure.

Nobusuke Kishi have been former bureaucrats and have attracted many ex-bureaucrat members of the Diet to their own factions. Likewise the majority of cabinet members have been ex-bureaucrats, and a similar tendency can be seen with regard to major officials within the LDP. Tables 1 and 2 show the number of ex-bureaucrats

Table 2. Number and percentage of ex-bureaucrats among major officials of the Liberal Democratic Party (up to July 1966)

Position	Total officeholders*	Ex-bureaucrats*	Percentage of ex-bureaucrats
Secretary-General	8	3	38
Chairman of the Executive Board	11	4	36
Chairman of the Policy Board	12	6	50
Chairman of the Financial Committee†	4	2	50
Chairman of the National Organization Committee	12	3	25
Chairman of the Publicity Committee‡	8	2	25
Chairman of the Diet Relations Committee	13	2	15
Chairman of the Party Discipline Committee	10	5	50
Total	78	27	35

* The same criteria were used to determine the number of major officeholders and ex-bureaucrats as in Table 1.
† Created in 1962.
‡ Created in 1959.

among major cabinet members and officials of the LDP. In Table 1, if the ministers of State were included in the calculation, the percentage of former bureaucrats would be higher. Although not indicated in Table 2, the majority of the vice-chairmen of the Policy Board, members of the Policy Council (Seisakushingikai), and various department chairmen have also been former bureaucrats. When the LDP leaders allocate members to the Diet's standing committees or corresponding departments of the party's Policy Board, ex-bureaucrats can usually get the assignments that roughly correspond to the bureaucratic posts they previously held. Because they provide a meeting point between the party and the bureaucracy, their presence is highly valued by both.

The Cabinet. When the administrative function of the government began to expand after 1955, the cabinet conspicuously revealed a lack of leadership and overall coordination in policy-making. The Provisional Administrative Investigatory Commission (Rinjigyōsei-chōsakai) has been conducting a thorough examination into the causes of the inadequacy and problems of the cabinet.[16] Probably the major impediment to the cabinet's functioning lies in the quality of the LDP itself.

Problems definitely exist in the political philosophies and leadership abilities of the prime ministers. Furthermore, as long as the government continues to attempt to function on the top of a constant power struggle within the ruling party, the establishment of effective prime-ministerial leadership will remain difficult. The Ikeda cabinet, which allegedly was stable in policy-making for a relatively long period and the Hatoyama cabinet with its "dual diplomacy" * were faction-balanced cabinets. Under these conditions, the prime minister could not afford flexibility in developing long-range policies. Cabinet change, a fast-working remedy for harmonizing the ruling party, often places unfit ministers in the cabinet.

Under the present cabinet system, the term of the prime minister, who is also the president of the LDP, is subject to review every two years, and the terms of the ministers and parliamentary vice-ministers (*seimujikan*) last usually no more than a year or so because of the practice of annual cabinet change. This presents a serious problem in the consistency and continuity of government policies. The ministers cannot responsibly guide their own ministries, with the result that they either "grandstand" to stay in office or follow an irresponsible "hit-or-miss rule," thinking "After all, I'll only be in office for one year. I can't expect much if I spread myself too thin. I'll try for the long shot." [17] A minister with such short tenure will not be able to exercise his best ability in guiding the policies of his ministry. He will merely represent the interest of his ministry at the time of compiling the annual budget for a new fiscal year, in that he is expected

* The Soviet Union did not sign the San Francisco Peace Treaty in 1951 and strongly protested the termination of the occupation of Japan. Premier Ichirō Hatoyama took an active interest in normalizing Japanese-Soviet relations and succeeded in concluding a joint declaration on October 19, 1956, which restored formal diplomatic relations between the two countries. The press characterized Hatoyama's foreign policies as the "dual diplomacy," because he tried to have active relations with the East while maintaining friendly relations with the West.

by his subordinates to secure as large an appropriation as possible. *Economic and Business Interests.* The financial community has increased its influence in the administration of government policies at the same time as its ties with the ruling party have been institutionalized. The term "financial" community is not necessarily synonymous with "economic" or "business" community. The major economic groupings which form the core of the financial community are four organizations centered in Tokyo and the Kansai Economic Association (Kansai Keizairengōkai).*

These organizations have three things in common: they represent the interests of big corporations, their objective is to defend the capitalistic system,[18] and they have relatively large memberships. It should be noted, however, that the four economic organizations often differ in their opinions and actions on desired policies and in their perceptions of existing problems and, as a result, seldom express a united position. For example, on October 3, 1952, prior to the creation of the LDP, the four organizations issued a joint resolution which expressed a desire for the establishment of stable government. While the Federation of Economic Organizations (Keidanren) enthusiastically supported the resolution, the Japan Federation of Employers' Associations (Nikkeiren) and the Japanese Management Association (Dōyūkai) were reportedly very restrained in their endorsements and critical of the proposed unprincipled merger.

It was during the latter part of the Yoshida administration that the financial community increased its interest and participation in political activities and eventually provided a major impetus for the downfall of the Yoshida cabinet as well as for the 1955 merger of the conservatives. The financial world even began to be openly involved in the selection of prime ministers,[19] thereby increasing its influence on the Liberal Democratic administration, particularly under Premier Hayato Ikeda, its favorite son.

About 1963, the Japan Federation of Employers' Associations and the Japanese Management Association reportedly started regular discussions with members of the LDP's Policy Board and Executive Board, which resulted in institutionalized ties between the party and

---

* The four major economic organizations are the Federation of Economic Organizations (Keidanren), the Japan Federation of Employers' Associations (Nikkeiren), the Japanese Management Association (Dōyūkai), and the Japan Chamber of Commerce.

the financial community. Although the Economic Council (Keizai-shingikai) and other advisory bodies of the government exist as a channel to express formally the demands of the financial community, the ties between the financial world and the bureaucrats concerned are presumably strong enough to preclude the need for any such formality.

Finally, brief reference should be made to other political forces in policy-making, such as opposition parties, local governmental units, interest groups, public opinion, and the mass media. Opposition parties and public opinion will be touched upon in subsequent sections.

As long as the Japanese governing structure continues to "allow only nominally the principle of separation of powers, thereby leading to a concentration of power," [20] local governments will remain restricted in any decision-making on their own matters as well as in their participation in the state's policy-making processes. The creation of the LDP and particularly the initiation of the Ikeda administration's regional development programs, part of the policy designed to achieve a high rate of national economic growth, have accelerated the dependence of local governmental units on the central government. Meanwhile, the local governments have increasingly taken on the characteristics of interest groups such as demanding various kinds of subsidies, thereby fostering a feedback mechanism which further intensifies the central government control.

As the keystone of the policy-making structure, the LDP should in theory strike a balance between the Diet and the cabinet-bureaucracy, but because of its weak and elastic character, it fails to function as such. As a result, even after the 1955 merger, the basis of the policy-making structure continues to be the bureaucracy. On this foundation rests the mutual interest of the LDP and the financial community, unaffected by intermediary institutions such as the cabinet or a deliberative council. The cohesiveness and mutual interaction among the LDP, the financial community, and the bureaucracy have continued to increase. On the one hand, their unity implies a top-heavy decision-making structure; on the other, the cabinet's lack of political leadership and inability to adjust policy have contributed to the growth of sectionalism in the bureaucracy and have also permitted the members of the ruling party to arbitrarily interfere in administrative matters, thereby weakening and diffusing the government's policy-making power. In short, the major characteristic of the decision-making structure after the 1955 merger seems to be the tendency for decision-making power to be concentrated in bureaucratic organizations.

The Policy-Making Process

The Executive Branch. It is extremely difficult to analyze the policy-making process within the executive branch of the government. The legal distribution of power and the formal procedures for policy-making can be found in various statutes,[21] but in the Japanese administration, where "authority and function do not necessarily coincide," [22] the actual decision-making process is obscure and complex. The common bureaucratic concealing of information and esoteric skill in formulating policies tend to cloud the eyes of the casual observer to even such phases of the decision-making process which are to some extent accessible to public observation, such as the policy planning of the investigatory or deliberative boards. Inasmuch as the real role and significance of these advisory boards are unclear, it is misleading to regard these phases as being representative of the whole process of policy-making activity. For example, although it might have been the result of many years of planning by the National Police Agency, a bill to revise the Police Procedure Law came as a complete surprise to the public when it was submitted to the Diet. Likewise, the people are often completely unaware of government decisions on important administrative measures until they are announced on television one day and put into practice the next. The major steps in the policy-making process under the LDP administrations will be traced, in the order of the development, drafting, and decision of policies in the executive branch of the national government.

Demands from the various segments of the citizenry make it necessary to formulate policies to satisfy them. Many proposals first surface when information concerning the involved issues has been gathered and analyzed and a method has been developed. A rather precisely formulated proposal is referred to as a policy outline or program. The policy development stage ends at this point.

The bureaucrats in each ministry are constantly and systematically engaged in the work under their jurisdiction, putting them in an advantageous position for gathering the information necessary for developing policies; ex-bureaucrats within the LDP, therefore, are in a more favorable position for making proposals than professional politicians. But it is one thing to say that they are in a position to collect information on public desires and demands, and entirely another to say that they are actually collecting it. The possibility always exists that instead of acting upon public demands, policy-makers are catering to bureaucratic opportunism. Recently, especially since 1960, the government has begun to show great concern about both opinion polls and public hearings, and each ministry, in its secretariat or in the investigatory section of its bureau, has likewise been trying to keep abreast of public opinion.

The gathering of data on public desires, however, does not by any means imply immediate conversion of such desires into policies. When establishing policy, public officials often have such selfish purposes as the expanding of their authority or regulatory function. (This type of policy-making will be referred to as "downward conversion" while that actually fulfilling public demands will be labeled "upward conversion.") Ideally, each bureaucrat ought to adjust conflicts in accordance with the public interest, but, in reality, the bureaucrats from time to time make policies that favor vested interests, as evidenced by all the various forms of corrupt activities in which the bureaucracy has been found to be involved.

As was manifested in the long-range economic plan initiated during the Hatoyama cabinet and the Ikeda cabinet's comprehensive development plan, the idea of large-scale planning was introduced into political decision-making after 1955, and for the first time a basic framework for the entire process of developing, drafting, and deciding a policy was provided. Indeed, a new type of policy-making emerged in Japan during this period.

A foreshadow of the economic planning in postwar Japan was a report, *Nihonkeizai saiken no kihonmondai* (The basic problems of Japanese economic reconstruction), prepared by a special investigatory committee of the Ministry of Foreign Affairs in March 1946. This was followed by *Keizaifukkōkeikaku* (The economic recovery plan), formulated in 1947 during the Tetsu Katayama cabinet (May 24, 1947–March 10, 1948) by Shūzō Inaba and other members of the Economic Stabilization Board (*Keizaianteihombu*) for use in requesting American recovery assistance. The idea of economic planning was temporarily out of favor under the Yoshida administration (Yoshida insisted on economic recovery under the principle of free economy and did not see the need for any type of government planning). When an economic crisis was created in 1954 by America's discontinuation of special procurements of Japanese products for the Korean War, Hatoyama began to doubt the principle of an unconditionally free economy. As a result, at the end of 1955, *Jiritsukeizai rokkanenkeikaku* (Six-year plan for a self-sufficient economy) became the government's first economic plan after World War II, although it did not go beyond the blueprint stage and did not exert any direct impact upon politics. Subsequent to *Shinchōki keizaikeikaku* (The new long-range economic plan), instituted at the end of 1957 by the Kishi cabinet, *Kōdoseichō shotokubaizō keikaku* (Plan for an economic growth rate and income doubling) was put into effect as a full-fledged economic plan by the Ikeda cabinet.

A series of economic policies were formulated, with the cooperation of scholars, by the staffs of the Economic Stabilization Board (Keizaianteihombu), the Economic Counsel Board (Keizaishingichō), and the Economic Planning Board (Keizaikikakuchō) *Nenjikeizaihōkoku* (Annual report on the state of the economy) (sometimes called *Keizaihakusho* or white paper on the economy), prepared each year since 1947 by the government's economists, has provided administrative agencies and the economic world with important data materials for a macro-analysis of the annual trends of Japan's economy and, theoretically, a source for developing new policies. In addition, since 1955, the Economic Planning Board has been submitting to the cabinet *Keizaimitōshi to keizai un'ei no kihontekitaido* (The fundamental attitude concerning economic prospects and operations), which the government has used as a policy guideline to formulate annual budgets.

This information and material for developing new policies has never been used effectively nor has a consistency of policies within or between concerned ministries been maintained. Consequently, long-range planning becomes situational planning and comprehensive planning turns into jurisdictional planning. This can be attributed to several factors: disregard of administrative planning techniques by the older legislative bureaucrats (the Economic Planning Board has been treated by other bureaucrats as if it were heretic); the persistency of bureaucratic sectionalism; and the intervention of the ruling party in the work of administrative agencies.

A policy outline is given more concrete substance at the drafting stage when a bill or ordinance is written. When a new policy entails a drastic change or requires a budgetary measure, it must take the form of legislation. With regard to many policies, however, which need only decisions by administrative agencies, the process differs from this point on. The drafting stage within each ministry ranges from the initial proposal to the final formulation by bureaucratic specialists. A final draft must be approved by a parliamentary vice-minister (*seimujikan*) in cases where the process is completed within a single ministry and by a conference of business vice-ministers (*jimujikan*) when a cabinet decision is required.

In Japan the drafting of a policy is carried out through the *ringi* system.* According to Kiyoaki Tsuji, the characteristics of the *ringi* system are as follows: all members of an organization participate in the process of deciding on proposals; circulation of a draft proposal throughout an organization will facilitate the flow of administrative information; and a high degree of cooperation can be achieved in administering a policy thus decided, since approval has already been obtained at all levels.[23] Although there are advantages to the system, it takes an unwarranted amount of time to secure final approval, thereby being inefficient; it also disperses decision-making responsibility, thus making it very difficult for high-level policy-makers to exercise direct control (conversely, even an incompetent can maintain his position by endorsing a policy as a mere matter of routine).

The next task is to coordinate and adjust policy alternatives. At all stages of developing and drafting a proposal, concerned ministries communicate and coordinate with each other. While both horizontal and vertical coordination of policy take place, the Legislative Bureau (Hōseikyoku), the Ministry of Finance, the Economic Planning Board, or the Administrative Management Agency (Gyōseikanrichō) undertakes, as a third party, the role of coordinator to dissolve conflicting interests or opinions among the various ministries. Furthermore, in the case of a policy that requires legislation, each ministry seeks the prior approval and support of the LDP in order to ensure smooth passage of the bill, and with important bills, the ministry will

---

* Under this Japanese decision-making procedure, a person initiates and drafts a policy idea, which is then deliberated by various higher-level decision-makers. Sometimes as many as ten different levels of decision-makers are involved before the policy is finalized.

also try to obtain the backing of the JSP and other opposition parties. The party relations section of each ministry (Seitōgakari) attempts to maintain connections with the appropriate departments of the Policy Board of the LDP. Since the end of the Occupation, the ruling party has assumed the powerful position formerly held by the GHQ,SCAP, and has gradually begun to interfere in technical matters of the administrative agencies. The LDP frequently collects political debts from the ministries in the form of concessions or subsidies. There is now a strong trend for the ruling party to directly negotiate with each ministry to jointly decide policies, instead of using the regular institution or organization within which such negotiation should take place.[24]

The criticism that a minister cannot exercise direct control over policies points to a problem concerning ministerial decision-making. Were a minister to veto a draft proposal approved by his subordinates who have many years of technical and administrative experience, not only would his entire bureaucratic force distrust him, but they might drive him out of office; hence, he is bound to rubber-stamp a draft proposal. Conversely, the system of *pro forma* approval of draft proposals enables incompetent ministers to remain in office. Herein lies one reason why national policy as a whole does not suffer from major changes, despite the alleged eccentricities of ministers who represent party factions. Since an unskilled minister spends half of his term studying matters pertaining to his own ministry, he is not likely to make decisions on very many substantive issues during that time. Conversely, a minister considered able and knowledgeable by the bureaucrats may promote the private interests of his own ministry in such a forceful manner that his decisions override other important considerations.

It is necessary for the cabinet to exercise strong leadership in policy-making in order to maintain administration unity and to implement well-planned, comprehensive policies. Various measures have been passed to promote the cabinet's coordination of policies, and it gradually has grown stronger since 1955. The entire executive branch of the government was significantly expanded in terms of both the quality and quantity of its personnel.[25] The cabinet still remains inadequate, however, and cannot exercise its leadership potentialities at all stages of the executive policy-making process. As detailed in *Rinji gyōseichōsakai daiichisenmonbukai daiippan hōkokusho* (Report by the First Section of the First Special Department of the Provisional Administrative Investigatory Commission), the cause of cabinet ineffectiveness must be sought in the coalition aspect of the ruling party, which precipitates the prime minister's difficulties in exercising leadership as well as promoting direct negotiations between the LDP and individual cabinet members, by bypassing the regular channel provided by the cabinet. The yearly difficulties over budget formulation and the establishment of the price of rice illustrate these problems.

The Diet. Budget formulation activities in the Diet can be regarded as one type of legislative policy-making in which the legislature deliberates and approves or rejects those policies which aleady have been decided by the executive branch and submitted to the Diet. Legal authority is thus conferred upon the policies that have been cleared through this process. In addition, legislative policy-making takes the form of private bills initiated by individual Diet members.

There is very little literature dealing with the entire policy-making process within the executive branch, but a fairly large number of studies, based upon both the formal Diet proceedings and actual observation of its legislative process, deal with various characteristics of policy-making in the Japanese legislature. A few problems concerning the legislative activity of the Diet have emerged since the formation of the LDP.

Legislative policy-making has decreased within the totality of national politics. The deliberation of bills in the Diet has been formalized because of the less central position of the Diet within the policy-making structure and the increased ties between the bureaucrats and the ruling party. After the 1955 merger, the Diet seldom performed its main function of deliberating bills, as it had done when it drastically modified the Subversive Activities Prevention Law in 1952.

The budgetary bill for the national government was amended each year by the Diet in 1952, 1953, and 1954, but never after the 1955 merger. The budgets prepared and submitted by the Ministry of Finance, however, have suffered major revisions by the ruling party itself. The 1956 budget was drastically amended by the LDP, which was campaigning in the election for the House of Councillors,[26] and the 1960 budget was tangled up until the very end of the Diet session by interfactional party struggles. Subsequently, deliberation of the annual budget has always occasioned disorder within the Diet.

Nonbudgetary bills pass through a series of deliberations and decisions. Beginning with the drafting stage, repeated deliberations are carried out with the appropriate departments of the Policy Board of the LDP. After approval by the concerned departments, the Policy Council (Seisakushingikai) and the Executive Board (Sōmukai), the bill ultimately receives the formal approval of the cabinet. Thus the various government policies are deliberated and decided upon, beyond any public supervision, outside of the Diet. As long as the ruling LDP maintains an absolute majority, the Diet's business will probably continue to be transacted in a party conference room in the attic. Indeed, anyone familiar with the inner workings of the LDP would contend that an LDP member who belongs to both a standing committee of the Diet and a department of the party Policy Board, having concurrent jurisdiction over the same issue will, as a rule, attend the meetings of the latter more often than those of the former.

Beginning with the Ikeda cabinet, more and more bills have been amended jointly by the LDP and opposition parties. What has been the role of the Diet and particularly the opposition parties in such circumstances? It has been suggested that the Diet performs an educational function when it deliberates bills in its committees and questions the administration's policies. In this context, the party reorganization of 1955, which brought about a serious confrontation between the LDP and the JSP, was useful. When the Hatoyama cabinet submitted various policies to the twenty-fourth session (December 1955–June 1956), the first regular session of the Diet to be convened after the reorganization, severe tensions arose between the two parties over the cabinet-sponsored bills, and the mood of this confrontation carried over into the next session of the Diet.

It must be noted, however, that the LDP and the JSP have jointly amended many bills in the Diet at the deliberation stage. Open hostility between the two major parties, an image which remains strong in the mind of the public after the twenty-fourth Diet session, has in fact been the exception, usually occasioned by a rigid LDP position on issues involving the Constitution, foreign policy, education, or law and order (particularly measures affecting labor unions). Most bills appearing before the Diet have been discussed in a cordial manner, and a compromise agreement has been worked out.[27] Compromise is likely on relatively nonideological issues, particularly bills related to the interests of specially designated industries (for example, the Environment and Sanitation Law) or bills related to regional interests (the Development Law).

Inasmuch as direct confrontation between the two parties occurs only when a "hawk faction" pushes the party leaders into an uncompromising position, it is not surprising that the Diet was relatively quiet during the Ikeda administration, when the party leadership was in the hands of moderate LDP members. The situation becomes heated when the moderate faction, not necessarily indifferent to the power struggle, joins the right wing to maintain the balance of power within the party. Afterward, quiet is soon restored. This cycle was repeated after the Ikeda cabinet, which was characterized by opposition parties cooperating with the LDP to amend bills. Granted that a hasty judgment should not be passed on the merits of this kind of situation, should not the increased number of jointly approved amendments be welcomed as rendering the policy-making process in the Diet more meaningful? According to some accounts given by Diet members, the LDP, when finding an opposition party's bill better than its own, either plagiarizes attractive portions of the bill to amend the government-sponsored bill before the opposition party has had a chance to formally propose it, or has a committee chairman present it in the form of a joint proposal. Table 3 indicates that no single bill presented by the opposition parties as a counterproposal to an LDP bill has received the Diet's approval. If the above account is true, there must be many chairman-sponsored bills which have actually been initiated by the opposition parties. An opposition-party bill has received Diet approval only when submitted in the form of a joint proposal cosponsored by the LDP.

The question of private bills proposed by individual members of the Diet should be touched upon briefly. On February 12, 1963, and each year thereafter the cabinet proposed to the Executive Board of the LDP that individuals be advised to refrain from proposing bills that would require an appropriation, cause a burden upon state funds, or create a revenue deficit after 1964. The establishment of the LDP had not stopped the continuing flow of private bills by Diet members who wanted to promote the interests of their constituents. Because of the government's commitment to a high economic growth rate, most private bills have dealt with regional development plans. Consequently, every part of Japan was covered by the net of special laws designed to promote regional economic development. This caused a member of the Policy Board of the LDP to complain that "this situation will, after all, render ineffective the special laws which put high priority on the development of selected regions." [28] Furthermore, many private bills are opportunistic and ignore long-range, comprehensive planning, though often receiving bipartisan support. Thus, as long as party politicians continue to intensify their demands, the request that governmental power in formulating budgets be vested in the hands of the ruling party must be repeated every year.

There was a noticeable movement within the LDP to increase the private bills (as seen in Table 4). In May 1966, Chairman Eiichi Sakata of the Organization Investigatory Committee (Soshikichōsakai) submitted to the president of the LDP a proposal for strengthening Diet-member–sponsored bills (*Giinrippō no kyōka nitsuite no kengon*). He pointed out that in light of the small number of bills submitted in the past by Diet members, it was necessary to prevent the members of the ruling party from becoming mere yes men for government-sponsored bills and that the policy deliberation in House committees should not be conducted between the opposition parties and bureaucrats, but between the parties. Consequently, he deemed it desirable from the standpoint of parliamentary politics to allow private budgetary bills as long as they did not affect the administration's fundamental or fiscal policies."[29] To avoid the negative effects of private bills, however, Sakata attached a condition that, as a rule, a bill be formulated by the appropriate department of the Policy Board and a necessary adjustment be made with the ministers concerned.

In the opinion of some Liberal Democratic members, Sakata's proposal had strong support among the LDP's rank-and-file members who are not afforded much opportunity to express themselves. Neither the JSP nor other opposition parties would oppose the strengthening of private bills. This kind of reform, once realized, would give the rank-and-file members of the ruling party a stronger sense of responsibility, a greater desire to acquaint themselves with and examine policies, and an increased opportunity to express themselves. It might also add some color and life to the Diet's committee debates which are currently dull gray with bureaucratic responses. At present, because the LDP lacks the ability to initiate policy ideas, proposals always originate with bureaucrats. Also, many Diet members concentrate their energy on economic and industrial development in their

Table 3. Number of bills submitted to the Diet by various parties (sessions 37–46)

Session	Parties introducing bills		No. bills submitted	No. bills passed
	Cabinet		25	23
37th (special) Dec. 5, 1960, through Dec. 22, 1960	House of Representatives	LDP	3	2
		JSP	2	0
		Chairman	2	2
	House of Councillors	LDP	0	0
		JSP	0	0
		DSP	1	0
		Chairman	0	0
	Total		33	27
	Cabinet		211	150
38th (regular) Dec. 26, 1960, through June 8, 1961	House of Representatives	LDP	8	2
		JSP	45(2)	0
		Chairman	7	6
	House of Councillors	LDP	4	2
		JSP	13	0
		DSP	18(1)	0
		Chairman	0	0
	Total		306(3)	160
	Cabinet		75(1)	68(1)
39th (extraordinary) Sept. 25, 1961, through Oct. 31, 1961	House of Representatives	LDP	7(1)	4
		JSP	23	0
		Chairman	4	4
	House of Councillors	LDP		
		JSP	(4)	0
		DSP	11(3)	0
		Chairman	1	1
	Total		121(9)	77(1)
	Cabinet		160(6)	138(2)
40th (regular) Dec. 9, 1961, through May 7, 1962	House of Representatives	LDP	10(4)	4
		JSP	34(13)	0
		Chairman	5	3
	House of Councillors	LDP	1	0
		JSP	8(4)	0
		DSP	7(4)	0
		Chairman	1	0
	Total		226(31)	145(2)

Note: Numbers inside parentheses indicate bills carried over from the previous session and are not included in the preceding numbers.

Table 3. (*continued*)

Session	Parties introducing bills		No. bills submitted	No. bills passed
	Cabinet		3(15)	3(8)
41st (extraordinary) Aug. 4, 1962, through Sept. 12, 1962	House of Representatives	LDP	(5)	0
		JSP	9(26)	0
		Chairman	2(1)	2(1)
	House of Councillors	LDP		
		JSP	1	0
		FPP	0	0
		DSP	7	0
		Chairman	1(1)	(1)
	Total		23(48)	5(10)
	Cabinet		11(4)	2(1)
42nd (extraordinary) Dec. 8, 1962, through Dec. 23, 1962	House of Representatives	LDP	(4)	0
		JSP	(31)	0
		Chairman	1	0
	House of Councillors	LDP	0	0
		JSP	0	0
		FPP	0	0
		DSP	(6)	0
		Chairman		
	Total		12(45)	2(1)
	Cabinet		185	158
43rd (regular) Dec. 24, 1962, through July 6, 1963	House of Representatives	LDP	11	2
		JSP	37	0
		Chairman	5	5
	House of Councillors	LDP	2	2
		JSP	19	0
		FPP	1	0
		DSP	12	0
		Chairman	0	0
	Total		272	167
	Cabinet		36	1
44th (extraordinary) Oct. 15, 1963, through Oct. 23, 1963	House of Representatives	LDP	2	0
		JSP	4	0
		Chairman	1	1
	House of Councillors	LDP	1	0
		JSP	0	0
		FPP	0	0
		DSP	0	0
		Chairman	0	0
	Total		44	2

Table 3. (continued)

Session	Parties introducing bills		No. bills submitted	No. bills passed
	Cabinet		13	11
45th (special) Dec. 4, 1963, through Dec. 18, 1963	House of Representatives	LDP	1	0
		JSP	2	0
		Chairman	2	2
	House of Councillors	LDP	0	0
		JSP	0	0
		FPP	0	0
		DSP	0	0
		Chairman	0	0
	Total		18	13
	Cabinet		174(2)	156(2)
46th (regular) Dec. 20, 1963, through June 26, 1964	House of Representatives	LDP	8(1)	5(1)
		JSP	32	0
		DSP	15	0
		Chairman	7	7
	House of Councillors	LDP	1	1
		JSP	14	0
		FPP	1	0
		DSP	1	0
		Chairman	1	0
	Total		254(3)	169(3)

constituencies as well as on the fixing of rice prices: the most effective means of getting votes. Therefore, these bills must be carefully examined before passage.

The policy-making processes in the executive and legislative branches of government, after the 1955 merger of the conservative parties, differ considerably, depending on the nature of the particular policy in question. Although a lack of sufficient information prohibits any conclusive judgment, two trends in the policy-making process have become conspicuous: the introduction of the idea of planned policy-making, and the formalization of the policy-making process in the Diet.

As has been described, the full-scale development of Japanese capitalism after 1955 forced the government to plan long- and short-

Table 4. Comparison between government bills and private bills in the House of Representatives (sessions 23–34)

Status of passage	Government bills	Private bills
Total number	865	287
Passed unanimously	592	102
Original draft passed	398	86
Unanimous votes with amendment	61	7
Unanimous votes with supplementary resolution	102	10
Unanimous votes with amendment and supplementary resolution	31	4
Decided by the majority votes	215	14
Original draft passed	128	13
Majority votes with amendment	46	1
Majority votes with supplementary resolution	29	0
Majority votes with amendment and supplementary resolution	12	0
Pending	58	168

Source: The Japan Socialist Party Policy Council, ed., *Riron to seisaku* (*Theory and policy*) (Tokyo: 1965), p. 121.

range policies. The idea was first introduced when the Ikeda cabinet, highly regarded by the financial community, developed long-range and comprehensive policies for a high rate of economic growth. Although highly successful in some ways, such policies were accompanied by adverse effects like rising prices, increasing differentials of income, a widening geographical gap in industrial development, and various kinds of pollution. Furthermore, the open-economy policy actively pursued by the Ikeda cabinet revived in a new form old questions regarding the proper size of industries and the need to prohibit excessive competition. The causes of these increasingly serious problems must be sought in the fact that Ikeda constantly gave preferred treatment to the larger businesses and that his policy was oriented toward economic issues and thereby lacked organic connection with noneconomic problems.

The rapid social and economic changes which have occurred ever since 1955 in Japan have demanded that national policies be made and resolutely carried out in comprehensive and long-range perspective. Fulfilling this demand would require strong political leadership capable of breaking the barrier of the ministries' bureaucratic sectionalism and adjusting the conflicting interests among various strata of the public. The cabinet, as the highest ruling body in national politics, is expected to assume that strong leadership, but in reality its members are constantly dependent upon the bureaucrats for policy ideas and formulation. The self-serving ruling party tends to overstep organizational jurisdiction and interfere with administrative agencies. These conditions tend to disperse policy-making in the service of bureaucratic sectionalism and private interest.

A second trend in policy-making after the 1955 merger is that the Diet has decreased its role in the total policy-making process, whereas direct negotiations and compromise between the administration and the LDP have increased. Diet members should exercise their own discretion, exclusive of that of administrative bureaucrats, in representing public demands and interests and in overseeing the various policies decided upon and administered by the executive branch of the national government. The Diet, however, appears to have accepted its self-imposed restrictions on the above functions, as manifested in the twenty-first session. In addition, during the smooth-running Diet sessions beginning with the Ikeda cabinet, the ruling and opposition parties have increased the number of jointly amended bills, thereby diminishing the formal role of the Diet to debate. Once again, in view of the fact that many of these amended bills served vested interests, the weakened Diet contains the same danger of contributing to the dispersion of administration as does direct intervention by the ruling party.

Thus, these characteristics of the policy-making process under the LDP administrations seem to be conducive to irresponsible policy-making and harmful to the public interest. The causes which hinder democratization and the rationalization of policy-making must probably be sought in the peculiar nature of the LDP.

Public Opinion, the Government, and the LDP

Further analysis of the policy-making process requires a study of the way in which the government and the LDP influence public opinion, an important input to decision-making. The government seeks public support in administering its policies and collects information concerning public reactions to them. Seeking public support and collecting information on public demands primarily take the form of manipulating and accommodating public opinion.

Public opinion is gradually becoming an important factor in Japanese politics. Both the government and the LDP are growing very sensitive to the importance of the mass media. The government's interest became particularly conspicuous after 1960, when the political consciousness of the Japanese people started to mature in response to the issues involved in the United States–Japan Security Treaty. The publicity and polls conducted by the government and the ruling party illustrate the importance ascribed to public opinion.

The Publicity Room of the Prime Minister's Secretariat (Sōrifukō-hōshitsu) and the Research Room of the Cabinet Secretariat (Naikakuchōsashitsu) correspond to similar sections in each ministry, designed to promote government publicity and to conduct research on public opinion.

In July 1960, during the Ikeda cabinet, the Publicity Department of the Deliberation Room of the Prime Minister's Secretariat was elevated in the organizational hierarchy and renamed. Its duties include informing the public of government policies and activities and holding public hearings to find out the opinions and demands of the people. For publicity purposes the government utilizes mass media, including radio, television, newspapers, weekly magazines, and official bulletins.[30] To obtain public feedback, the government uses such methods as the monitoring of public reactions to government action,[31] public hearings, and opinion polls.[32] The Publicity Room of the Prime Minister's Secretariat coordinates its activities with the publicity section of each ministry and employs various prefectural agencies as well.

The Research Room of the Cabinet Secretariat was first established in April 1952 in the office of the Prime Minister's Secretariat, as suggested by Taketora Ogata.[*] It alarmed various quarters which feared a revival of the prewar Cabinet Infomation Bureau (Naikakujyōhōkyoku). The revised Cabinet Law of August 1957 moved the Research Room from the Prime Minister's Secretariat to the Cabinet Secretariat. The Cabinet Law and the Cabinet Secretariat Organization Ordinance assign the Research Room the following three functions: collecting and analyzing information on important cabinet policies; coordinating with concerned administrative organs with respect to the preceding function; and publicizing matters pertaining to its own jurisdiction. With respect to collecting information, the Re-

* Taketora Ogata (1888–1956) was a president of the former Liberal Party and an acting president of the LDP.

search Room conducts opinion polls of the public and intellectuals. It selects 50 to 200 intellectuals, representing various academic circles, solicits their opinions on designated topics, and publishes its findings as the "survey of the intellectuals' opinions." [33] It also has commercial pollsters conduct surveys on various public issues.

An examination of available opinion polls indicates that the Publicity Room emphasizes testing public reaction to specific policies while the Research Room selects broader topics with which to work, and that the findings of the two are reported to both the cabinet and the ministries concerned.

In addition to these two specialized agencies, various kinds of councils and investigatory committees exist within the prime minister's office and each ministry to collect information and opinions that can be used in developing government policies. The Administrative Management Agency (Gyōseikanrichō) and the Local Administrative Supervisory Bureau (Chihōgyōseikansatsukyoku) are designed to receive complaints and grievances from the public.

Since November 1966, the Publicity Committee of the LDP has had under it the bureaus of education and propaganda, intelligence, publications, the party bulletin, and culture, as well as a political directory center.[34] The committee itself was established as part of an organizational expansion in 1959.[35] One of the goals set forth in its guidelines for 1960 was to establish a party publicity system under which "publicity, policy, and organization will be organically united at the party's central level" and "coordination between publicity activities and organizations will be promoted at the local level." [36]

The committee's strong determination to strengthen the party organization and its readiness to compete with the popular movement led by the JSP, in anticipation of the proposed ratification of the revised United States–Japan Security Treaty, can be detected in the following policy statement: "In the light of the conspiratorial propaganda advocated by the International Communist Movement and the corresponding movement of domestic leftist forces, we must particularly try to arouse public opinion to protect democracy and parliamentary politics and contribute to the establishment of a peaceful Japan by overcoming the danger of violent revolution." The policy statement also emphasized the use of various media and the necessity of having party policies and guidelines treated in a correct and favorable manner at both the national and local levels. Premier

Kishi tried to manipulate the mass media with the support of the LDP and their prefectural associations, which had protested against mass-media usage in the latter part of May 1960, and even with the co-operation of the United States Embassy. From then on, the publicity activities of the LDP appear to have gradually expanded and strengthened. But a reading of the 1966 publicity guideline indicates that "the systematic publicity activities within the party are still weak," and that "individuals in charge of publicity should be assigned in each party organization, so that materials for public relations and party directives might be promptly and adequately disseminated to the lowest echelons of the party." [37]

The fact is that the retardation of development of the various party branches was precipitated by the prosperity of the citizens' associations for individual candidates. As long as the LDP fails to function as an intermediary between public demand and national politics, there will be no flow of policy ideas from below. While research for developing policy ideas is primarily conducted by the Policy Board, it has a long way to go before it can bring forth policies which reflect the public will. The only incentive now for policy development stems from the representatives' passion for getting votes and the former bureaucrats' desire for control.

The government and ruling party both began to launch full-fledged publicity campaigns and public hearings after the Ikeda era. The Kishi administration actively used mass media for the publicity it needed to push the revision of the security treaty, but it was not until the formation of the Ikeda cabinet that both the government and ruling party, compelled by the impact of the popular movement in connection with the security treaty, seriously initiated publicity campaigns and public hearings. Ikeda stressed popular appeal and tried to address varied and wide audiences. Likewise, the LDP adopted the policy to "give its propaganda a popular image with the cooperation of the mass media." [38] A family edition of the LDP newspaper was created. It is also noteworthy that Ikeda tried to be identified with the people by making frequent television appearances. Television was spreading at a spectacular rate at that time.[39] Although usually an ineffective speaker, when Ikeda spoke to the people on the television screen, he was somewhat successful in his energetic attempt to create an image as a sincere and trustworthy statesman.[40] It is generally felt that his success owed much to the skillful direction of his aides.[41]

The publicity and research activities of the government and ruling party will increasingly utilize television, radio, newspapers, magazines, and other forms of mass media. The press is traditionally guaranteed a measure of free expession, but there is a great danger that the broadcasting industry will be controlled by the government, since it seems to be economically weak and dependent on the government which controls the air waves. The government already appears to be using the mass media energetically for a new type of mass psychology, exemplified by the "Micchie" boom,[42] instead of manipulating the mass media the way it did in prewar days.

Notes to Selection 1

1. The major political forces in the Japanese policy-making structure would include, among others, the Diet, political parties, the bureaucracy, local governmental units, interest groups, and the mass media.

2. Interparty changes are exemplified by the formation of the Democratic Socialist Party (January 1960) and the Fair Play Party (Kōmeitō) (November 1964), as well as the decline and disappearance of the Green Breeze Party (Ryokufūkai) (June 1965). Examples of intraparty changes are the increased influence of ex-bureaucrats in the cabinet, particularly since the Ikeda administration (July 1960–November 1964), and the growing strength of the dove factions who wanted to avoid intraparty confrontations within the LDP.

3. Maurice Duverger, *Les Régimes politiques,* 6th ed. (Paris: Presses Universitaires de France, 1961).

4. This policy was adopted in the tenth session of the Diet on the basis of reports and recommendations made to the chairmen of both houses by a group of Diet members who had visited the United States in 1950 to study the American legislative system. According to this policy, as adopted in Japan, the ruling party is given a chance to examine bills to be submitted by the cabinet and select from them private bills which will be introduced by Diet members. Then the ruling party is called upon to submit the bill to the Diet, after the government has drafted it and made necessary preparation for the legislation. With this application to Japan of the American practice of delegating legislative power to the executive branch of government, the number of bills submitted by the members of the ruling party increased to 32 in the tenth session. But it decreased drastically each successive session, partly due to an inconvenience of the method, until the fifteenth session in which it was discontinued. Tatsuo

Satō, "Hōritsu ga umareru made" [Coming of law into being], *Hōritsu Jihō,* January 1953.

5. For example, in the sixteenth session of the Diet the Antitrust Law was revised, and such important bills as the Veterans' Pension Law, the Criminal Procedure Law, and the Tax Law were greatly amended. Likewise, in the nineteenth session, in which the revision of the Police Procedure Law was proposed, the Liberal Party, the Progressive Party, and the Japan Liberal Party added a joint amendment thereto.

6. Especially important were the revision of the Anti–Subversive Activity Law in the thirteenth session and two education laws in the twentieth session.

7. As a result of the second revision of the Diet Law in the second session (December 1947–July 1948), the Joint Committee on Legal Statutes had lost the power to make recommendations to the cabinet. Inejirō Asanuma, the chairman of the Diet Steering Committee, who proposed the revision of the law, failed to give a reason for the revision. *Dainikai kokkaishūgi'in kaigiroku* 70gō [Proceedings of the second session of the House of Representatives, no. 70].

8. The revised Diet Law in the second session reduced an open debate to once every three weeks.

9. Secretariat of the House of Councillors, *Kokkaihō kaiseikeika gaiyō* [Summary of the passage of the revised Diet Law], 1959, p. 287.

10. Kiyoaki Tsuji, "Kanryōkikō no onzon to kyōka" [Fostering and strengthening the bureaucratic structure], in Yoshitake Oka, ed., *Gendai Nihon no seiji katei* [The political process in modern Japan] (Tokyo, 1958), p. 112. He lists the following factors as contributing to the expansion of bureaucratic forces during these reform periods: the indirect government by the Occupation force; the alleged neutrality of the bureaucrats, a myth which had grown in the minds of the people since the Meiji era; and the failure of the ruling political party to effectively remove bureaucratic dominance in politics.

11. The administrative state is described as a form of the nation-state corresponding to the stage of monopolistic capitalism. Around 1955, with a great increase in the administrative function in Japan, postwar capitalism appeared to have developed on a full scale.

12. The Executive Board members strongly criticized a conciliatory attitude which Minister Matsuda took in negotiating with the representatives from the Japan Teachers' Union (Nikkyōso) on the issue of the proposed evaluation of teachers' work efficiency. *Mainichi,* February 28, 1960.

13. In 1964, when the established price of rice was unprecedentedly high, Munenori Akagi, the Minister of Agriculture, told the press that "I was surprised by the high price, but Finance Minister Kakuei Tanaka

must have been surprised even more than I was." This price-fixing took place one day before a general election. *Asahi,* September 9, 1964.

14. Robert A. Scalapino and Jyunnosuke Masumi, *Parties and Politics in Contemporary Japan* (Berkeley: University of California Press, 1962), Table 3 in Appendix.

15. Jyunnosuke Masumi, "1955nen no seijitaisei" [The political structure in 1955], *Shisō,* June 1964, pp. 64–65.

16. See *Rinji gyōsei chōsakai dai'ichisenmonbukai dai'ippan hōkokusho* [The report of the first section of the first special department of the Provisional Administrative Investigatory Committee], September 1963.

17. Remark by Seijyūrō Arafune, the Minister of Transportation. *Mainichi,* August 10, 1966, evening edition.

18. The opposition movement to the Small and Medium Enterprises Organization Law (Chūshōkigyō Dantaisoshikihō) of March 1957 best illustrates this. *Sankei,* March 13, 1957.

19. For example, it is reported that on September 6, 1966, Taizō Ishizaka, the chairman of the Federation of Economic Organizations, and Aiichirō Fujiyama, the chairman of the Japan Chamber of Commerce, met with Nobusuke Kishi, the secretary-general of the LDP, and conveyed the wish of the financial circle for the resignation of Premier Hatoyama. The History Study Association, ed., *Sengo nihonshi* [Postwar Japanese history] (Tokyo, 1961), vol. 3, pp. 117–118. The financial community is reported to have strongly supported Kishi, Ikeda, and Satō for the premiership.

20. See Suruki Akagi, "Gyōseisekinin no riron to kōzō" [Theory and structure of administrative responsibility], *Shisō,* June 1965, p. 18; see also the special feature, "Jichitai to chiikiminshushugi" [Local self-government and regional democracy], *Shisō,* May 1961; Nikō Kawanaka, "Chihōdantai nitaisuru chūōseifu no atsuryoku" [The pressure of the central government upon the local autonomy], *Hōritsu Jihō,* July 1955, pp. 41–48.

21. The distribution of power is stipulated in the Cabinet Law, the National Administrative Organization Law, and others; distribution of power and decision-making procedures at ministerial levels are stipulated in various regulations and ordinances.

22. Kiyoaki Tsuji, "Decision-Making in the Japanese Government: A Study of Ringisei," in Robert E. Ward, ed., *Political Development in Modern Japan* (Princeton, 1968), pp. 457–475.

23. Ibid.; and Nikō Kawanaka, *Gendai no kanryosei* [Modern bureaucracy] (Tokyo, 1962).

24. According to Masao Maruyama of Tokyo University: "The modern organization and institution, by nature, contain a danger of becoming rigid and inelastic because their original functions cease to work. Furthermore, the area is often very wide in which social adjustment takes place

from the beginning without the intermediary of such organizations" in Japan. He thus points out the tendency for problems to be resolved directly, without the intermediary of the organization or institution. Masao Maruyama, *Gendaiseiji no shisō to kōdō* [Thought and behavior in modern Japanese politics] (Tokyo, 1956), vol. 2, p. 431.

25. The Committee of Cabinet Members (a round-table conference) and a coordination organ therefore were established to discuss designated matters.

26. The Ministry of Finance proposed an increase in national railroad fares and the consumer price of rice to make up for the deficit created by food management budgets, but the LDP leaders stopped it for fear of the impact of such increases upon voters.

27. According to an account given by an informant in the Diet, 73 percent of all bills from the thirty-eighth through the fortieth sessions were passed by unanimous votes of all parties. See also The Japan Socialist Party Policy Council, ed., *Riron to seisaku* [Theory and policy] (Tokyo, 1965), p. 122.

28. *Asahi*, August 9, 1964.

29. *Mainichi*, May 28, 1966.

30. The Publicity Room publishes the graphic *Photo, Kaisetsu: Seifu no mado* [Window of the government], the gazette appendix, *Shiryōban* [Materials], *Kabeshashinshimbun* [Wall photo], *Seifukunkōbutsu geppō* [Monthly index to government publications]. The Publicity Room of the Prime Minister's Secretariat, *Shigoto no aramashi* [Outline of works] (Tokyo, 1966), pp. 8–9.

31. In June 1962, the government initiated a poll in which it sought the opinions of 455 respondents chosen from various social backgrounds on various national topics about ten times a year. In July 1966, for example, a poll was taken on the subject of one hundred years of the Meiji era.

32. According to *Shōwa 40nendo kōhōkōchōkatsudo* [Publicity and public-hearing activities in 1965], published by the Publicity Room, 21 public-opinion polls were conducted on the government's policies and general trends. The Publicity Room selects government policy topics at the request of each ministry and decides on questionnaire items with the consultation of concerned departments and bureaus; it selects topics and decides on questionnaire items on general trends with the ministries. It also conducts polls when the government urgently needs information on current topics.

33. It had the Domestic and International Survey Association (Naigai jōsei chōsakai) conduct these polls, for example, in May 1966 on "Communist China" and in August on "What do you expect of the Satō cabinet?"

34. It is an organ to compile the directory for distributing publicity materials.

35. The organizational development of the LDP was divided into three stages: an initiation period (1955–1957), an expansion period (1958–1959), and a strengthening period (1961–1966). As a result of intensive efforts for expansion, its party organizations covered almost all areas in Japan by the end of 1960. The Liberal Democratic Party, ed., *Jiyū-minshutō jyūnen no ayumi* [Ten years of experience for the LDP] (Tokyo, 1966), pp. 213 ff.

36. The Liberal Democratic Party, *Wagatō no kihonyōkō* [Basic platform of our party] (Tokyo, 1960), pp. 42 ff.

37. The Liberal Democratic Party, *Wagatō no kihonhōshin* [Basic policies of our party] (Tokyo, 1966), pp. 118 ff.

38. The Liberal Democratic Party, *Wagatō no kihonhōshin* (Tokyo, 1962), p. 75.

39. According to *NHK nenkan* [Japan Broadcasting Corporation yearbook, 1965], television viewing grew at the rate of 11.0% in 1958, 23.2% in 1959, 64.8% in 1962, and 83.0% in 1964.

40. He appeared on an NHK program, "Discussion with the Prime Minister," which started in the fall of 1961.

41. For example, his cold-looking gold-rimmed glasses were replaced by ones with tortoise-shell frames.

42. In October 1958, public opposition to the government's attempt to revise the Police Procedure Law increased. Subsequently, when Premier Kishi abandoned his plan to have the law revised by a forceful manner, the growing antigovernment sentiment subsided somewhat among the public. In the midst of this political tension, the Imperial Household Conference announced on November 27 the engagement of the crown prince with Miss Michiko Shōda, daughter of Hidesaburō Shōda, the president of Nisshin Flour Mill Company. The press and other mass media gave her the nickname "Micchie" and enthusiastically reported their engagement as a symbol of the democratized imperial household, in that the prince met the commoner through playing tennis and was to marry her for love. Their wedding ceremony on April 10, 1959, marked the apex of the public jubilation. The "Micchie" boom was very effective in decreasing public dissatisfaction with a series of reactionary policies imposed by the Kishi administration.

The Small and Medium-Sized Enterprises Organization Law*

NAOKI KOBAYASHI

Planning the Legislation

Initiation and Debate. Those who were involved in the planning for the Small and Medium-Sized Enterprises Organization Law (Chūshōkigyō Dantaisoshikihō), hereafter referred to as SMEOL, are not always in agreement on who originated the bill and when and how it took place. Bureaucrats, members of the ruling and opposition parties, and members of the interest group, the Japanese Political League of Small and Medium-Sized Enterprises (Nihon Chūshōkigyō Seijirenmei) (JPLSME), all claim that they dominated the planning stage of the bill. Such conflicting claims for credit are not necessarily based on the egocentric or dogmatic ideas of the participants, but may very well be the result of the complexity of the legislative process and the various perspectives thereon. If the official drafting of a bill is to be regarded as the first step of legislation, then the origin of the SMEOL can be clearly traced to the establishment by the House of Representatives, in June 1956, of the Small and Medium-Sized Enterprises Promotion Council (Chūshōkigyō Shinkō Shingikai). But if we were to probe into the historical antecedents of the SMEOL, we could go back as far as the Employment Security Law of 1952 and the Small and Medium-Sized Enterprises Cooperative Union Law of 1949, or even the Guild Law in the Meiji era. In Japan, it is the bureaucrats who have traditionally exercised initiative and assumed the major role in legislation. Nonetheless, if the force which guides

---

* This selection is taken from "Chūshōkigyō dantai soshikihō no rippōkatei," in *Tokyo daigaku kyōyōgakubu shakaigaku kiyō* (The Social Science Bulletin, Faculty of Liberal Arts, the University of Tokyo), vol. 7 (1958), pp. 34–55, 84–96. Translated and reprinted with permission of the author.

the bureaucrats to draft a piece of legislation exists elsewhere, that which gives the impetus to represent social demands and to put them in the policy-making structure can be discovered. According to Tameji Kawakami, the director of the Small and Medium-Sized Enterprises Agency (Chūshōkigyōchō), Yasuhiro Nakasone, an LDP member in the House of Representatives, proposed the creation of the Small and Medium-Sized Enterprises Promotion Council in order to cope with the precarious economic conditions among Japan's small enterprises. Outside the Diet, Gisuke Ayukawa* and the JPLSME, which he heads, responded to the complaints of businessmen about the inadequacy of the Employment Security Law and the Small and Medium-Sized Enterprises Cooperative Union Law and launched a well-organized and heavily financed campaign for the passage of their version of the SMEOL.

The formal inauguration of the JPLSME in April 1956 was preceded by the work of a preparatory committee, which met in December 1955 and compiled a list of policy objectives including "the passage of a law to strengthen the unity of small and medium enterprises." In May 1956, the JPLSME published its first draft of an outline of the Small and Medium-Sized Enterprises Organization Bill, apparently referred to at a meeting of the Small and Medium-Sized Enterprises Promotion Council. The JPLSME, which was created as a pressure group, increased the area of its activities as its organization expanded. It is highly probable that the JPLSME's draft and its lobbying activities greatly influenced the content, form, and timing of

---

* Gisuke Ayukawa was born in 1880 in the Yamaguchi prefecture. After studying engineering at Tokyo University, he studied metal casting in the United States. In the prewar period, he built the Nissan Conglomerate by amalgamating Nissan Automobile Manufacturing Company, Hitachi Manufacturing Company, Japan Mining Company, Nissan Chemical Company, Japan Oil Company, Japan Refrigerator Company, Japan Coal Company, Nissan Fire Insurance Company, and many others. During World War II, he served as an industrial consultant to the Manchukuo as well as being a member of the House of Peers. After he was released from the Sugamo War Criminal Prison, where he had been detained as a suspect, he worked during the Kishi administration as the top economic advisor to the cabinet. He was elected to the House of Councillors both in 1953 and 1959, but when his second son, a successful candidate to the House of Councillors, was charged with having violated the Election Control Law, he and his son resigned. He was not only the president of the JPLSME and the Japan Political League of Agriculture and Fishery (Nihon Nōsangyō Seijirenmei), but also a consultant or chairman of several companies including Nissan Industrial Company.

the government's SMEOL bill. Indeed, until shortly before the formation of the Small and Medium-Sized Enterprises Promotion Council, the administrative agencies had neither thought of anything like the SMEOL nor attempted to unify the Small and Medium-Sized Enterprises Cooperative Union Law and the Employment Security Law. Even when the textile industry expressed a desire for the amalgamation of the regulatory union and the cooperative union by the means of the Employment Security Law, the Small and Medium-Sized Enterprises Agency supported the status quo and disapproved of any move toward the amalgamation.[1] The rapid change in the government's attitude cannot be fully understood unless the activities of both the JPLSME and the bureaucrats are examined. Apart from the question of whether or not Gisuke Ayukawa exerted "pressure from above," the JPLSME's draft proposal undoubtedly had a significant impact upon the legislative process of the present law. What Ayukawa called "the boiler of the Japanese Political League of Small and Medium-Sized Enterprises" constituted the main source of energy with which to push the bill through the Diet.

The influence of the JPLSME was not so great, however, as to completely dominate the planning of the government's bill. Ayukawa's proposal for nearly unconditional and compulsory union membership was severely criticized from the beginning by leading bureaucrats and was so much modified in the government's bill as to arouse great dissatisfaction within the JPLSME.[2] There is no evidence to indicate that strong pressure was applied by the JPLSME on the bureaucrats of the Small and Medium-Sized Enterprises Agency. According to Kenkichi Matsuzaki, director of the JPLSME's Policy Bureau, at the legislation stage political pressure directed at the Diet and the major parties is more effective than that directed at the bureaucrats. It appears that the Small and Medium-Sized Enterprises Promotion Council was not a direct target of the interest-group activities and was able to perform its duties in a relatively neutral manner. Just like many other councils created by the government at that time, however, a problem did arise concerning the selection of its members.[3]

The question of how to organize the small and medium-sized enterprises was handled by the fifteen-member second department of the council. Except for its chairman, Professor Atsutarō Yamanaka of Hitotsubashi University, every member of the department came from the top echelons of the business community. Apart from the criticism that consumers and small enterprisers were not represented on the council, there were no allegations of political bias regarding the selection of the council's members. The council was given only six months to deliberate the issue and had to get down to business promptly. Twelve meetings were held between August 3 and December 24, 1956, when the final proposal was submitted by the council. Various problems in strengthening the organization of the small and medium-sized enterprises were studied. It is noteworthy that the opinions presented by each council member at the second meeting in mid-August contained rather positive suggestions for strengthening the organization of the small enterprises. Indeed, the Small and Medium-Sized Enterprises Promotion Council's final draft, which considerably weakened the requirements for compulsory union membership and strengthened collective bargaining, more closely resembled the JSP's version of the SMEOL than that of the government.[4] The formulation of the draft that later became the government bill started in full scale around November 1956 without waiting for the final proposal of the Small and Medium-Sized Enterprises Promotion Council.

Submission of the Bill to the Diet. The cabinet submitted to the Diet on April 5, 1957, the SMEOL bill, a first draft of which had been worked out by the Cooperative Union Section of the Small and Medium-Sized Enterprises Agency nearly nine months before, approximately six months after the Small and Medium-Sized Enterprises Promotion Council had completed its proposal and two months after the JSP had submitted their version to the Diet. Where was the bill prior to submission to the Diet? What kind of examination was it given? Did the government have any special reason for suddenly submitting the bill at the last minute of the twenty-sixth session, when it was obvious that deliberation time would run out?

On the first day of the legislature's deliberations, Takeo Tanaka, a JSP member, was highly critical of the government:

The method used by the government to submit its own bill is extremely unfair. What was the government doing after the Small and Medium-Sized Enterprises Promotion Council had presented its proposal last October? I was told that the Legislative Bureau of the cabinet and the Fair Trade Commission strongly opposed the government's bill on the ground that it might be in violation of the Constitution and that opposition from economic interests caused disagreement and confusion within the ruling party. That's why the government was forced to delay presenting the bill until today. Our JSP bill was presented on February 13, but it was ignored for nearly two months and in fact deliberation of our bill was obstructed. The Kishi cabinet will not have any excuse against a charge that it was not determined to resolve basic problems of the small and medium-sized enterprises (applause).

Opposition interest groups such as the National Consumers Liaison Association (NCLA) (Zenkoku Shōhishadantai Renrakukai) attribute the government's delay to their effective opposition to the bill. But it appears that a more basic reason can be found in the need for "cautious deliberation" to adjust differing opinions within the government and the LDP.

Both the Fair Trade Commission (Kōseitorihikiiinkai) and the Legislative Bureau of the cabinet expressed doubts about the legality of the SMEOL as early as October 1956, when the Small and Medium-Sized Enterprises Promotion Council was still working out a draft proposal. Both government agencies feared that it would violate the Antitrust Law and even the Constitution. The opinion of the Fair Trade Commission received much attention in the newspapers and also was published separately on December 12, 1956. A summary of the commission's points follows. Regulating all kinds of enterprises and compelling every enterpriser to join a union will be inappropriate, however necessary unions may be to organize small and medium-sized enterprises; regulating nonunion members by a loose standard will restrict legitimate activities of nonunion members and will infringe upon the interests of consumers as well; it will be difficult to make big enterprises agree to collective bargaining and conclude a collective agreement favorable to small and medium enterprises. Such a collective agreement, even if effective, will contain the danger of bringing about other cartels and defeat its own purpose. Furthermore, if the competitor is another small or medium enterpriser, conflict will merely be aggravated.

The Fair Trade Commission, which was considered a guardian of the Antitrust Law, expressed stiff opposition to a bill of strong regulatory nature. The extent of their opposition to the bill, particularly concerning the first point above, is reflected in the remarks which Masatoshi Yokota, chairman of the commission, made at a plenary meeting of the House of Representatives on April 5, 1957:

The Fair Trade Commission has studied with care the original draft of the SMEOL. After much deliberation we proposed certain amendments that would bring the bill more in line with the policies of the Small and Medium-Sized Enterprises Agency and other concerned agencies and that would make it less likely to conflict with the Antitrust Law. On the problem of compulsory membership, however, no consensus was reached. I hope that the Diet will carefully deliberate on this point.

He went on to testify at the plenary meeting of the House of Representatives on April 16:

Our amendments were brought before the conference of vice-ministers after no consensus had been reached on this point among the agencies. . . . Contrary to our practice, our director attended the meeting and explained our position. . . . But the proposal was submitted to the Diet without this issue being solved.

A similar objection arose within the Legislative Bureau of the cabinet because the bureau suspected that the stipulation in the government bill providing for compulsory union membership would violate the freedom of association guaranteed in the Constitution. Much of the few months prior to the presentation of the government's bill to the Diet appears to have been spent gaining bureaucratic support including that of the ministries of Agriculture and Welfare. As pointed out before, though, the bill was submitted with no consensus on the question of compulsory membership, a crucial issue which the opposition parties were going to attack later.

The government's bill was drafted by the Small and Medium-Sized Enterprises Agency in the summer of 1956, without waiting for the council's recommendation. At almost the same time, the JPLSME announced a third draft of its version, which included strong regulation of union membership as suggested by President Gisuke Ayukawa. The JPLSME threatened to present its own bill to the Diet unless its proposal on the issue of compulsory membership was incorporated somehow into the government version of the SMEOL. Subsequently, compromises were reached at a meeting of the Small and Medium-Sized Enterprises Special Council of the LDP, attended by department and section chiefs of the government and Kenkichi Matsuzaki from the JPLSME. The decision to have the government present the bill undoubtedly shows that the JPLSME reluctantly conceded to the relatively moderate government position concerning compulsory membership. The government in return agreed to adopt the title of the bill as proposed by the JPLSME.

Furthermore, both the government and the ruling party could not disregard big business, which formed the backbone of the conservative government. Big business could not be indifferent to the proposed SMEOL inasmuch as it would be directly affected by the organization of small and medium-sized enterprises, particularly in collective bargaining. The more the government accommodated the demands of the JPLSME, the more it had to take into account the interest of big business. According to the remarks made by the vice-director of the Federation of Economic Organizations, "Ever since the government began to prepare the present bill, we have carefully studied both private and government opinions." On March 12, after meeting with the government, its standing committee came to the judgment that the government bill "would be damaging to the principle of capitalistic economy," and that "it would inform the government and the Diet of its opposition to the bill." [5]

There is no way of knowing how the Federation of Economic Organizations conveyed its decision to oppose the government's bill or how the government explained its position. Nonetheless, it seems that the government succeeded in avoiding a confrontation with the big-business group by considerably modifying its position on union negotiation (as compared with the JSP's version of the bill) and conferring upon the unions a strong collective-bargaining power. Although representatives of the Federation of Economic Organizations and the Kansai Economic Association did testify before the Diet and an investigatory committee to express their opposition to the strong regulations that would impinge upon the principle of free competition, the ironing out of differences that the government had undertaken prior to the presentation of its own bill to the Diet prevented these big-business groups from marshaling all their forces against the government's bill.

Thus, prior to formal debate in the Diet, the bill had gone through a political process of negotiations and compromise and had become enmeshed in the complex of conflicting interests and tensions both in and out of the government and the ruling party.

Even before the government submitted its bill to the Diet various interest groups were heatedly debating the idea of legislating the SMEOL. Indeed, for a half-year after October 1956, the noise of such debate was deafening. Press coverage of the bill in this period was often critical. Such major newspapers as *Asahi, Yomiuri, Maini-*

chi, Tokyo, and *Tokyo Times* regularly reported detailed analyses and editorialized on the developments of the issue. With the exception of *Nihon Keizai Shimbun* (Japan economics), the major newspapers voiced opposition to the SMEOL on the basis that the restriction of business by such a stringent law would adversely affect the consumer in Japan. According to some sources, they were also concerned about the impact of the SMEOL upon the management of the newspaper business, in that the proposed law would encourage the middlemen in the industry, who deliver papers to the public, to unite and demand collective bargaining with the management. Thus, it seemed that under the guise of protecting consumers the newspaper owners engaged in a vigorous campaign against the bill in cooperation with other opposition groups like the NCLA. But self-interest does not seem to be the only ground for their opposition. For example, *Mainichi's* position was ambivalent in that it criticized the bill from the standpoint of the consumers' interest while editorially acknowledging "the right of the organized small and medium enterprises to negotiate." Nonetheless, public opinion was all the more aroused when the press was drawn into the struggle.

Decision-Making Process within the Parties and the Diet

Just as interest groups' attitudes toward the SMEOL reflected complex and conflicting social interests, intra- and inter-party tensions reflected the ideological differences of Diet members and their varying assessments of constituent interests. A compromise between the ruling and opposition parties, when effected in the absence of sufficient intra-party consensus within the JSP, led to split voting by the JSP members of both Houses.

Decision-Making Process within the LDP. Although the government had reached a compromise with the JPLSME and had coordinated various opinions of the concerned bureaucrats, an objection was raised from within the LDP. Katsuichi Yamamoto, an LDP member in the House of Representatives, bitterly attacked the government bill on the ground that "the proposed SMEOL would bring about an undesirable change in the economic bases of our country." By reiterating the critical view held by the Fair Trade Commission in 1956, he argued that the bill would unduly control the free economy and that it would be better to aid small and medium-sized business enterprises through reduced taxes and other financial measures. He supported the consumer-oriented view of the NCLA and other opposition groups. The LDP leadership as well as the interest groups favoring the bill were reportedly surprised by his further remarks that the JSP bill, which opposed a free economy, was actually more liberal than that of the government that claimed to uphold a free economy. This happened when the government was about to settle the question of the formal title of the bill and whether the bill should be submitted as government-sponsored or private. It was also shortly after the JSP had presented their bill. While Yamamoto's remarks may have encouraged the JSP and other opposition groups they had little effect within the LDP. According to one of the party's proponents of the bill, Yamamoto was not speaking for big business and had little influence with his colleagues.

On the basis of the final compromise worked out with the JPLSME and the study made at the February 16 meeting of the Small and Medium-Sized Enterprises Special Council within the LDP, "both the government and the LDP have reportedly agreed to have Kūshō Ogasa, a Liberal Democrat, propose a bill which would combine the government's bill and the JPLSME's proposal." Mikio Mizuta, the minister of International Trade and Industry, kept insisting, however, on a government-sponsored bill which was finally accepted at a cabinet meeting held toward the end of March. According to one newspaper, "This bill was unusually controversial even before its presentation to the Diet . . . , and probably because of its highly political nature it took the bill an unexpectedly long time to be accepted within the LDP." Indeed, it was so difficult to unite the LDP behind the bill that the JSP's bill was submitted earlier.

In the course of a Diet interpellation on April 5, 1957, Takeo Tanaka stated in part: "I understand that at the March 26 Executive Board meeting of the LDP, which witnessed flaring tempers and business being transacted in mass confusion, it was decided to submit the bill in its original form with the understanding that it would be modified in the Diet." But it is interesting to note that the JSP, to which Tanaka belonged, experienced more internal disunity at the twenty-seventh session than did the LDP. As far as the government's bill was concerned, the relatively weak opposition launched by big business, including the Federation of Economic Organizations, was a factor which successfully pushed forward the present legislation without serious difficulties. With the exception of the insurance companies that joined the minister of Finance to vigorously oppose that portion of the government's bill which would create the Fire Safety Cooperative Union (Kasaikyōsai Kyōdōkumiai), no other opposition by big business seriously divided the LDP into supporters of big business and those of small and medium business. Another factor favorable to the proponents of the government bill can be found in the committee system under which it is difficult for ordinary Diet members to understand such complicated bills as the SMEOL.

Decision-Making Process in the Diet: Confrontation and Compromise between the LDP and the JSP. The JSP submitted their version of the SMEOL fifty days earlier than the government, which rushed its bill to the Diet after the lapse of two-thirds of the twenty-sixth session. The debate on the two versions of the SMEOL was characterized first by confrontation between the LDP and the JSP and eventually culminated in a compromise bill. With a general election in the offing, both parties were obliged to give the appearance of being "supporters of small and medium enterprisers" in the face of anti-SMEOL movements in and out of the parties, and a compromise had to be reached lest they should be blamed for the failure to pass a law for the less fortunate segment of Japanese business.

The major contentions of each version of the SMEOL, particularly with respect to compulsory membership and collective bargaining, had been presented on the Diet floor by the end of the first month of debate. The controversy in the twenty-sixth session of the Diet reached its climax during the "golden week" * of May 1957. Starting in the first part of April, both parties were bombarded by interest-group activities for and against the present legislation. Pressed to find a compromise solution, both parties energetically worked throughout the holidays of May 2–4. They selected a bipartisan subcommittee which formulated a jointly modified bill including the following main points: (a) a new title for the bill; (b) the increased duty of big business or nonunion members of small and medium enterprises to respond to the union's demand for negotiation;[6] (c) the degree of economic depression shall be determined by the Small and Medium-

---

* April 29 (the Emperor's birthday), May 3 (Constitution Day), and May 5 (Children's Day) are national holidays, and the Japanese workers can have three days off in addition to the regular weekly day off. The press has referred to this as the "golden week" for the workers.

Sized Enterprises Promotion Council;[7] (d) those small and medium enterprisers who cannot comply with an order to join a union shall be allowed to remain as nonmembers;[8] (e) the establishment of the Fire Safety Cooperative Union and Business Cooperative Subunion (Jigyōkyōdōshōkumiai);[9] and (f) the exclusion of the Agricultural Cooperatives, the Fishing Cooperatives, and the Livelihood Cooperative Association (Seikatsukyōdōkumiai) from complying with the order for collective bargaining.[10] The government's bill was accepted in substance while the JSP succeeded in modifying the compulsory membership clause and amending the Cooperative Union Law. On this point seeds were sown for further trouble within the JSP.

It was two days after the closing of the twenty-sixth Diet session that the Executive Board of the LDP and the Diet Liaison Committee of the JSP finally worked out a jointly amended bill. The Financial Department of the LDP's Policy Council (Seisakushingikai Zaimukai) attempted in vain to remove from the modified bill the JSP's proposal for the Fire Safety Cooperative Union, and finally, in the afternoon of May 7, 1957, the committee passed and sent the joint proposal to the House of Councillors. In the upper house the JSP was strongly opposed to the compulsory membership clause, and the LDP members of the Financial Committee, who represented the interest of the Ministry of Finance, and the local administrative commissioners (Chihōgyōseiiin) also favored revision of the proposed Fire Safety Cooperative Union. Therefore, the plenary session of the House of Representatives reconvened at the last minute of the session (i.e., 11:50 P.M. on May 18) and voted to extend the session another day for the leaders of the two parties to continue their negotiations. But in the end the lower house shelved the jointly amended SMEOL bill, while passing an environmental sanitation law and defeating a bill designed to revive the national foundation day.

The Commerce and Industry Committee of the House of Councillors continued its deliberation on the legislation throughout the off-session period of the Diet and conducted public hearings between June and October 1957 at Sapporo, Sendai, Kanazawa, Osaka, Nagoya, and Fukuoka. At the same time, the various interest groups continued their activities. The Diet began its twenty-seventh extraordinary session on November 1, 1957, with the debate on the proposed SMEOL, but in the midst of vigorous petitioning and lobbying neither the government nor the JPLSME could expect easy pas-

sage of their bill. Heated debates, although mostly repetitious, reached
their climax on November 12 when the leaders of the two parties
disagreed with each other over the question of whether or not the
bill should be modified for the second time. The JSP leaders held a
Central Executive Board meeting on the same day and tried in vain
to persuade the party's members in the House of Councillors to vote
for the bill as initially modified, whereupon the JSP members were
split in both houses. Nonetheless the SMEOL was passed in its
initially modified form in the plenary meeting of the House of Councillors on November 13, 1957, and in the plenary meeting of the
House of Representatives on the following day. What was the reason
for the JSP, ahead of the LDP in presenting their version of the
SMEOL, to have been so split that JSP members in the upper house
voted one way while their colleagues in the lower house voted the
other?

Decision-Making Process within the JSP. The JSP has always
demonstrated its concern over the problems of small and medium-
sized enterprises. "As the first step in achieving an improved division
of labor among small and medium enterprises under the socialistic
planned economy," the JSP made it its basic policy to "correct the
unbalance between the big and small enterprises." Based on this
fundamental policy, the Socialists, in the fall of 1956, promulgated
three bills: a bill designed to secure industrial fields for small and
medium enterprises, a bill to organize small and medium enterprise,
and a bill to regulate commerce. These bills, presented to the Diet in
February 1957, proposed that the problem of the small and medium-
sized enterprises be approached in such a comprehensive manner as
to solve the contradictions of Japanese capitalism and that comprehensive legislative measures be initiated from a more systematic perspective. Granted that these JSP bills were probably given some
thrust by the JPLSME and, consequently, were largely motivated to
boost the JSP's strength in the forthcoming general election for the
House of Councillors, still they are based on the JSP's five-year economic plan and call for strengthened collective bargaining as opposed
to compulsory membership as proposed by the LDP and the JPLSME.

The JSP did not seem to have definitively solved the question of
whether small and medium-sized enterprises in Japan should be regarded essentially as an "ally" of the Socialist front or as an anti-
revolutionary force. Therefore, a basic disagreement arose between

the left and right wings of the party over whether the JSP should be a "party for a class or the people," a disagreement which was exposed to the public when the JSP cast split votes in the Diet on the jointly modified version of the SMEOL. The split voting reflected not so much a lack of party discipline as the inability to form a theory incorporating small and medium business and the SMEOL into the Socialist doctrine. On the one hand, the JSP was praised by the NCLA who said that "we must express our deep respect for the views held by the men of good sense in the House of Councillors"; on the other hand, the party was bitterly attacked by the pro-SMEOL interest groups. Whatever the internal circumstance may have been, it must have been embarrassing for the JSP to vote one way in the House of Councillors and the other way in the House of Representatives. Criticism against the JSP for its lack of discipline and unity, however unfounded, must have been a hard blow to the party.

The JSP's left wing, dominated by labor unions and powerful in the House of Councillors, expressed strong dissatisfaction with the compromise bill which their colleagues in the House of Representatives had worked out with the LDP. When they failed to drastically revise the bill, particularly with relation to the deletion of the compulsory membership provision in Article 55, the left-wing members were obliged *in toto* to vote against the bill. Chōzaburō Mizutani and Ikkō Kasuga, the JSP's main proponents of the SMEOL, "reached a compromise with the LDP in the House of Representatives too soon, when the rank-and-file members could not make up their minds" and, moreover, they later failed to unify party opinion behind themselves. A further analysis suggests that consensus probably could not have been reached even had they been granted more time because of the different backgrounds of the JSP members in the Commerce and Industry Committee of the House of Councillors. Mizutani and Kasuga came from the small and medium-sized enterprises and also had personal ties with the JPLSME whereas other JSP members did not, and this created different approaches to the bill. Kasuga first expressed dissatisfaction with the jointly revised bill in the House of Councillors and tried in vain to further modify it. On one occasion, he confessed the difficult situation he was in by stating: "We are not satisfied with the jointly revised bill, but we would like to have it passed as it is, rather than having no bill passed, just as the real mother of the baby in King Solomon's trial would give up her baby to save its life." This remark seems to aptly reflect the condition under which the JSP had to compromise with the LDP in the House of Representatives. The agony of the split voting reveals the peculiar nature of the JSP as well as of the SMEOL itself and depicts the complex and difficult process of intra- and inter-party compromise surrounding this legislation. By taking advantage of the Diet rule that deliberations cannot be regarded as formal proceedings unless stenographically recorded, a chairman of the Commerce and Industry Committee of the House of Councillors thwarted the LDP's motion to quickly terminate the committee's interpellation of the bill. After two weeks of deliberation, which witnessed this quasi-filibustering against the ruling-party members of the committee, the SMEOL, in its jointly modified form, was passed through the House of Councillors, still containing many problems for both the political parties and interest groups to solve after its enactment.

Notes to Selection 2

1. The agency's reasons were as follows: First, whereas the regulation of small and medium businesses is meaningless unless the big enterprises are also controlled, cooperative economic activities stipulated in the Cooperative Union Law try to solve only internal problems of the small and medium-sized enterprises, and thus it is difficult to unify these two unions charged with different functions. Second, whereas unions under the Cooperative Union Law do not necessitate any regulation over non-union members, the regulatory unions under the Stabilization Law would make it indispensable. Third, some types of business are impossible to unionize and treat uniformly. Finally, the regulatory union covers a wide area, while the cooperative union is, by nature, not only limited to a small area but also differs in function. (This information was obtained from the Promotion Section of the Small and Medium-Sized Enterprises Agency.)

2. For example, the opinion of administrative agencies around October 1956 was manifested in the following remarks made by Tameji Kawakami, the director of the Small and Medium-Sized Enterprises Agency. Speaking about the framework of the bill, he stressed the need for strengthened organization for all the small and medium enterprises, but added that "the interest of small enterprises and the public interest must fully be balanced" (*Tokyo,* October 3, 1956). He was critical of the

JPLSME, saying that "it would be improper to unconditionally force union membership. . . . Should we not let the government decide on the issues of compulsory membership and the regulation of nonunion members in case of depressions as stipulated in the provision of Article 29 of the Stabilization Law?" (*Asahi,* October 2, 1956). A government bill which Kōshō Ogasa and Tameji Kawakami later prepared was "of their own making to the extent it followed this line of thought." Ayukawa was "disappointed" by the government's idea inasmuch as he failed to make Kawakami change his mind on the question of union membership. Kenkichi Matsuzaki, *Dantaihō hayawakari* [Handbook of organization law], Preface.

3. According to the Enabling Act, which established the Small and Medium-Sized Enterprises Promotion Council: "The prime minister shall appoint the members of the council from those who possess a wide knowledge and experience in the small enterprises or from men of learning and experience." A list of candidates selected by the Small and Medium-Sized Enterprises Agency, which was doing the administrative work for the council, was finally approved. But, for some reason, the prime minister's appointees included 23 members who had not been selected by the agency. Although the prime minister's power to appoint was given by the Enabling Act, there seemed to be somewhat irregular "political" consideration in the actual selection of the members. Compared with the selection of members to the Constitutional Commission, however, the selection of membership in the present case was fair.

4. A comparison of the government bill and the JSP's bill follows.

Government Bill	JSP Bill
Definition of Small and Medium Enterprise	

Government Bill	JSP Bill
Small and medium-sized enterprises shall include, unless otherwise stipulated in a government ordinance, the enterprises with fewer than 300 full-time employees in industry, mining, and transportation, and fewer than 30 in commerce and services. An automated enterprise with fewer than 300 employees may be regarded as a big enterprise, whereas an enterprise with more than 300 employees may be regarded as small or medium-sized enterprises, as in construction.	An enterprise with fewer than 200 full-time employees (or fewer than 30 in commerce and services) and less than $27,778 of capital shall be defined as a small or medium-sized enterprise. The qualification for membership in a Labor Enterprise Cooperative Union shall be fewer than 10 employees (or fewer than 2 in commerce and service).

Government Bill   JSP Bill

Classification of Unions

There shall be the Business Co-operative Union, the Trust Cooperative Union, the Commerce and Industry Union, etc.

There shall be the Business Co-operative Union, the Labor Enterprise Cooperative Union, the Enterprise Coordination Cooperative Union, etc. The Labor Enterprise Cooperative Union shall deal with finance and taxation of petty enterprises and the Fire Safety Cooperative Union shall legalize the existing voluntary cooperative system.

Establishment of Unions

A union can be established only when excessive competition within the same type of business is likely to cause unstable business conditions in a designated area. Except for a Union of Stores, districting of unions may not overlap. No less than one-half of the same type of small and medium-sized enterprises are necessary to form a Commerce and Industry Union. Union membership can be extended to a big enterprise provided that more than 50 percent of their work is performed by small and medium-sized enterprises and that no less than two-thirds of the same kind of enterprises in the same area and more than two-thirds of all union members are engaged in small and medium-sized enterprises.

In view of the fact that the Small and Medium Enterprises Stabilization Law, the Import and Export Control Law, the Machinery Industry Promotion Provisional Law, the Food Hygiene Law, and the Environment Hygiene-Related Law designate 85 types of business, the Business Coordinating Cooperative Union shall be established by small and medium-sized enterprises engaged in the kind of businesses designated in these laws. It is also required that no less than one-half of the same type of small and medium-sized enterprises in the same area and that no less than two-thirds of all union members be in small and medium-sized enterprises.

The general meeting of union members may pass a resolution to admit big enterprisers into their union. The Fire Cooperative Union shall have no less than $2,778 of capital, and no fewer than 1,000 members.

Government Bill	JSP Bill

Function of Unions

The Commerce and Industry Union shall regulate and economize businesses and is capable of concluding a union agreement. It is a cooperative union without capital stock, and other unions are with capital stock. Petty enterprises without holding capital stocks may be admitted into a cooperative union.

The Business Coordinating Co-operative Union shall conduct collective bargaining, economic and regulatory activities, and is capable of concluding labor agreements. It shall be a cooperative with capital stocks.

Collective Bargaining

A party to collective bargaining with representatives from the Commerce and Industry Union shall comply in good faith with the latter's request for bargaining. The other party to negotiation shall be big enterprisers who transact with union members, or nonunion members of the same type of small and medium-sized enterprise. A competent minister can advise either party to negotiation to start collective bargaining.

A party to bargaining with representatives from a union must comply with the latter's request to negotiate unless there is a justifiable reason to the contrary. A conciliation of disputes can be requested, upon unsuccessful negotiation, to the Small and Medium-Sized Enterprises Coordinating Committee which, in turn, prepares an arbitration proposal and advises both parties to accept it.

Collective Agreement

A collective agreement shall become effective upon the approval of a competent minister.

A collective agreement, when concluded, must be reported to an administrative agency. The parties to an agreement can request a competent minister to approve of its validity. The Antitrust Law shall not be applicable to the collective agreement concluded between the union of subcontractors and a contractor to improve their relationship, which is approved by a competent minister, or to the one which is concluded between a member

Government Bill   JSP Bill

Collective Agreement

and nonunion members in the same
type of business. (Since there is no
method other than collective agreements, many privileges are granted
to the collective agreement.)

Order to Join the Union

A minister may order, after a hear-   No provision.
ing, nonmembers of the Commerce
and Industry Union to join the
union in order to correct instability
caused by the latter, provided that
(1) no fewer than three-fourths of
those engaged in small and medium-sized enterprises in the same
area be union members; (2) no
fewer than three-fourths of the
same type of enterprises in a designated area be small or medium-
sized; and (3) no less than one-
half of the production in a given
commodity be made by small and
medium-sized enterprises in a designated area. Nonunion members
shall be deemed to have become
members fifteen days after such an
order has been issued.

Regulation of Business Activities of Nonunion Members

A minister may, after a hearing,   No provision.
regulate business activities of the   The aforementioned collective
enterprises when he judges that   agreement shall suffice for this pur-
voluntary regulations by the Com-   pose. Unlike the regulatory order
merce and Industry Union cannot   in the government's bill, this is a
correct instability caused by non-   civil contract. A hearing must be
union members of the Commerce   held prior to the arbitration. An
and Industry Union. It is required   arbitration, when successfully
that the Commerce and Industry   reached, shall be tantamount to a
Union be of such a nature that the   collective agreement concluded and
same type of enterprises can join   approved by a competent minister.

Government Bill   JSP Bill

Regulation of Business Activities of Nonunion Members

and that a considerable portion of the same type of business be conducted by the small and medium enterprises.

Order for Deliberation and Conciliation

(1) "The Small and Medium-Sized Enterprises Stabilization Council" shall investigate, at the request of concerned ministers, the regulatory function of the Commerce and Industry Union. (2) "The Central Small and Medium-Sized Enterprise Conciliatory Council" and "Small Enterprises Conciliatory Council" in each prefecture shall investigate, at the request of concerned ministers or governors, matters concerning union agreements.

"The Central Small and Medium-Sized Enterprise Coordination Committee" and the "Local Small and Medium-Sized Enterprise Coordination Council" shall conduct arbitration and conciliation of disputes arising in connection with the union's collective bargainings and agreements.

5. *Mainichi,* March 13, 1957.

6. Article 29 stipulates that the "management shall agree to negotiate in the absence of a justifiable reason to the contrary."

7. Article 42, Section 3.

8. Article 55, Section 4.

9. Revised Cooperative Union Law.

10. In a subcommittee meeting, the LDP gave the JSP a commitment to the effect that the proposed bill, in its actual operation, would be interpreted to exclude these businesses from the list of parties who must comply with the union request to negotiate, but it did not have any intention of putting it in writing. Later the Legislative Bureau of the House of Representatives codified it in order to clarify the logical construction of law. The fact that, after several protests to the Socialists, the Liberal Democrats gave in seems to indicate a peculiar influence of "printed" words over legislation in that once printed as code, this provision was, however unwillingly, accepted by the LDP.

Interest Groups in the Legislative Process*

NAOKI KOBAYASHI

Pro-SMEOL Interest Groups

An outstanding characteristic of the legislative process of the Small and Medium-Sized Enterprises Organization Law was the intense and spectacular activity of interest groups, particularly the JPLSME. From the very beginning, Gisuke Ayukawa, the head of the former Nissan Automobile Corporation, invested $1,250,000 and exercised charismatic leadership in the JPLSME. Some anti-SMEOL groups have argued that Ayukawa invested such an enormous sum of private funds and devoted himself to the problems of the small and medium-sized enterprises, which appeared to be irrelevant to his own, because of political ambition. Ayukawa, however, claimed that he had found the key to Japan's economic recovery while he was in the Sugamo Prison.[1] He was convinced that the only way for Japan's small and medium enterprises to eliminate endemic excessive competition, and to break through the "depressed and miserable social condition," would be "to organize themselves, both labor and management, so that their political force might be able to effectively influence the national legislature for the improvement of their business." He promptly set out to form an "interest group comparable to the General Council of Trade Unions of Japan (Sōhyō)," the most powerful labor union. At the beginning, there was a suggestion to establish a political party, but an interest group was preferred because, in the opinion of Ayukawa, "in the country's present condi-

* This selection is taken from "Chūshōkigyō dantai soshikihō no rippōkatei" in *Tokyo daigaku kyōyōgakubu shakaigaku kiyō* (The Social Science Bulletin, Faculty of Liberal Arts, University of Tokyo), vol. 7 (1958), pp. 62–84. Translated and reprinted with permission of the author.

tion, it would be most effective and adequate for small and medium business to form an interest group and work on the government and political parties in an open and straight-forward manner." After having studied interest groups in the United States as well as seeking advice from Teiji Yabe and others, Ayukawa formed a 1,500-member preparatory group late in 1955, followed by the formal establishment of the JPLSME at a convention held in Hibiya Park, Tokyo, on April 11, 1956, with 4,200 present. The first of seven policy goals, adopted at the Hibiya meeting, dealt with the enactment of an organization law for the small and medium enterprises, and a campaign to achieve this goal was immediately set in motion.

Forms of Interest-Group Activities. A variety of tactics and strategies that the JPLSME employed as an interest group were based upon the pressure principle, as interpreted by Ayukawa. He explained his theory as follows:

In physics there is a principle of Charles and Boyle. . . . If you continue to heat water which has turned into vapor inside a boiler, then the pressure will inevitably rise. Because the volume inside the boiler is fixed, the pressure will rise with the temperature. I wondered what would happen if I applied this principle of physics to solve the problems of the small and medium enterprises. The former principle is physics, and the resultant one, of my own invention, is psychological. Compare the pressure volume inside the boiler to the invariable number of votes cast. Suppose the number of small and medium enterprises is 200,000, then, even if vigorous campaigns were waged, it would be impossible to gain more than 200,000 votes. Sometimes the votes to gain would be less than 100,000. In order to maximize our votes we must apply as much heat as possible. If the small enterprises are strongly determined, then, naturally the pressure will rise. Would it not be good if we made full use of this pressure in politics?

Since the JPLSME is a pressure group, it would not do any good if the pressure is too low. It is most important to heat it up and achieve something with the pressure. Pressure would not be effective unless it were applied to the opponent's crucial points. Even if it is as strong as dynamite, it will be useless if it is thrown into jello or mud. It will not go off unless the object it hits is hard and resistant. If we put pressure on public officials upon whom the electoral process has no effect, then they will simply come to us with their empty thank you's. After all, we should bring our gifts to our own representatives for whom votes speak. The people in each region should make small boilers. If they keep a fire burning so that the pressure is heightened, they can aim it at the local representatives. It will not matter whether they are conservative or liberal. I will make a big boiler by accumulating your own pressure and turning it on the party leaders. Isn't this a good idea? [2]

Based on Ayukawa's principle, the JPLSME's activities concentrated on an expansion of the organization, which would in turn raise the pressure energy, and the concerted exertion, both in Tokyo and the prefectures, of pressure upon the Diet members. Throughout the twenty-sixth and twenty-seventh sessions of the Diet, the JPLSME used many varieties of the method.

On May 24, 1956, shortly after its initiation, the JPLSME in its policy bureau completed and published its first draft of the SMEOL. On August 24, it published its third draft which, after several modifications with the technical assistance of the Legislative Bureau of the House of Councillors, was in a nearly completed form and distributed it to the quarters concerned. First the JPLSME attempted to have the LDP and the government submit it to the Diet in the form of a private bill. Ayukawa exerted pressure on the top leadership when a compromise was attempted between the JPLSME's third draft and the government's bill. The former, strongly advocating the idea of compulsory membership in a small and medium enterprisers' union to discourage nonunion members, was not adopted in its original form but was undoubtedly incorporated into the latter. Furthermore, the JPLSME's third draft, which precipitated not only the government's bill but also the JSP's bill and many other private bills, contrasted with the bills proposed by the Japan Chamber of Commerce, the All Japan Small and Medium-Sized Enterprises Council, and the National Small and Medium-Sized Enterprises Cooperative Unions' Central Association, none of which was given much attention or had much influence over the government's bill.

The JPLSME constantly employed the pressure generated by the massive number of votes controlled by its large membership. Particularly, its local members turned the old and usually inadequate method of petition and appeal into a "very effective" pressure on their Diet representatives. The JPLSME, through petition, created human waves of 300,000 members at very important stages of legislation and sent a large number of petitioners to the Diet, especially the house Commerce and Industry Committee. The JPLSME, convinced of the "decisive power" of petitioning, had various Diet members from different constituencies present a pamphlet on the petition concerning the legislation of the Small and Medium-Sized Enterprises Organization Law to the chairmen of both houses at the twenty-sixth session of the Diet. As of May 9, 1957, at the beginning of the debate on the SMEOL, 61 percent of the members of the House of Representatives and 47 percent in the House of Councillors transmitted the total of 1,476 letters of petition. In addition, the JPLSME's local organizations kept sending telegrams and letters to the national legislators to compete with anti-SMEOL groups such as the NCLA. Form letters, rather than the separately prepared petitions, were made at the JPLSME headquarters and distributed to the local offices. The principle of diminishing returns made petitioning less effective in proportion to the amount of money spent for it. If the petitioning contributed to the success of the JPLSME at all, it is probably because the petitioning, which has the same effect as the monetary lure in an election, was effectively tied to the overall strategy of winning legislators' votes.

Furthermore, personal petitioning was also actively employed in both the twenty-sixth and twenty-seventh sessions of the Diet. During the two sessions, as many as one hundred people were mobilized every day, marched to the buildings where Diet members were staying, and often succeeded in committing legislators to the SMEOL. They also occupied all the spectators' seats in the various committee meetings in the Diet and vigilantly watched the activities of committee members. On November 7, 1957, at the climax of the SMEOL deliberation, the JPLSME held an emergency meeting of national representatives in the building of the House of Councillors and confirmed many legislators' support for the bill. Indeed, the group's energetic and incessant pressure activities took the opposition groups by surprise.[3]

Since its first rally at Hibiya Park on December 4, 1956, the JPLSME had held a demonstration march in metropolitan Tokyo as well as many conventions designed to expand its branch organizations. This kind of convention was thought to have the dual effect of boosting the morale among rank-and-file members, thereby raising Ayukawa's "boiler pressure," and of demonstrating their strength to the public. These conventions also presented an opportunity which legislators from many constituencies could not afford to miss. When a Diet member made a speech at a JPLSME convention, showing sympathy with and support for the SMEOL, he usually made certain commitments for the legislation. Furthermore, a convention resolution pledging the passage of the SMEOL not only "enhanced the morale of JPLSME workers" but also attracted the political parties' attention. Particularly when these conventions were held simultaneously on a nationwide basis, they had an increased effect, like a chain reaction. Indeed, they were held one after another in thirty-five cities during the latter part of October 1957. The success of the JPLSME can be attributed to its sizeable campaign fund, which helped to transform the large organization into a high-pressure tool, and a close collaboration with other interest groups. It enabled small and medium businessmen to demonstrate their "strong desire" to interested Diet members and obtain from them a positive commitment to or at least sympathy for the present legislation.

The opinion poll conducted by the JPLSME in June 1956 on all candidates for the House of Councillors had the dual effect of increasing the candidates' interest in the small and medium enterprises and putting psychological pressure upon them by asking their opinion of the proposed SMEOL. Although it did not have as direct an effect as petitioning, the opinion poll was a unique method of the interest-group activity. The result of the poll was that out of 342 candidates, 277 favored the bill, 2 opposed it, 60 reserved their answers, and 3 did not reply. Among the 127 successful candidates, 109 favored the bill, 1 opposed it, 15 reserved their answers, and 2 did not answer. Later, when the JSP voted against the jointly amended SMEOL in the House of Councillors, the JPLSME, on the basis of this opinion poll, felt that the JSP members had for the most part fallen back on their commitment. The truth was, however, that the JPLSME never placed much faith on legislators' commitment to the bill but simply hoped that the opinion poll would encourage both the LDP and the JSP to include in their campaign platforms the adoption of a small and medium-sized enterprises organization law of one sort or another. (A timely opinion poll conducted by an authoritative pollster presumably is effective in influencing respondents' decisions, although it is very difficult to measure objectively the degree of such an influence.)

The president of the JPLSME, who occupied a conspicuously influential position within the big-business community, performed a major role in increasing the interest group's influence. How he worked behind the scenes on the government and the LDP is not entirely clear, but through his effective leadership within the JPLSME and his direct ties to the top political leaders, he is said to have actively solicited the support of the leaders of the Federation of Economic Organizations as well as transmitting the JPLSME's own draft bill to the government.

On August 14, 1956, Ayukawa met with the members of the LDP's National Organization Committee (Zenkokusoshikiiinkai) at the Akasaka Prince Hotel and requested passage of the JPLSME's draft bill in the twenty-seventh session of the Diet; on October 29, prior to the convening of the session, he told a press conference that "at the next session of the Diet, the SMEOL ought to be passed by all means." An "institutional linkage" probably existed between Gisuke Ayukawa and Premier Nobusuke Kishi. Judging from their intimate relationship dating back to the Manchurian period, the appointment of Kishi, influential among the bureaucrats in the Min- istry of Transportation, to the LDP presidency and the premiership was believed to have provided Ayukawa with a very effective avenue through which to communicate with the government and the LDP. Indeed, Ayukawa's strong influence was referred to by Teiji Yabe at a Commerce and Industry Committee meeting of the House of Councillors on May 16, 1957. Ayukawa's close association with the LDP, undisputedly cooperative in nature, was something for which an opposition interest group like the NCLA could not possibly hope. The pressure "pipe line" originating from Ayukawa's "boiler" ex- tended to every corner of the legislative machinery and, despite its short existence, was able to achieve better results than an ordinary interest group could ever aspire to.

The Organization and Political Posture of the JPLSME. Ayukawa attributed the victory of the SMEOL to the highly effective pressure tactics used by the JPLSME. He argued that the continued increase of pressure is a prerequisite for small and medium-sized enterprises to revitalize their business. "There are 120 constituencies in Japan. It is necessary to turn the outlet of a highly pressurized boiler on the lawmakers in each election district and make them become of some service. This task will require more than anything else a strengthened organization on our side." [4] The resolution of the JPLSME's national convention held toward the end of 1957 had stressed the same point: "The JPLSME should try to form one branch organization in each constituency for the House of Representatives and maximize the political power of the small and medium enterprises at the forthcoming general election." [5]

In its effort to expand the organization, the JPLSME passed a resolution on December 9 setting up an unrealistically high goal of mobilizing three thousand specially trained members and recruiting five million new members in half a year. The JPLSME, as a pressure group, was fully aware of the power of organization. It was consolidating its suborganizations throughout the country but, despite its expected membership of ten million by the end of 1957, created 214 branches with a total membership of three hundred thousand. Consequently, it felt the need for devising a method of rapidly expanding its organization. The concrete measures devised included demonstration meetings, publicity programs, and campaigns to double or triple its membership.[6] As Taizō Ishizaka, the chairman of the Federation of Economic Organizations, admitted, "the medium and small enterprises are as hard to organize as imported rice is difficult to make a ball of," [7] * and it is even more difficult to make the small and medium enterprises a viable interest group comparable to powerful labor unions. Unlike the other small and medium-sized enterprise organizations, the JPLSME was composed of organized, active members capable of being mobilized for lobbying and other interest-group activities in the legislative process. It is highly doubtful, however, whether or not the JPLSME will be able to break through the thick wall of apathy surrounding medium and small enterprisers and transform them into as large a pressure group as the General Council of Trade Unions of Japan, which has five million members.

The JPLSME has already demonstrated, though, a real power in the legislation of the SMEOL and has become so large that it cannot be disregarded. Its political posture and the future course of its actions must be taken into account. Despite its professed political neutrality, the JPLSME obviously shows its proximity to or inclination toward the conservative LDP, as evidenced in several different ways. Although the amount of a political contribution may not always indicate the proximity of the donor to the recipient party, the fact that Ayukawa contributed fifty million yen to the LDP and one million

---

* The Japanese sometimes press a handful of cooked rice inside their palm and shape it in a ball. Before eating, they put some pickle inside the rice ball and wrap it with seasoned laver. Imported rice is believed to be less pasty and more difficult to make a ball of than is domestic.

yen to the JSP seems to reflect his personal preference of the former to the latter. The JPLSME regarded the LDP as an ally during the SMEOL struggle and directed its interest-group activities primarily at the ruling party; in contrast, the JPLSME occasionally demonstrated antipathy toward the left wing of the JSP. Due to the close relationship between Premier Kishi and the JPLSME's president, Ayukawa, dating back to the pre-1945 period, the JPLSME was strongly tinged with conservatism. Some people, by putting together these factors, charge that the strengthening of the JPLSME was tied to the attempt to create a stable conservative government, but it is difficult to predict how the passage of the SMEOL will change the JPLSME as an interest group.

Moderately Pro-SMEOL or Neutral Interest Groups. So far emphasis has been placed on the JPLSME, but there existed within the small and medium-sized enterprises' community other interest groups which pushed forward the SMEOL. Many economic interest groups have existed much longer than the JPLSME and have performed important economic activities. It was primarily their sense of duty that kept many economic organizations from being actively engaged in any political pressure activities, including the legislative process of the bill. As some economic interest groups gradually came to support the proposed SMEOL, a slight tension and distrust of the rapidly expanding JPLSME began to manifest itself, thereby confusing the small and medium enterprises' circle.

The League of Japanese Small and Medium-Sized Enterprises Organizations made its initial objective to improve the management of the small and medium enterprises as well as to gain assistance for cooperative unions and did not hesitate to become a political force in order to solve a wide range of problems confronting small enterprises. In the case of the enactment of the Department Store Law, it exerted pressure on Diet members. A merger with the JPLSME for the common cause of the SMEOL failed as a result of tension concerning the chairmanship of the merged organization. The League of Japanese Small and Medium-Sized Enterprises Organizations (Nihon Chūshōkigyō Dantairenmei) subsequently took a somewhat indecisive position in that it would maintain close contact and present a united front with the JPLSME but would not merge with the latter at the loss of its identity. It was also of the opinion that instead of unnecessarily expanding organization, it would develop its own

SMEOL draft while steadily advancing the policy of the National Small and Medium-Sized Enterprises Cooperative Unions' Central Association.

The National Small and Medium-Sized Enterprises Cooperative Unions' Central Association (Zenkoku Chūshōkigyōtō Kyōdōkumiai Chūōkai) is an economic organization designed for improving management through the cooperative union system and was created as a result of the revision of the Cooperative Union Law in July 1955. It differs radically from the JPLSME inasmuch as its policy "excludes any involvement in political activities." A highly emotional conflict arose between the League of Japanese Small and Medium-Sized Enterprises Organizations and the JPLSME in March 1956 when Masataka Toyota, chairman of both the League of Japanese Small and Medium-Sized Enterprises Organizations and the National Small and Medium-Sized Enterprises Cooperative Unions' Central Association, took a very critical view of the proposed SMEOL, particularly with respect to the bureaucratic control of nonunion members and the method of collective bargaining. Based on the judgment that the existing Employment Security Law would suffice in coordinating and regulating the businesses, the National Small and Medium-Sized Enterprises Cooperative Unions' Central Association did not at the beginning support the proposed SMEOL, which in its opinion, would not be of much significance. When Shinji Yoshino assumed the chairmanship, however, following Toyota's resignation in May 1957, his close cooperation with the JPLSME became conspicuous. In fact, Yoshino, speaking at a JPLSME convention, stressed his "determination to act side by side" with them.[8] Thus, it was apparently after May 1957 that the National Small and Medium-Sized Enterprises Cooperative Unions' Central Association began to render active support to the SMEOL, but in view of the fact that its vice-chairman, Tatsuzō Shiozawa, was an advisor for the JPLSME, some people speculated that cooperation must have started much earlier.

The All Japan Small and Medium-Sized Enterprises Council (Zennihon Chūshōkigyō Kyōgikai) is a progressive interest group among the strongly conservative small and medium-sized business circle. With the objective of attaining economic democracy, the activities of the All Japan Small and Medium-Sized Enterprises Council include educating the public, gathering necessary information and materials, and making policy proposals to the government and the

Diet. Its bipartisan membership prevented the interest group from reaching an internal consensus on the proposed SMEOL or a joint program with the JPLSME. On the one hand, many of its leaders joined the JPLSME, but on the other, there were men like Seizaburō Tsukahara who strongly opposed the bill, and it was unlikely for this type of group to compromise in order to keep internal unity. The majority faction, however, took a favorable view toward JPLSME's proposal, and many members in their individual capacities participated in the latter's activities.

Actively Pro-SMEOL Interest Groups. The three groups described above, while critical of legislating the SMEOL, either came to support it in a half-hearted manner or to take a politically neutral position. Many small and medium-sized enterprise organizations, however, worked actively with the JPLSME. Eight organizations especially, including the National Cooperative Unions' Central Association (Zenkoku Kyōso Chūōkai), the Federation of All Stores (Zenshōren), and the Federation of Japan Specialty Stores (Nissenren), got together with the JPLSME prior to the twenty-seventh session of the Diet and pledged to make concerted efforts for the present law. Outside the small enterprises circle, the Tokyo Chamber of Commerce requested the government and the Diet on October 17, 1956, to "enact a small and medium enterprises organization law," and the Japan Chamber of Commerce, at its meeting on November 21, expressed a similar opinion. With both tradition and prestige behind them and virtually free from any tie to the JPLSME, these two chambers of commerce probably had a small but significant influence on the decision-making process. Intensive research into the role of the lower echelon of guilds, other associations of stores and retailers, as well as numerous professional organizations has yet to be conducted.

Anti-SMEOL Groups

National Consumers Liaison Association. A second characteristic of the interest-group activities surrounding the present legislation is found in the active anti-SMEOL campaigns which the National Consumers Liaison Association (Zenkoku Shōhishadantai Renraku-kai) (NCLA) lodged with the cooperation of other organizations. The Federation of Japan Livelihood Cooperative Unions (Nihon Seikatsukumiai Rengō)[9] regarded the JPLSME's draft SMEOL and the creation of the Small and Medium-Sized Enterprises Promotion Council as being an unreasonable infringement upon the consumers' interest. The Housewives Federation (Shufuren), the General Council of Trade Unions of Japan (Sōhyō), the Congress of Industrial Unions of Japan (Sanbetsu), and the School Livelihood Cooperatives (Gakkōseikyō) held a meeting at the assembly hall of the Housewives Federation on December 24, 1956, where they developed a unified campaign program and agreed to try to stop the passage of the present bill.[10] This was followed by the first liaison conference in the beginning of January 1957 where representatives from sixteen organizations passed a joint resolution to oppose the legislation of the SMEOL and immediately thereafter set out for petition canvassing. The NCLA bulletin reveals the well-prepared action programs adopted at the January conference and reports as follows:

The Anti-SMEOL Campaign Method

1. The mass-education campaign: (a) Flyers are to be distributed throughout the country via each participating organization; (b) nationwide signature campaigns are to be waged; and (c) each organization will hold seminars to train its local members.

One hundred thousand copies of the flyer were printed for initial distribution. Forms for the signature campaign were sent to the printer. The posters were requested. The Federation of Livelihood Cooperative Unions has worked out itineraries for the local seminars.

2. Measures aimed at the LDP and the government: (a) Negotiations with the Policy Board of the LDP, the Policy Council Central Headquarters of the JSP, and the Commerce and Industry Committee of both houses; (b) negotiations with the Small and Medium-Sized Enterprises Agency, the Ministry of International Trade and Industry, the Fair Trade Commission, the Ministry of Welfare, and the Ministry of Agriculture.

These negotiations began in the latter part of 1956. On January 9, 1957, we listened to the opinions of the research section head of the Fair Trade Commission and other persons concerned.

3. The recruitment of scholars who will assist the preparation for public hearings. It is important to explain to them the NCLA's main objections to the proposed SMEOL. We already secured consent from two or three scholars.

4. Contact with the mass media: We met with the reporters from the *Asahi,* the *Yomiuri,* the *Sankei,* the *Tokyo,* the *Fujin Times,* and the *Kyōdō Press* today.

5. A nationwide meeting of consumers: It was decided to hold a na-

tionwide meeting of consumers who oppose the SMEOL on February 26 at the Kyōsaikai Building in Tokyo. We are going to marshall all our efforts centering around the anti-SMEOL gatherings of participating organizations culminating in the proposed nationwide meeting of consumers. The meeting will be preceded by a public hearing with representatives of the JPLSME, the Small and Medium-Sized Enterprises Agency, the Fair Trade Commission, and scholars attending.

6. We should have each participating organization set up a consumer liaison group in each prefecture following the same set-up as in Tokyo. For example, in the Kansai district there already exist some attempts to form such liaison groups. We will help local organizers to accelerate the proposed national meeting.

The anti-SMEOL campaign method was decided as above, but concerning the nature of the consumer's liaison group there were differing opinions: the Housewives Federation wanted to push its anti-SMEOL campaign among the small and medium enterprises as well, so that it would not be misunderstood as a sect of consumers, the General Council of Trade Unions of Japan wanted to see the formation of an alliance of a wide range of groups including those small and medium enterprisers who opposed the SMEOL. It was decided after weighing these opinions that for the moment the NCLA, by its very nature, should be consolidated as a group of consumers and that it should push the opposition campaign by close contact with the anti SMEOL groups of the small and medium enterprises.[11]

Thus, a wide range of campaigns were actively conducted both in and out of the Diet from February through April 1957. The NCLA executive secretaries analyzed existing situations once every month and adopted various tactics which were presumably learned from the experiences of the General Council of Trade Unions of Japan. The booklet containing sample letters of petition as well as the names and addresses of the people to whom the petitions should be sent, distributed to the participating anti-SMEOL groups, reveals only a fragment of the NCLA's activities.[12] The March 7 handout of the NCLA indicates the following activities:

Activities inside the Diet
1) We plan to speak to the Special Subcommittee for the Small and Medium-Sized Enterprises Organization which was created in the Commerce and Industry Committee of the House of Representatives with Seiji Katō (a JSP member) as its chairman; 2) a participating anti-

SMEOL group in each prefecture should send petitions to its Diet members; 3) each group should resort to "human-wave" tactics of petitioning; 4) six or seven witnesses should be sent to the Diet's public hearing to be held in the first part of April; 5) letters of petition should be sent to both houses; and 6) we should try to make the Diet take time in its debate on both of the SMEOL bills so that it will not be able to finish its debate by the end of the current session of the Diet.

Activities outside the Diet
1) Recruitment of housewives for distributing flyers on the streets. (An additional 100,000 copies are being printed.) It may be necessary to have them make campaign speeches on the streets; 2) discussions with the small and medium-sized enterprises organizations; 3) the arrangement of debates on radio and in the press; 4) preparation for a brief summary of our opinion on the proposed SMEOL and open letters of inquiry to be distributed to all Diet members, men of learning and experience, and press reporters.

Activities at the local level
1) Activities similar to those of the central organizations should be initiated to influence local legislative bodies; 2) discussions with local small and medium enterprisers should be held in order to undermine the opponents' local solidarity; 3) each interest group should be urged to form local consumers associations; 4) a national convention of local delegates should be held in the middle of April in order to make a final effort against the present legislation.

Inside the Diet, the NCLA was conspicuous in its attempt to persuade the rank and file of the JSP as well as energetically negotiating with its leadership. Likewise, outside parliament, it worked closely with other organizations through its bulletins, resolutions, and opinion papers, while contacting the public by distributing posters and flyers and making speeches from moving cars.[13] It also staged demonstrations by holding consumers' meetings three times: February 26 and November 5, 1957, on a nationwide scale, and April 17 on an emergency basis. Thus the NCLA engaged in a kind of interest-group activity which this sort of consumer organization had never before undertaken. According to the evaluation of the NCLA, the public and press campaigns which it launched were primarily responsible for not only delaying the presentation of the government's bill, but also for arousing public opinion so that the bill was shelved at the end of the twenty-sixth session. The NCLA campaign presented a new chapter in the history of Japanese interest groups in that it succeeded in organizing consumers, a difficult-to-define group, and in unifying the anti-SMEOL groups, as well as arousing much interest in and criticism of the present legislation.

But, in spite of its interest-group activities, the NCLA failed to defeat the bill. Primarily designed as a morale-booster for its rank-and-file members was the NCLA official's claim that "we can stop the bill's passage with one final burst of strength" or that "our movement has attested to the fact that before the sound judgment and strong determination of the people, the task of turning back the clock is insurmountable, no matter how much money Ayukawa is willing to spend." The fact that the SMEOL was enacted seemed to demonstrate that mobilizing and organizing the consumers is far more difficult than organizing small and medium-sized enterprises and that even with the use of skillful techniques the opposition campaign had its own limits.

The Federation of Japan Livelihood Cooperative Unions and the Housewives Federation,[14] the two mainstays of the NCLA, were far from developing effective political pressure activities. The NCLA's campaign fund of $3,611 in 1957, with its breakdown of $2,222 contributed by the Federation of Japan Livelihood Cooperative Unions, $833 from the Housewives Federation, and $556 from the sales proceeds of cooperatives of big enterprises, was a small sum contrasted with the JPLSME's campaign funds of $2,778,000. This led the anti-SMEOL groups to argue that they had to fight with their own fists against the well-financed JPLSME.[15] If these opposition groups, handicapped from the beginning, were no match for the JPLSME, it was not so much the lack of campaign funds as their weak organization that was fatal to the cause. As previously mentioned, it is a very difficult task to unite consumers and attempt to organize them for their own interest. It was probably inevitable from the very nature of the SMEOL that the NCLA's slogans like "opposition to price-fixing by the government" and "opposition to bureaucratic control" could not appeal to the public enough to block passage of the bill. It was also unavoidable that despite the attendance of as many as 800 members at the NCLA's national convention held on February 26, continuous support came from just a handful of groups centering around NCLA director Kin'ichi Katsube and several individuals from the Housewives Federation and that a big interest group like the General Council of Trade Unions of Japan did not actively push the opposition movement.[16] Resolutions and petitions to the Diet were constantly sent out, but their effectiveness was substantially undermined by the counteractivities of the JPLSME and could not produce the kind of achievements which might have been expected for an organization with an impressive and good-sounding title like the NCLA. But the NCLA's spectacular activities did add another characteristic to the present legislative process in that they were directed toward an extremely amorphous and fluid type of social stratum and succeeded in raising critical public interest in the SMEOL. Particularly, given the special political significance attached to the law in question, the NCLA will perform an overseeing function even after enactment.

Right after the enactment of the SMEOL, the NCLA rediscovered that "the Japanese consumer movement was organizationally and politically weak" and accused both the government and the LDP of having neglected the consumers' interest and public opinion. Since Ayukawa predicted that the passage of the present bill is merely a prelude, the interest-group activities appear to be continuing, particularly those concerning the legal interpretation of the SMEOL.

Other Anti-SMEOL Groups. Those interest groups which opposed the SMEOL did not necessarily act in concert with the NCLA. The Association of Department Stores and various agricultural organizations indicated their opposition to the bill. The Japan Small and Medium-Sized Enterprisers' Fraternity (Nihon Chūshōkigyōsha Dōyūkai) staged an independent anti-SMEOL campaign, at the same time cooperating with the NCLA. The Federation of Economic Organizations and the Kansai Economic Association, two major representatives of the big capitalists, did not accept the antimonopoly ideology of the NCLA but opposed the SMEOL as a whole.

The Small and Medium-Sized Enterprisers' Fraternity is a small gathering of "hand-picked members" (to use the expression of Seizaburō Tsukahara, a central figure in this organization) and claims "fifty years of experience in the small and medium enterprises." Although it has been regarded as one minority faction within the All Japan Small and Medium-Sized Enterprises Council, the nature, ideology, and financial sources of this interest group are not clear.[17] For its small membership, it conducted a very active anti-SMEOL campaign by publishing newsletters, petitioning the Diet, and even distributing flyers through chartered helicopters. One pamphlet labeled "down with the SMEOL" lists the following attitudes of this economic group: opposition to the idea of strengthening only small and medium enterprises; strong opposition to compulsory union membership; opposition to control by bureaucrats or union bosses; and correction of policies giving a preferential treatment to big enterprises. Although it advocated a voluntary organization by enterprisers themselves, the Small and Medium-Sized Enterprisers' Fraternity seemed to have had neither a clearly formulated ideology nor the capability of making campaign policies. Its policies had an anti-monopolistic and libertarian appearance in their opposition to control by union bosses and bureaucrats, but were neither socialistic nor laissez-faire.

Although Kenkichi Matsuzaki of the JPLSME cynically stated before the Commerce and Industry Committee in the House of Councillors that "Tsukahara's group, compared with the ten million membership of the JPLSME, would not be large enough to be seen even in a microscope," [18] the failure of the Small and Medium-Sized Enterprisers' Fraternity was not so much the result of its small membership as its unclear position on the present bill and lack of strength needed to organize the anti-SMEOL movement effectively. The fact is that the anti-SMEOL circle was not able to organize effective interest groups comparable to the rapidly expanding JPLSME. Tsukahara's remarks reflected the mentality of Japan's small and medium enterprisers when he testified before the Diet that "the small and medium enterprisers were so hard pressed by thir day-to-day works that they were totally unaware of the proposed SMEOL being submitted before the Diet . . . nor were they informed of what was going on." The failure of Tsukahara's small, hand-picked opposition group to develop a clearly defined position seems to reflect the general apathy of Japan's small and medium enterprisers.

The anti-SMEOL campaign by the Federation of Economic Organizations and the Kansai Economic Association was not conducted by any conspicuous methods except for the Diet testimonies and the newspaper accounts of the decisions of their boards of directors. In the Kansai Economic Association, the Osaka branch raised the strongest objection to the present bill. In March 1957, the Kansai Economic Association reportedly sent many petitioners to Tokyo to protest the scheduled presentation of the government's bill to the Diet, while the Federation of Economic Organizations was fearful of antagonizing the small and medium enterprisers if it decided to take an active part in the anti-SMEOL campaign. Thus, when Ayukawa told the group of selected members from the Federation of Economic Organizations on May 5 that "although the method of collective bargaining was not desirable, it would be an unavoidable social and not economic policy," the chairman of the federation, Taizō Ishizaka, replied that "the Federation would not overtly oppose the SMEOL." The Kansai Economic Association, on the one hand, held the critical view that this bill "runs counter to the economic system which puts a priority on the consumer and contains a grave danger to Japanese exports, the lifeline of the nation's economy." On the other hand, it conceded that this type of legislation would not constitute a menace to the big enterprises and "would probably be a necessary social policy." [19] Thus, the ultimate enactment of the SMEOL was definitely aided by the decisions of the General Council of Trade Unions of Japan, the Federation of Economic Organizations, and the Kansai Economic Association not to undertake vigorous campaigns against the legislation.

Notes' to Selection 3

1. Gisuke Ayukawa, *Wagakuni no chūshōkigyō o ikasumichi* [A way to vitalize small and medium enterprises in our country] (pamphlet), December 15, 1955.
2. "The Japanese Political League of Small and Medium Enterprises" (A newsletter published periodically by the JPLSME), August 15, 1957.
3. Ayukawa's contribution to the JPLSME amounted to as much as $1,229,000 by the end of 1957. How much of this sum was used directly for interest-group activities is unknown. Pamphlets published by some anti-SMEOL groups generally state that JPLSME's pressure-group activities would have been impossible without the ample funds supplied by Ayukawa. It was at that time that the National Consumers Liaison Association bemoaned its campaign fund of $3,600 as compared to the JPLSME's $1,400,000.
4. "The JPLSME," January 1, 1958.
5. "The JPLSME," December 15, 1957.
6. The JPLSME played their campaign song (as corny as most) dur-

ing the "JPLSME Hour" on the Japanese short-wave radio station and also distributed campaign buttons.

7. *Sunday Mainichi*, November 24, 1957.

8. "The JPLSME," December 15, 1957.

9. Its chairman was Sadao Nakabayashi.

10. The National Consumers Liaison Association was composed of a wide range of consumer groups. It included the Livelihood Cooperative Unions with the local council of labor unions at their center, various employees' cooperatives operated by the welfare section of big enterprises (such as the All Textile Association), the Housewives Federation, the Women's Democratic Club, the Federation of All Japan Women's Organizations, the Livelihood Association, and the Study Group of Women's Problems. The "Records of the Consumer Movement" reports that as the officials of the NCLA gradually changed its main policy from the solution of consumers' day-to-day complaints to an antimonopolistic stand, those organizations which by nature or for internal reasons could not take clear political stands dropped out of the opposition movement. For example, except for the Housewives Federation, many women's organizations had neither a full understanding of or much interest in the movement and remained as nominal participants to the NCLA.

11. *Shōdanren Sokuhō* (The NCLA bulletin), no. 1, January 19, 1957.

12. How actively various organizations, both central and local, responded to the NCLA's request to send petitions is unknown, although the NCLA's Director Kin'ichi Katsube maintains that such petitions reached a considerable number. According to the NCLA's experiences, typewritten official statements and handwritten petitions were both relatively effective, but telegraph messages and telephone calls had adverse effects. Petitions were sent to anti-SMEOL leaders as well, including Mikio Mizuta, the minister of International Trade and Industry, and Gisuke Ayukawa, the chairman of the JPLSME, and the LDP members of the House Commerce and Industry Committee. The NCLA officials neither expected nor achieved any result from the petitions sent to these opponents.

13. For example, 300,000 flyers were distributed in April 1957.

14. The activity of the Housewives Federation (chairwoman, Mumeo Oku) in the present legislation cannot be overlooked. Beginning in October 1956, when the government's bill was being discussed in the Small and Medium-Sized Enterprises Promotion Council, the group often raised opposition to the strongly regulatory bill and, along with the Federation of the Livelihood Cooperative Unions, submitted on December 18, 1956, petitions to the Small and Medium-Sized Enterprises Agency. Further-

more, Akiko Mimaki, the vice-chairwoman, debated with some opponents in the *Mainichi,* a daily paper, on December 30, 1956. While the Livelihood Cooperative Unions were opposed to the bill, primarily to protect their interests against their business "enemies," the Housewives Federation purported to represent solely consumer interests and displayed their symbol of a man-size spoon, adding a spectacular aspect to the entire campaign. Much persuasive pressure, however, could not be expected of a weak organization which was resorting to a highly emotional method, symbolized by such slogans as "milk for ten yen [three cents] and reduced TV prices." The JPLSME was of the opinion that "toward the end of 1956, the Housewives Federation evaded any serious discussion with us on the ground that they did not understand the bill and had to study it first and merely conducted an emotional opposition." Although there was no doubt about the intention of the federation, it would have been very difficult for an interest group which lacked an understanding of the nature of the legislation and interest-group activities to expand their action front and pose a serious threat to the JPLSME. This bill provided a good trial for the Housewives Federation, which had received much attention at a time when the effect of organizing women for political purposes was being debated.

15. *Shōdanren Sokuhō* (The NCLA bulletin), no. 7, April 4, 1957.

16. The opinion of the General Council of Trade Unions of Japan concerning the present bill seemed somewhat subtle and different from that of the Federation of Economic Organizations. In an extraordinary session of the Diet, the council actively negotiated with the JSP leaders but did not seem to have been so much concerned about the issue as the Livelihood Cooperatives or the Housewives Federation were. Masaharu Irie, the small and medium enterprises department chief of the council, did not consider the present legislation to be the best solution, as the following excerpt from the minutes of the Commerce and Industry Committee of the House of Councillors (no. 34, May 15, 1957) reveals: "First, profits of monopolistic capitalists should be restricted. Also other measures should be taken to regulate their activities. Second, any benefits deriving from these restrictions should be utilized in supporting small and medium enterprises. . . . We, the workers, are just as much concerned about the excessive competition as the small and medium enterprisers are. Does a major problem of excessive competition among the Japanese not lie in the low wages?" In testimony given on the same day, however, before the Commerce and Industry Committee of the House of Councillors, Sadao Nakabayashi, the chairman of the National Consumers Liaison Association, criticized the bureaucratic control contained in the bill and emphasized the need for positive measures to voluntarily

organize small and medium enterprises in enhancing their position. In this respect, the NCLA did not completely oppose this type of legislation.

17. According to the newsletter of the Japanese Management Association, Katsuichi Yamamoto (an LDP member of the House of Representatives), Akira Kazami (a JSP member and a committee member of the U.S.S.R.–Japan Association), and Shichirō Hozumi (a JSP member) were included as associate members, thus manifesting a multiparty character. It had some ten chairmen including Yasuo Nakano, the chairman of the Political Committee, but judging from the attendance at monthly meetings, the association had approximately twenty members and was receiving funds from various department stores.

18. The opinions of Kenkichi Matsuzaki of the JPLSME and Seizaburō Tsukahara, witnesses in the Diet, reveal the interesting attitudes of the two opposing groups. Matsuzaki contends that "small and medium enterprises of all kinds support the JPLSME" and that "the worry of Tsukahara is illusory," while Tsukahara stated that this type of group (the Japanese Management Association) was created in order to give the silent public the opportunity to speak out and pleaded that his group deserved attention because it was made up of flesh and blood. While Matsuzaki insisted on stressing the weight his remarks should carry because of his strong organizational backing, Tsukahara, who felt inferior to the JPLSME, took a defensive attitude, showing thereby the power differentials between the two interest groups, even though Tsukahara looked down on the JPLSME as the "grouping of some sinister persons."

19. The same thing can be said of the anti SMEOI statement submitted to the government and the Diet jointly by nine big-business organizations including the Association of Department Stores, the Association of Coal Mines, the Federation of Iron and Steel, and the Association of Textiles. The statements to oppose the compulsory union membership and the strengthened bargaining power of the union and the fear of bureaucratic control closely resemble that of the NCLA.

PART II

PUBLIC OPINION
AND VOTING BEHAVIOR

Editor's Introduction

A large number of the Japanese people are either uninformed about or indifferent to many public issues. Naoki Kobayashi, for example, after administering opinion polls to small and medium businessmen in Tokyo, found that as many as 43 percent of the respondents neither knew about the proposed Small and Medium-Sized Enterprises Organization Law nor took any interest in it. He attributes the high rate of indifference to political apathy and lack of time to keep informed about even those bills that directly affect their own businesses. Likewise, according to a press poll in 1970 (*Asahi*, June 23, 1970), 27 percent of the male and 46 percent of the female respondents were not interested at all in the United States–Japan Security Treaty, and 30 percent of the male and 30 percent of the female respondents were only slightly interested. Furthermore, most individuals, even if they do hold strong opinions on specific public issues, do not articulate them. If these opinions, then, have any influence on decision-makers, it is probably due to the impact of public-opinion polls rather than to any overt public action. The potential strength of the polls lies in the fact that decision-makers sometimes act as if public opinion did actually make a difference; in particular, any public opinion that might be perceived as a threat can be a potent force in influencing policy-making. Although governmental leaders are becoming increasingly sensitive to some expressions of public opinion, in practice the Japanese elite are not accustomed to accommodating opponents' views.

The public depends on other political forces for formulation of opinion, leadership, and communication. Various groups and individuals such as former party leaders, well-known businessmen, ex-bureaucrats, and leading scholars tend to become spokesmen of public opinion. The mass media serve to transmit public opinion to

91

policy-makers as well as formulating or influencing it themselves. But articulated opinion does not necessarily accurately reflect mass opinion, nor does it always have equal access to decision-makers. The opinions of some individuals and organizations are more influential than others. It should be remembered, then, that public opinion represents interests and influences policy-making to only a limited extent in Japan, as in all other Western democracies.

Voting behavior and public opinion are related since, in effect, an election is a public-opinion poll and voting is one of several means of measuring public opinion. The present electoral system has been widely criticized as contributing to factionalism within the parties, thereby adversely affecting policy-making leadership. The system is also said to favor local rather than national electoral issues and to emphasize the personality of candidates rather than policy alternatives. In the light of this criticism, Selections 4 and 5 analyze the relationships between voting behavior and the nature of the two major parties, as observed in opinion polls and voting studies.

The LDP, with an estimated membership of 632,322 as of July 1970, attracts approximately three-fourths of the rural votes. Rapid economic development and urbanization in postwar Japan have reduced the agrarian segment of the working population from 47 percent in 1948 to 18.7 percent in 1968. But the agrarian electorate continues to represent the largest single bloc of votes for the conservative party. Two factors have helped to maintain their strength. First, the present type of apportionment for the House of Representatives tends to overrepresent the rural votes. The membership of the House is set at 491 (including Okinawa), and under the "medium-sized" election districting, each district sends from three to five members, with the exception of the single-member district of the Amami Islands. Although the term of office for members of the House of Representatives is set at four years, the cabinet has dissolved the House much earlier. Even after a partial reapportionment in 1964, which added five new electoral districts and gave nineteen new seats to five of the most underrepresented metropolitan areas, the actual political value of the "one man, one vote" principle differed greatly, with rural votes weighing several times as much as metropolitan votes. In the 1969 general election, for instance, a candidate in the third electoral district in Osaka was defeated when he had a popular vote of 121,424, whereas a candidate in the second district in the Chiba prefecture was elected with only 31,899 votes. Second, the percentage of eligible voters who actually vote is much higher in rural than in urban areas. Social mores in rural areas which disapprove of nonvoting partly account for the higher rate of voter turnout.

Given the agrarian electorate's preference for the conservative party, how have industrialization, urbanization, and subsequent socioeconomic changes affected their voting behavior? Hiroshi Suzuki (Selection 4), addressing himself to this question in the Ishikawa prefecture, found a measure of interrelationship. In the Noto district, where socioeconomic changes have been slow, a traditional form of electoral behavior, involving considerations of personal and geographic propinquity with candidates, persists in a new form and thereby continues to provide the LDP with *jiban* or "safe" districts. In the Kaga district, however, where industrialization and urbanization have contributed to the rapid decline of the agrarian population, a transformation is under way. Gradually the former *jiban,* nurtured by personal efforts of local bosses, are being broadened into modern, less stable, but more intensive political organizations, centering especially around organized labor. A candidate's votes are often rather evenly spread throughout the constituency; some candidates cannot rely entirely on their safe districts but must gain votes in additional areas to ensure their victory. In either case, each candidate must campaign heavily because increasing emphasis is being placed on criteria that represent the voter's evaluation of his own interests rather than on his personal relations with the candidate or local bosses. While socioeconomic changes have been partly responsible for the breakdown of safe districts for some conservative-party candidates, Suzuki argues, the persistence or revival of traditional voting behavior among the agrarian electorate still offsets the effects of such changes. Further research, by Norio Ogata and Michitoshi Takabatake at Rikkyo University and Jun'ichi Kyōgoku at Tokyo University, is being conducted on the role of *jiban* in voting behavior, through the use of multivariate analysis or principal factor solution.

The JSP, with membership of 36,000 as of August 1970, has its popular base in urban areas, among organized labor and intellectuals. In Selection 5, Joji Watanuki analyzes the voting and other political behavior of Japanese labor. His findings, derived from opinion polls using multivariate techniques, reveal different party preferences. As expected, managerial workers prefer the LDP while white-collar workers and field workers largely support the JSP. Blue-collar (or sales and services) workers split their support between the LDP and the JSP. Furthermore, Watanuki holds that as white-collar and blue-collar worker groups increase in size and political weight, the liberal and progressive tendencies of Japanese workers will become increasingly conspicuous. It remains to be seen, however, how such a trend would affect the Socialists' votes.

Selections 6 and 9 deal with parts of public-opinion polls conducted by a twenty-five-man team in both 1965 and 1966. The team interviewed respondents selected at random from various social strata throughout Japan and Okinawa and had their data cross tabulated by an HITAC 5020 at the computer center of Tokyo University. In Selection 6, Nobuyoshi Ashibe reports his findings of public opinion in selected areas of civil liberties in Japan. Post-1945 Japan has witnessed much civil-liberty–related legislation, besides which, the courts, headed by the Supreme Court with the newly acquired power of judicial review, have been energetically concerned with the protection of civil rights and civil liberties. Overall, his analyses indicate that, despite the rapid socioeconomic changes taking place in Japan, the people's consciousness of their own constitutional rights and liberty is slow to change, so that a modern, liberal consciousness and the traditional, conservative one coexist in the minds of many Japanese.

Electoral Behavior in a Conservative Stronghold: A Case Study of the Ishikawa Prefecture*

HIROSHI SUZUKI

The Ishikawa prefecture† has long been regarded as a stronghold of Japan's conservative parties. This article attempts to probe the electoral structure in that prefecture by analyzing the popular votes cast for the successful candidates of both conservative and progressive parties in the seven general elections for the House of Representatives between 1949 and 1963.

Voting behavior, among other variables, has a close relationship to the industrial structure of an election district. Electoral behavior is not so much a direct reflection of economic variables as an intertwining of complex factors ranging from major issues, political and social conditions, value orientations and political consciousness of the electorate, the slate of candidates, and the degree of competitiveness, to the weather on election day. Most past studies have dealt with voting behavior in only a few elections and consequently have failed to discover variables, particularly electoral psychology, which can be found only by following a succession of elections.[1] In the light of the recent trend toward group research and the use of historical or statistical methods, this study employed political and sociological ap-

---

* This selection is taken from "Hoshu seitō no jiban ni mirareru tokuhyō bumpu jōkyō: Ishikawaken no bawai," in *Kanazawa daigaku hōbungakubu ronshū: Hōgakuhen* (Journal of Law, Kanazawa University), vol. 14 (1967), pp. 113–135. Translated and reprinted with permission of the author.

† Ishikawa prefecture is situated approximately 250 miles northwest of Tokyo, facing the Sea of Japan.

proaches. An examination of the relationship between conservative votes and the industrial, particularly agricultural, structure in the Ishikawa prefecture reveals that the conservative hold on the prefecture is weakening, but, of course, this finding should not be hastily generalized to all other conservative strongholds.

Industrial Structure

The main industry in the Ishikawa prefecture is agriculture and small and medium light industries, particularly textiles. The prefecture's agriculture, primarily aquatic rice, is hampered by the bad weather. Its arable land average of 1.89 acres per farmer is smaller than the national average of 2.18 acres. It has the largest number of small farmers among the three far-northern prefectures, but has ranked high in the nation's rice production mainly owing to improved agricultural technology. Silk and rayon textile industry and light textile machinery manufacturing form the main nonagricultural industry there, but 93.8 percent of the 9,931 companies in the prefecture employ fewer than 29 workers.

In the prewar period, the small textile industry, as a major driving force behind the nation's export business, and, in the early postwar period, the rapidly increased rice production constituted the mainstay of the prefecture's industry. But, under a new policy to develop an economy centering around the heavy chemical industry, both the small textile industry and agriculture, with their meager, individual-based capitals, rendered the prefecture underdeveloped in the nation's industry after 1955.

The change which started at that time in the industrially weak prefecture cannot be overlooked. According to Table 1, showing the population shift in different types of industries in the prefecture, the

Table 1. Population shift in different types of industries (in percentage)

Industry	Nationwide			hikawa prefecture		
	1955	1960	1962	1955	1960	1962
Primary	41.1	32.6	30.2	45.0	37.1	31.9
Agriculture	37.9	29.7	28.1	41.6	34.9	29.9
Secondary	23.8	29.2	31.0	23.5	28.5	31.4
Tertiary	35.1	38.2	38.8	31.5	34.4	36.7

ratio among the primary, secondary, and tertiary industries was approximately 5:2:3 in 1955, but changed to 3:3:4 in 1962, thus approaching the national average. The population in the primary industries, parficularly agriculture, rapidly shifted to the secondary and tertiary industries. Small and medium farmers with fewer than 1.7 acres could not live solely on their income from agriculture, and they were forced either to look for an additional job or change to nonagricultural work (see Table 2). Table 3 indicates a tremendous growth in the number of farmers holding an additional job.

Table 2. Comparison of farmers' income between farming and nonfarming sources (in percentage)

Area	Farming income	Nonfarming income
Entire prefecture	38.3	61.7
Kaga district	44.3	55.7
Noto district	32.4	67.6

Table 3. Percentage of farmers engaged exclusively in farming and farmers holding additional jobs

Type of employment	1946	1955	1960	1962
Exclusively farming	45.5	21.0	18.7	10.0
Additional job in primary industry	37.1	43.6	40.7	34.1
Additional job in secondary industry	17.4	35.4	40.6	55.9

The rapid decrease of agricultural population and corresponding increase of farmers holding secondary jobs is a nationwide trend. As far as the Ishikawa prefecture was concerned, however, there was a considerable difference between the Kaga and Noto districts in the size of the agricultural population. As Table 4 shows, the population ratio among the three types of industry in 1960 was approximately 3:2:4 in the Kaga district and 6:2:2 in the Noto district. Also, a larger percentage of farmers have been engaged exclusively in farming in the Noto district, which has had traditionally small numbers of full-time farmers. In the Kaga district the tendency for farmers to get an additional job has increased at a faster rate than in the Noto district, thereby contributing greatly to the transformation of the agricultural structure in the prefecture.

Table 4. Size of the population engaged in different types of
industries in the two districts of the Ishikawa prefecture, 1960
(in percentage)

Industry	Entire prefecture	Kaga district	Noto district
Primary	37.1	27.0	55.9
Agriculture	34.9	25.9	51.6
Secondary	28.5	33.4	19.6
Tertiary	34.4	39.6	24.5

The two districts also differ in terms of the type of extra jobs
held by farmers. In the Kaga district the farmers permanently employed in secondary or tertiary industries are 54 percent and manual
laborers hired on a day-to-day basis amount to 28 percent, while
in the Noto district those farmers who are self-employed in forestry,
fishery, or seasonal work make up an overwhelmingly high percentage.
Since, however, farmers in the Kaga district are employed mostly in
small and medium enterprises, their income is not always stable.

Thus, the Noto district accounts for the weak nonagricultural industrial basis of the Ishikawa prefecture, whereas the rapid change of
the prefecture-wide agricultural structure owes much to the Kaga
district. Various measures have been taken to narrow the gap in the
industrial development of the two districts, but regional development
plans, hampered by undesirable geography and weather, have not
progressed as fast as the prefectural leaders have wished. Furthermore,
the local government, forced by its poor financial condition, often
has to turn to the national government for assistance, which, in turn,
enables the conservative party to maintain and advance its electoral
hold by playing on the local government's expectation that the ruling
conservative party's candidates to the Diet would secure appropria-
tions for industrial development in their constituencies.

General Elections

The Kaga district, the first election district, and the Noto district,
the second election district, are each assigned three members in the
House of Representatives. The number of eligible voters in the 1963
election were 383,640 in the Kaga district and 237,844 in the Noto
district, with eligible voters per Diet member being 127,000 in the
former and 79,000 in the latter. Since the 1949 general election, the

Kaga district increased its eligible voters by approximately 100,000 and the Noto district by 5,000. Thus, the two districts are very different in terms of total eligible voters and eligible voters per Diet member.

The voter turnout in the 1963 general election for the prefecture was 74.1 percent (75.32 percent for men and 73.05 percent for women), which was slightly higher than the national average of 71.14 percent. As for the rest of the country, it was the lowest turnout of the seven general elections. According to Table 5, however, the 1963

Table 5. Percentages of voter turnout

Area	1949	1952	1953	1955	1958	1960	1963
Kaga district	76.10	84.70	82.50	84.60	82.51	77.33	68.10
Noto district	76.10	80.10	10.70	78.60	76.28	82.04	83.77
Entire prefecture (average)	76.10	82.40	81.70	82.00	79.94	79.25	74.10
Nation (average)	74.04	76.43	74.22	75.84	76.99	73.51	71.14

voter turnout in the Noto district (a postwar record high of 83.77 percent) exceeded that of the Kaga district (a postwar record low of 68.1 percent), as in the 1960 general election. Also, for the first time in the Noto district the female voters (84.88 percent) exceeded the male voters (82.37 percent) in the 1963 election. The increased voting rate in the Noto district, particularly the high degree of female voter turnout, probably resulted not so much from heightened political consciousness among the voters as from the hard work of election campaigners.

As Table 6 shows, in the 1960 general election the progressive party's candidates in the Kaga district rapidly increased their votes, surpassing their conservative opponents. In the 1963 general election the conservatives came back, but in Kanazawa city, which had 55 percent of all eligible voters in the Kaga district, the progressive votes (52.4 percent) exceeded the conservative ones (47.6 percent) by a wider margin than in 1960. Conversely, in the Noto district, since 1949 the progressive votes remained in the neighborhood of 10 percent of all the votes cast, while the conservatives maintained their overwhelming predominance.

In the 1949 general election the progressives in the Kaga district elected two of their candidates: Ryōichi Oka (medical doctor) of the

Table 6. Conservative and progressive party votes in the Kaga and Noto districts and Kanazawa city (in percentages)

Area	Party	1949	1952	1953	1955	1958	1960	1963
Kaga district	Con-servative	63.9(1)	76.8(3)	69.7(2)	67.8(2)	69.8(2)	49.2(2)	54.2(2)
	Pro-gressive	36.3(2)	23.2	30.3(1)	32.2(1)	30.2(1)	50.8(1)	45.8(1)
Noto district	Con-servative	88.6(3)	89.4(3)	94.4(3)	95.7(3)	85.1(3)	85.9(3)	89.2(3)
	Pro-gressive	11.4	10.6	5.6	4.3	14.9	14.1	10.8
Kanazawa city	Con-servative	53.9	66.9	59.4	60.6	64.7	48.4	47.6
	Pro-gressive	46.1	33.1	40.4	39.4	35.3	51.6	52.4

Note: Figures inside parentheses indicate the number of successful candidates.

JSP, and Sakujirō Nashiki (lawyer) of the Japan Communist Party (JCP). The conservatives managed to elect only one, Eiichi Sakata (ex-bureaucrat of the Ministry of Agriculture and Forestry) of the Democratic Liberal Party. In 1952 Masanobu Tsuji (independent), a former staff member of the Imperial Headquarters from Enuma county, created a great confusion in the Kaga district, where both the conservative and progressive parties had to adjust their slate of candidates to compete with the strong new opponent. The JCP, which had greatly increased its seats in the Diet in the 1949 election, was completely defeated. Likewise, R. Oka of the JSP was defeated by M. Tsuji. Thus, M. Tsuji's election along with other successful candidates (E. Sakata of the Liberal Party and Eiji Takebe [Director of All Japan Sightseeing Associations] of the Progessive Party) radically redrew the 1952 election map of the Kaga district. M. Tsuji continued to conduct popular and effective election campaigns and was elected four consecutive times until 1959 when he moved to the House of Councillors by getting the third highest number of votes in the nationwide constituency. R. Oka (JSP) made a successful comeback in the 1953 general election and steadily gained votes thereafter. E. Sakata, defeated by M. Tsuji in the 1955 election, managed to regain votes and continued to be elected. The Kaga district has not experienced any radical change in the slate of candidates since Tsuji switched to the House of Councillors, and currently the LDP (conservative party) holds two seats and the progressives hold one.*

The three seats in the Noto district remained in the hands of the conservatives, Shūji Masutani (lawyer), Yoshio Minami (ex-bureaucrat of the Ministry of Commerce and Industry), and Tamaki Ōmori (civil and construction engineer). No new candidates from either the conservative or progressive parties were elected. Thus, the Noto district was a very solid area for some incumbent conservatives and, to that extent, a powerful fortress for the conservative parties. Starting with the 1960 general election, however, the conservatives' hold began to break when a new candidate from the same conservative party drew an unexpectedly large number of votes, although not enough for election. Finally, in the 1963 general election, their bastion partially collapsed when another new candidate, Sakonshirō Inamura (construction company owner), defeated T. Ōmori.† The record-breaking voter turnout, particularly that of women, and an unprecedentedly large number of election-law violations in the Noto district seem to reflect the fierce and sometimes underhanded attempts to get voters to the polls in 1963. The high rate of voting probably indicates many voters' protests against the senior Diet members who had been tenaciously holding on to their election strongholds. But the mere expression of desire for new Diet members, unless accompanied by criticism of specific legislation by the incumbents, would give politicians the chance to manipulate voters fairly easily.

Voting Patterns

The following six members of the House of Representatives were elected more than five times in the seven general elections in the

---

* In the 1967 general election incumbents Eiichi Sakata (LDP) and Shigeo Imura (LDP) were re-elected, but Tetsuo Katsuragi, a new independent candidate, defeated the incumbent JSP member, Ryōichi Oka. Since Katsuragi later joined the LDP, the progressive parties lost all seats in the Kaga district. In the 1969 general election, the incumbents were all defeated and replaced by new members, Yoshiaki Mori (independent), Yukio Betsukawa (LDP), and Keiwa Okada (LDP). The results of these two elections seem to indicate highly unpredictable voting behavior in the Kaga district.

† In the 1967 general election, incumbent LDP members Shūji Masutani and Sakonshirō Inamura were re-elected, but a new LDP candidate, Misoji Sakamoto, defeated the incumbent Yoshio Minami. The 1969 general election returned three LDP incumbents to the House.

Ishikawa prefecture between 1949 and 1963: Eiichi Sakata (lost in 1955), Masanobu Tsuji (elected consecutively between 1952 and 1958), and Ryōichi Oka (lost in 1952) in the Kaga district; Shūji Masutani and Yoshio Minami (both elected consecutively between 1949 and 1963), and Tamaki Ōmori (defeated in 1953 and 1963) in the Noto district.

According to Tables 7 and 8, Shūji Masutani's votes in both

Table 7. S. Masutani's votes in his safe election districts

	Fugeshi county (including Fugeshi city after 1955)	Suzu county (including Suzu city after 1955)	Votes in both counties	Total votes in Noto district	Percentage of his total votes received in both counties
1949	20,895	5,845	26,740	39,393	67.8
1952	26,513	9,878	36,391	49,588	73.3
1953	25,355	10,163	35,518	45,703	77.7
1955	25,749	9,502	35,251	49,381	71.3
1958	25,527	9,653	35,180	55,849	62.9
1960	26,199	9,262	35,461	53,906	65.7
1963	21,806	10,239	32,045	44,191	72.5

Table 8. Votes received by S. Masutani, Y. Minami, and T. Ōmori in Fugeshi and Suzu counties

Area	Candidate	1949	1952	1953	1955	1958	1960	1963
Fugeshi county	S. Masutani	51.4%	61.6%	58.6%	57.1%	56.0%	52.7%	46.0%
	Y. Minami	5.5	3.7	3.5	4.3	2.8	3.9	4.7
	T. Ōmori	13.4	15.3	17.7	15.5	9.0	6.2	8.0
	Total eligible votes cast	40,592	43,745	43,266	45,049	45,489	49,667	49,542
Suzu county	S. Masutani	26.4%	42.7%	45.1%	43.9%	45.1%	43.1%	47.6%
	Y. Minami	2.4	1.7	1.6	2.0	1.0	3.1	8.7
	T. Ōmori	7.1	12.3	14.7	15.0	7.3	5.4	7.4
	Total eligible votes cast	22,089	23,117	22,510	21,632	21,377	21,466	21,485

Fugeshi county (his home county, which incorporated Wajima city after 1955) and the adjacent Suzu county (which incorporated Suzushi city after 1955) fluctuated very little, between 62.9 percent and 77.7 percent, throughout the seven general elections. Also he received approximately 50 percent of the total votes cast in both counties. Furthermore, Masutani's votes remained more or less 20 percent in Kashima county and Nanao city respectively and less than 10 percent in Hakui and Kahoku counties. It seems to follow that both Fugeshi and Suzu counties are S. Masutani's safe election districts.

Tables 9 and 10 show that in both Hakui county (his home county,

Table 9. Y. Minami's votes in his safe election districts

Hakui county (including Hakui city after 1955)	Kahoku county	Votes in both counties	Total votes in Noto district	Percentage of his total votes received in both counties
1949	18,141	6,013	24,154	31,980	75.5
1952	18,677	12,310	30,987	39,636	78.1
1953	17,523	12,159	29,682	39,095	75.9
1955	18,073	15,074	33,147	42,043	78.8
1958	20,960	14,794	35,754	41,938	85.2
1960	22,391	14,635	37,026	43,889	84.3
1963	15,865	13,756	29,621	37,365	79.2

Table 10. Votes received by S. Masutani, Y. Minami, and T. Ōmori in Hakui and Kahoku counties

Area	Candidate	1949	1952	1953	1955	1958	1960	1963
Hakui county	S. Masutani	2.5%	2.1%	1.3%	2.8%	7.0%	6.8%	3.1%
	Y. Minami	48.9	45.6	42.3	46.3	54.3	52.7	35.9
	T. Ōmori	16.6	9.7	11.5	15.1	16.6	14.6	9.0
	Total eligible votes cast	37,064	40,915	41,360	39,009	38,569	42,478	44,129
Kahoku county	S. Masutani	3.1%	4.2%	3.0%	4.4%	18.5%	16.0%	9.8%
	Y. Minami	18.2	35.8	34.9	39.9	43.5	39.8	43.3
	T. Ōmori	9.6	11.1	8.6	11.8	15.1	11.9	8.2
	Total eligible votes cast	33,091	34,379	34,761	37,720	33,965	36,684	31,751

which incorporated Hakui city after 1955) and the adjacent Kahoku county, Yoshio Minami throughout the seven elections gained consistently between 75.5 percent and 85.2 percent of all the votes he received in the Noto district and approximately 45 percent of all votes cast in these two counties. Conversely, he scored only 15 percent of the votes cast in Kashima County and about 5 percent in all other places, thus finding his own strength primarily in Hakui and Kahoku counties. As Table 10 indicates, in 1963 when a new candidate ran from Hakui city along with Y. Minami and others, Minami's votes dropped by as much as 17 percent (from 52.7 percent in 1960 to 35.9 percent), but the drop did not affect his victory. The accompanying list of figures shows that in Nanao city (his home city) and

Ōmori's votes in his strongholds (Nanao city and Kashima county) in relation to his total votes

Year	Percentage
1949	49.1
1952	48.9
1953	50.8
1955	53.7
1958	50.8
1960	54.2
1963	53.9

Kashima county, both of which were surrounded by the safe districts of S. Masutani and Y. Minami, Tamaki Ōmori's votes approached 50 percent of his total votes in the Noto district. Therefore, Nanao city and Kashima county can be regarded as Ōmori's safe districts, where he received approximately 40 percent of the total votes cast. But, because he was less secure in those areas than Masutani and Minami were in their strongholds, Ōmori had to rely upon scattered votes in other areas. His votes reached a peak in 1955 but soon began to decline, culminating in his defeat in 1963 when he received only 35.6 percent of the votes in Nanao city and 22.2 percent in Kashima county (see Table 11).

According to Table 12, the ratio between Eiichi Sakata's votes in Enuma county (his home county, which incorporated Kaga city after 1958) and his total votes in the Kaga district declined from 33.7 percent in 1949 to 23.2 percent in 1963, mainly because his votes in the county did not change significantly while in the entire district they steadily increased. Furthermore, Table 13 shows that the ratio between Sakata's votes in Enuma county and the total eligible votes cast in the Kaga district was 46.5 percent in 1949, dropped to 30.5 percent in 1955, and gradually rose again until 1963, when it reached 57.0 percent. He received approximately 10 percent of the votes cast

Table 11. Votes received by S. Masutani, Y. Minami, and T. Ōmori in Nanao city and Kashima county

Area	Candidate	1949	1952	1953	1955	1958	1960	1963
Nanao	S. Masutani	31.3%	30.2%	21.2%	25.9%	30.1%	22.8%	17.9%
city	Y. Minami	8.9	8.2	8.7	6.4	4.0	3.1	2.8
	T. Ōmori	35.8	42.9	48.1	59.0	45.1	42.6	35.6
	Total eligible votes cast	15,875	17,511	17,159	22,992	22,349	24,615	25,889
Kashima	S. Masutani	21.4%	18.9%	16.8%	22.3%	22.6%	16.4%	11.7%
county	Y. Minami	13.5	17.4	20.5	20.1	17.3	14.1	10.8
	T. Ōmori	38.6	32.6	38.2	43.9	35.8	29.5	22.2
	Total eligible votes cast	26,528	29,662	29,250	24,949	21,731	24,346	25,363

Table 12. E. Sakata's votes in his safe district (Enuma county)

	Enuma county (including Kaga city after 1958)	Total votes in the Noto district	Percentage of his total votes received in the county
1949	14,556	43,171	33.7
1952	11,892	41,504	28.6
1953	11,927	47,572	25.0
1955	11,284	42,468	26.5
1958	14,166	53,033	26.7
1960	17,225	64,125	26.8
1963	17,367	74,796	23.2

Table 13. Votes received by E. Sakata, M. Tsuji, and R. Oka in Komatsu city and Enuma county

Area	Candidate	1949	1952	1953	1955	1958	1960	1963
Komatsu	E. Sakata	20.5%	15.5%	15.7%	17.7%	24.7%	23.6%	38.1%
city	M. Tsuji	0*	27.2	18.5	43.1	19.6	0*	0*
	R. Oka	10.7	5.1	10.1	15.3	18.4	15.7	27.4
	Total eligible votes cast	24,965	30,396	31,184	31,053	45,133	46,993	38,837
Enuma	E. Sakata	46.5%	32.3%	32.7%	30.5%	43.8%	51.1%	57.0%
county	M. Tsuji	0*	37.7	31.4	48.1	28.7	0*	0*
	R. Oka	10.1	4.6	9.5	11.3	9.5	15.1	23.3
	Total eligible votes cast	31,305	36,729	36,434	36,924	34,608	33,463	30,258

* M. Tsuji did not run in 1949, 1960, and 1963.

in Kanazawa city and about 20 percent in all other cities and counties. Thus, Enuma county, seemingly a safe district for Sakata, was not actually so solid as to ensure his election when compared with the strongholds of S. Masutani and Y. Minami in the Noto district. Indeed, in the four general elections between 1952 and 1958 his stronghold was shaken by the "Tsuji whirlwind," and in 1955 he was defeated. After Tsuji switched to the House of Councillors, Komatsu city and Ishikawa county, both of which were adjacent to Enuma county, went to Sakata.

Except in Enuma county (his home county) where his votes remained in the neighborhood of 30 percent, Masanobu Tsuji's votes were extremely unstable. As Table 14 shows, M. Tsuji's votes in

Table 14. M. Tsuji's votes in Kanazawa city and Enuma county

	Kanazawa city	Percentage of his total votes received in the city	Enuma county (including Kaga city after 1958)	Percentage of his total votes received in the county	Total votes in the Kaga district
1952	27,598	42.5	13,848	21.3	64,912
1953	20,624	41.1	11,449	22.8	50,090
1955	33,082	39.5	17,785	21.2	83,696
1958	19,097	41.9	9,935	21.8	45,582

Enuma county accounted for only 21 percent of the total votes cast in the Kaga district, not sufficient to ensure his victory. During his four elections, his votes floated between 83,000 in 1955 and 45,000 in 1958. The floating votes he picked up in Kanazawa city, which amounted to more than 40 percent of the total votes there, were presumably a significant factor leading to his four consecutive successful elections. After he suffered a slight stagnation in the 1958 election, he switched to the House of Councillors and ran from a nationwide constituency in 1959; he was elected with the impressive numbers of 84,000 votes in the Ishikawa prefecture and 683,000 in Japan, thereby attracting much attention throughout the country.

Ryōichi Oka, a JSP member, was the only candidate from any progressive party elected six out of seven times. As Table 15 shows, throughout the seven general elections including the 1952 election in which he was defeated, his votes in Kanazawa city (his home city) always reached more than 60 percent of his total votes in the Kaga

Table 15. R. Oka's votes in Kanazawa city

	Kanazawa city	Total votes in the Kaga district	Percentage of his total votes received in the city
1949	25,379	40,148	63.2
1952	20,442	31,453	64.9
1953	36,615	54,593	67.0
1955	32,890	53,577	61.3
1958	29,666	49,342	60.1
1960	39,456	61,411	64.2
1963	44,499	74,507	59.7

district and thus represented the main source of his continued success. Although more than 25 percent of the total eligible voters in Kanazawa city voted for R. Oka, they did not constitute an overwhelmingly large portion of his total votes in the Kaga district, as compared with the votes of Masutani and Minami in their safe districts. Before 1953 he received less than 10 percent of the votes in Komatsu city and Enuma county and about 15 percent in both Nomi and Ishikawa counties, but after 1955 his votes in those areas showed a considerable increase while there was no significant increase in his votes in Kanazawa city.

Three voting patterns emerge with respect to the six lower-house members examined so far. First, the cases of S. Masutani and Y. Minami in the Noto district represent a pattern in which the candidate received as much as 60 to 80 percent of the total votes cast in his solidly safe district while collecting scattered votes from the rest of the constituencies. T. Omori's votes are a weaker example of the same pattern, in that he managed to maintain only 50 percent in his safe districts and had to rely heavily on other parts of his constituency for victory. The cause of Ōmori's defeat in the 1963 election was not so much a decrease of his votes in his strongholds as in the other districts.

Second, M. Tsuji's votes form a different pattern, inasmuch as they were spread nearly even in each county and city in the Kaga district rather than being concentrated in any safe districts. Indeed, his four consecutive victories are attributable to the floating votes rather than fixed votes in a safe district, which tends to provide a candidate with strong reserve votes.

Third, the votes gained by E. Sakata and R. Oka form a transitional pattern from the first to the second (see Tables 16 and 17).

Table 16. Votes received by E. Sakata, M. Tsuji, and R. Oka in Kanazawa city

Candidate	1949	1952	1953	1955	1958	1960	1963
E. Sakata	11.7%	9.1%	11.8%	9.7%	8.1%	12.4%	14.7%
M. Tsuji	0*	23.7	16.9	25.8	13.1	0*	0*
R. Oka	25.6	17.5	30.1	25.6	20.4	28.8	33.1
Total eligible votes cast	98,924	116,581	121,536	128,148	145,029	133,276	134,187

* M. Tsuji did not run in 1949, 1960, and 1963.

Table 17. Votes received by E. Sakata, M. Tsuji, and R. Oka in Nomi and Ishikawa counties

Area	Candidate	1949	1952	1953	1955	1958	1960	1963
Nomi	E. Sakata	17.9%	21.3%	24.5%	22.6%	30.6%	26.7%	41.5%
county	M. Tsuji	0*	26.4	19.9	31.9	14.8	0*	0*
	R. Oka	14.4	14.1	17.7	19.9	15.1	13.5	21.8
Total eligible votes cast		28,272	27,281	27,273	27,461	18,529	18,975	18,310
Ishikawa	E. Sakata	21.9%	20.7%	23.1%	18.7%	26.4%	33.5%	41.5%
county	M. Tsuji	0*	19.6	16.4	28.3	12.5	0*	0*
	R. Oka	15.3	9.5	15.7	16.7	13.5	17.8	22.5
Total eligible votes cast		31,061	40,624	41,446	37,604	38,857	38,430	36,658

* M. Tsuji did not run in 1949, 1960, and 1963.

The only difference between the two is that rural votes made up the base of Sakata's pattern at an early period but later caused a transformation in which his votes spread evenly throughout his constituency, whereas urban votes comprised the base of Oka's first pattern which gradually changed to the second. E. Sakata came from a rural area and received many farmers' votes, traditionally the single largest source of support for the conservative parties, but R. Oka, as a Socialist from a city, ran on the strength of the organized labor and liberals in urban areas.

Among the three voting patterns the first seems to give a candidate a fixed and stable base of support. The second pattern, characterized by M. Tsuji's floating votes, has an inherent weakness in that unless a candidate develops a spectacular campaign technique to capture the voters' interest in each election, stagnation and apathy will soon offset his original explosive popularity. A transitional pattern can ensure some stability as long as reasonably large and fixed votes are secured in some safe districts while relatively evenly spread votes come from the rest of the constituency.

The Voting Pattern and the Agricultural Community

The fact that the first pattern of voting was found in the Noto district while the second and transitional patterns were seen in the Kaga district cannot be fully explained without analyzing, among other factors, the industrial and agricultural structures and characteristics of each district. The relationship between the three voting patterns and the industrial structure of the Ishikawa prefecture will be examined on the basis of a survey conducted immediately after the 1963 general election.

As Table 4 indicates, as high as 55.9 percent of the population in the Noto district is engaged in primary industry, with 51.6 percent of that being in agriculture. Although a very large number of farmers hold an extra job, an overwhelmingly large portion of them are either self-employed in forestry or fishery or become migrant workers during off-seasons. The Noto district, where many farmers are excluded from the secondary and tertiary industries, exhibits an extremely low degree of population mobility and is much less urbanized than the Kaga district. The strong ties based on geographical propinquity and kinship that still persist in the Noto district are reinforced by the low degree of social mobility and urbanization. According to Table 18,

Table 18. Results of poll on criteria for voting (percentage of respondents)

Area	Party affiliation	Party and candidate	Candidate's qualification	Cannot say one way or the other	Do not know
Kaga district*	37.7	13.4	31.1	7.2	10.6
Noto district†	19.3	15.6	44.7	4.1	16.3
Totals	30.6	14.2	36.2	6.2	12.8

* 469 respondents.
† 294 respondents.

19.3 percent of the voters in the Noto district chose their candidates on the basis of the candidate's party affiliation, whereas 44.7 percent of them voted on the basis of the candidate's qualifications, and the majority of the candidate-oriented voters preferred a local candidate. Voting preference in the Noto district is strongly affected by a voter's ties with the candidate based on geographical and personal propinquity, neither one of which has anything to do with the qualifications expected of a political representative. This voting behavior in the Noto district largely accounts for the votes gained by some conservative party members who through their services oblige their constituents to vote for them.

Among various other adverse effects upon voters' free decision-making, the community mores of mutual agreement among voters, deriving from strong ties based on geographical closeness and kinship, have persisted in such traditional organizations as community and town associations in the Noto district. A survey has indicated that the practice of mutual agreement among voters has decreased considerably in the Noto district, but recently has revived in the form of citizens' associations for electing individual candidates. Not only village or town associations but also agricultural and fishing cooperatives provide places where the local influentials can take the initiative in organizing most of the citizens' associations. Citizens' associations, which have the appearance of voluntary gatherings of local voters, tend to create the false image of spontaneity among local residents while actually preserving the traditional agreement among voters and molding solid support for certain candidates.

This voting behavior in the Noto district, coupled with the agricultural dominance there, largely accounted for the solid support given to some conservative representatives. But, to the extent that a new conservative candidate, Sakonshirō Inamura, defeated the conservative incumbent T. Ōmori in 1963, the party's solidarity was gradually breaking down. As previously mentioned, Ōmori's votes formed only a weak base, and accordingly he had to depend on districts other than his own safe districts. The candidacy of S. Inamura and the increased voter expectation for new representatives led to the decrease of Ōmori's strength in his safe districts and his eventual defeat. S. Inamura was first elected with less than 6 percent of all eligible votes cast in S. Masutani's stronghold and approximately 20 percent in the strongholds of both Y. Minami and T. Ōmori, thereby dealing the fatal blow to Ōmori who had to rely on votes in areas other than his own safe districts. Inamura, a construction company owner, had opened the first recreation center in the area in 1962. In the rural Noto district, which had a large primary-industry population but only a few public entertainment facilities, his recreation center offered an ideal place for many women and elderly people to relax. Inamura thus succeeded in capturing many votes and in competing with incumbent Diet men who had nurtured their safe districts for years by means of their geographical or personal ties with voters.

The second, evenly scattered vote pattern and the transitional pattern seen in the Kaga district are again very closely related to the industrial, and particularly agricultural, structure there. The rapid population decrease in primary industry, especially agriculture, and the urbanization of agricultural villages through the influence of commercial and industrial cities like Kanazawa and Komatsu have gradually weakened or even destroyed the candidate's geographical and personal ties with his electorate.

The source of a candidate's support in the Kaga district has become more diversified than that which was based on geography or kinship, for instance, the floating votes of M. Tsuji, the organized, conservative votes of E. Sakata, and the organized, liberal votes of R. Ōka. M. Tsuji directed his election campaign toward apathetic voters in agriculture, forestry, small and medium businesses, and urban areas, and his vigorous and effective campaigning stirred up a "Tsuji whirlwind," making out of floating votes, as he put it, an "amorphous organization" throughout his constituency. Tsuji, a former staff member of the Imperial Headquarters, adopted as his campaign program the neutrality of Japan with a self-defense force and an anti-American, anti-Russian, and anti-Yoshida stand. He tried to arouse the voters' military sentiment by building a campaign office building which resembled the former military headquarters at the war front. He decided not to have any nationally known statesmen speak in his support, but his spectacular campaigning always drew a great deal of popular attention. By winning each election with massive votes, he altered one corner of the political map in the Kaga district and thereby disrupted the conservatives' safe districts.

At the beginning, E. Sakata's votes reflected the first voting pattern with a base in the agricultural area, particularly his own county. Partly due to the "Tsuji whirlwind," however, he could no longer depend on the strength of his safe districts. As he began to cultivate the organized votes of both the agricultural cooperative union, which increasingly assumed the character of an interest group by demanding a high rice price for producers, and other primary industries which had spread throughout his constituency, his votes began to gradually spread out more evenly with the conservative and organized votes forming his main strength.

Organized labor and liberals in and around Kanazawa city used to constitute R. Oka's main source of support, but, in parallel to the increase of farmers who held extra jobs, his strength began to gradually penetrate the rural areas. Consequently, unorganized and liberal voters began to emerge in the Kaga district, where the agricultural votes were traditionally either floating and susceptible to demagoguery or the organized, conservative votes of agricultural cooperative unions. Whether the unorganized, liberal vote in the Kaga district will become or remain scattered greatly depends on the further structural change of the district.

Conclusion

Political and sociological approaches have been used here to construct electoral patterns and then to analyze the relationship between these patterns and the industrial and agricultural structure in the Ishikawa prefecture, one of the bastions of the conservative party. Since the structure of the agricultural community is extremely complex and constantly changing, the findings in the present study cannot be considered final. Nonetheless, the three distinctive patterns which emerged in the analysis of votes of the six representatives seem to reveal both a traditional and a more modern voting behavior coexisting in the Ishikawa prefecture. The breakdown of this conservative territory seems to point to a quasi-modernization, inasmuch as it is so far confined to the replacement of one conservative candidate by another. As the candidate's geographical and personal ties with his voters become weaker and weaker in an agricultural community, those conservative candidates who have been easily elected on the strength of such ties in a safe district will have to somehow reinforce their support. In the Kaga district especially, where no candidates have secured a solid base pattern of voter support, it becomes imperative for both conservative and progressive party candidates to secure fixed numbers of organized votes; no less important in affecting the result of an election are the floating or scattered votes. In conclusion, the transformation of the existing parties and the active campaigning by new candidates among the employees of small and medium enterprises and the white-collar class as well as farmers holding extra jobs seem to have contributed to the breakdown of safe districts for some conservative candidates.

Note to Selection 4

1. Ishikawa Prefecture Election Control Commission, ed., *Ishikawa-kenmin no seiji'ishiki to tōhyōkōdō no jittai* [Political consciousness and voting behavior of the Ishikawa residents], March 1964.

The Voting Behavior and Party Preference of Labor*

JŌJI WATANUKI

The purpose of this study was to analyze the voting behavior and party preference of labor on the basis of several public-opinion polls which were conducted during the past few years, either individually by the present writer or jointly with the League for Fair Elections (Kōmeisenkyo Renmei).[1] Respondents, selected by random sampling from all eligible voters in Tokyo and Japan, answered a questionnaire while being interviewed. The term "labor" here does not refer to organized labor but rather to workers in general. Studies of labor in certain geographical areas, of labor unions, or of specific enterprises may determine some characteristics of a narrowly defined labor aggregate but cannot be generalized to labor in Tokyo and Japan as a whole. Conversely, the present findings will not account for the behavior of a particular labor group in a particular location, but this shortcoming can be minimized by subclassifying labor in terms of income, union membership, size of the business enterprise, and so forth.

First the respondents were randomly sampled, eligible voters of both sexes over twenty years of age, and they were classified according to the type of work in which they engaged in the following four categories: (1) managerial workers; (2) specialists, technicians, and clerical workers; (3) workers in sales and services (but security workers are classified in category (2) above); and (4) workers in production, transportation, communication, and mining, skilled as well as

---

* This selection is taken from "Rōdōsha no tōhyō kōdō to seitō shiji taido: Ikutsuka no chōsakekka kara," in *Nihon rōdō kyōkai zasshi* (Journal of the Japan Labor Association) (1969), pp. 14–23. Translated and reprinted with permission of the author.

unskilled. The four categories of employees will hereafter be referred to as managerial workers, white-collar workers, workers in sales and services, and field workers, respectively.

Managerial workers are usually classified as white-collar workers in the broad definition of the term, but Marxist theoreticians would place them at a lower level of the ruling class in opposition to the labor class.* Even some non-Marxists like Ralf Dahrendorf would argue that managerial workers possess a delegated authority and serve the interests of the ruling class. Furthermore, it has been empirically proven in various press opinion polls that managerial workers tend to differ in their views from specialists, technicians, and clerical workers.

White-collar workers, as defined in the present study, manifest a wide variety of characteristics with regard to working conditions and the size of their employing institution. Theoretically, white-collar workers do not possess the means of production. Moreover, this group is not in the ruling position in a big organization in the Dahrendorf fashion nor is there much possibility of their reaching it or even expecting to reach it. In this sense, white-collar workers do not differ much from the three other categories of employees. It may be meaningless or even impossible to distinguish this group on the base of the power relationship and the ownership of the means of production, but the category of white-collar workers remains meaningful as long as various social strata are to be classified by taking into account total living opportunities, way of life, and pattern of thought. Empirically, the white-collar workers differ to a statistically significant degree from other categories of labor in terms of voting behavior and political and social consciousness.

A distinctive voting behavior and political consciousness of workers

* According to the predominant and orthodox Marxist view of the Kōza (intellectuals) faction, the Meiji restoration was a bourgeois democratic revolution which moved Japan into the first stage of a capitalistic country, while in the prewar and early postwar periods Japanese capitalism was supported by its imperial system under which monopolistic capitalists and landlords, as the ruling class, exploited and oppressed Japanese workers and farmers. The Kōza faction advocated a bourgeois democratic revolution to overthrow the ruling class and to prepare the way for a socialist revolution. Later, however, this faction began to regard American "imperialism" as the cause of Japanese capitalism and accordingly changed its immediate objective to a national liberation to save the Japanese people from American "imperialism." The Rōnō (workers and farmers) faction, however, assumed that Japan was already in the stage of socialist revolution and advocated more radical views of Marxist ideology.

in sales and services has previously been found, and it has been predicted that with the likelihood of increase in their number, this group will be of more importance in the future when one is examining the political behavior of big-city dwellers.[2] No Marxist theoreticians would insist on a sales and services category, but among those scholars who actually have used it on the strength of their empirical data are Solomon B. Levine, who has noted that this group is called "gray-collar workers" in the United States, and Saburō Yasuda, a sociologist who refers to this group as "yellow-collar workers." Both designations, however, seem somewhat unsavory and are not popularly used. The press and public-opinion pollsters do not usually treat these workers as a separate category of employees but if specialists, technicians, and clerical workers (that is, the white-collar workers) are to be classified separately, then workers in sales and services should be treated likewise, at least empirically. Public-opinion polls on various elections conducted by the Central Research Company (Chūō-chōsasha) at the request of the League for Fair Elections used to treat sales and services workers as part of the field workers, but, starting with its poll on the sixth unified local election in 1967, the category has been added to their questionnaire. Finally, no special remarks seem to be necessary regarding the category of field workers.

Both objective and subjective attributes of employees in the four different categories will be utilized as variables of the voting behavior and party preference of labor, and the findings will also be compared with those of all the eligible voters in Tokyo and Japan. In the rest of this article, the term "labor" will primarily refer to the categories of (2) white-collar workers, (3) sales and services workers, and (4) field workers, while the category of (1) managerial workers will be used to draw comparisons with the other three labor classes.

Attributes of the Four Kinds of Employees

A macro-interpretation or prediction of election results requires more than the collection of data on political consciousness, voting behavior, and other characteristics of various social strata. The size of each social stratum must be known, because a large social group with a large number of voters can affect the outcome of the election.[3]

Estimated sizes of each group in three sample surveys in Tables 1 and 2 are considerably different from the findings of a government

Table 1. Survey and census statistics on the size of labor classes in metropolitan Tokyo (in percentage)

| | Employees | | | | | |
Source of figures	Self-employed	Family employed	Managerial workers	White-collar workers	Workers in sales and services	Field workers
Survey 1*	27.3	6.2	7.4	23.7	15.8	19.4
Survey 2†	30.0	4.3	9.2	18.6	11.6	26.1
Census‡	14.8	2.7	8.2	24.1	12.5	37.7

* Survey 1 consists of male job holders in the Tokyo survey of April 1967 conducted by the League of Fair Elections. Valid samples numbered 417.

† Survey 2 consists of male job holders in the March 1968 Tokyo survey conducted by the Political Consciousness Study Group (Seijiishiki Kenkyūkai). Valid samples numbered 372.

‡ The census used 1 percent of respondents in the 1965 census, and its classification was based on positions held by male workers 15 years of age and over.

census. Even after marginal errors have been corrected, the size of the self-employed group is larger and that of field workers is smaller in each of the three surveys than in the census. The cause of such discrepancies is generally suspected to lie in the survey technique employed. When interviewed face to face, a respondent tends to answer in a manner that makes his social prestige, educational background, and occupation sound more impressive than they really are. The government census employs two methods: one in which a member of the family fills in the questionnaire, and the other in which a census taker fills in the questionnaire by interviewing any member of the family. Our surveys used a third method in which a census taker fills in the questionnaire by interviewing a specific family member whose opinions were being sought, rather than any family member. Regardless of the survey method employed, however, respondents tend to present themselves in the best possible light.

Another cause of different findings on the size of social strata can be found in the fact that the government census classifies as employees a large number of either the self-employed or family employees. After the subcategory of "those who work at home" in the 1965 census has been reclassified into self-employed and family employees, the size

Table 2. Survey and census statistics on the size of labor classes in Japan (in percentage)

Source of figures	Self-employed in agriculture or fishery	Family employed in agriculture or fishery	Self-employed in commercial or industrial services	Family employed in commercial or industrial services	Employees			
					Managerial workers	White-collar workers	Employees in sales and services	Field workers
Survey 3*	21.5	3.2	20.8	3.8	4.7	21.3	8.0	16.7
Census†	13.1	4.8	12.0	2.4	4.7	18.7	7.3	37.0

* Survey 3 consists of male job holders in the July 1968 national survey by the League of Fair Elections. Valid samples numbered 1,047.

† The census used 1 percent of respondents in the 1965 census, and its classification was based on positions held by male workers 15 years of age and over.

of each labor category in the census comes closer to the findings in the three surveys (see the accompanying list).

Results of reclassification of "those employed at home" into "former middle class" in Tokyo (1960 census)

Classification	Percentage
Former middle class	33.5
New middle class	26.9
Workers in sales and services	7.1
Labor	32.5

But the 1965 census classifies labor into four groups (employees, company officials, the self-employed, and family employees) and cannot be reclassified in the same manner as the 1960 census which classifies occupations into nine types including "those employees who work at home."

Thus, surveys 1, 2, and 3 seem to reflect more adequately than the government's census the size of social strata. The fact is that the ratio between field workers and white-collar workers is currently 1:1 and that workers in sales and services represent a relatively large portion of Tokyo labor.

Some of the findings in Tables 3 and 4 showing the objective attributes of labor both in Tokyo and Japan are available in statistical reports, but some others are made known only through the three surveys.

First, most noticeable are the different degrees of union membership in each category of employees. A high correlation of membership with voting behavior, party preference, conservative or progressive ideology, and political interest has been found previously.[4] A union member is usually more liberal and more interested in politics than a nonmember. According to Table 4, the nationwide average rate of union membership is 39.6 percent which, despite 95 percent reliability and ±3.6 percent sampling error, appears to be a little higher than the rate of union membership estimated in *Rōdōkumiai kihonchōsahōkoku* (the government's labor union basic survey report). Causes of the different findings on union membership are probably twofold: (1) distortions due to uncollected responses (resulting in low degrees of union membership among them) and false answers from respondents; and (2) distortions due to the watered-down responses given to the labor union basic survey's questionnaire. Even with these distortion factors taken into account, the union mem-

Table 3. Objective attributes of labor from the 1968 Tokyo survey on international consciousness (in percentage)*

Attribute	Managerial workers	White-collar workers	Sales and services workers	Field workers	Size of group within all eligible voters
Sex					
Male	100.0	63.9	64.2	81.5	45.5
Female	0	36.1	35.8	18.5	54.5
Age					
Early 20's	0	27.8	13.4	16.8	12.7
Late 20's	5.9	13.9	37.3	16.0	14.9
30's	23.5	38.0	23.9	25.2	29.8
40's	41.2	11.1	13.4	23.5	19.1
50's	17.6	5.6	10.4	12.6	11.7
Over 60	11.8	3.7	1.5	5.9	11.8
Education					
Elementary	2.9	17.6	34.3	65.5	41.0
Secondary	29.4	54.6	47.8	32.8	41.1
Higher	67.6	27.8	17.9	1.7	17.6
Monthly income of respondent					
Less than $83	0	25.9	31.3	22.7	23.2
$83 to $139	5.9	30.6	31.3	31.9	28.6
$140 to $278	38.2	37.0	37.3	42.0	38.4
$279 or more	55.9	4.6	0	2.5	8.2
Monthly income of respondent's family					
Less than $83	0	7.4	14.9	10.1	5.6
$83 to $139	5.9	20.4	13.4	25.1	16.2
$140 to $278	32.4	42.6	41.8	51.9	45.4
$279 or more	61.8	26.8	6.0	5.3	25.0
Number of employees where respondent works					
1 to 9	0	6.5	22.4	13.4	4.8
10 to 99	20.6	30.6	25.4	40.3	13.2
100 to 999	29.4	19.4	29.9	15.1	8.9
Over 1,000	50.0	43.5	19.4	24.4	13.5
Union membership					
Member	14.7	40.7	10.5	29.4	27.7
Nonmember	61.8	17.6	29.9	19.3	25.6
Nonunionized	23.5	41.7	59.6	51.2	46.7
Total†	(34)	(108)	(67)	(119)	(902)

* Since the response "unknown" is excluded from the above table, the total figure in each column does not reach 100 percent.
† Numbers in parentheses indicate total respondents.

Table 4. Objective attributes of labor from the 1968 national survey (in percent-age)*

Attribute	Mana-gerial workers	White-collar workers	Sales and services workers	Field workers	Size of group within all eligible voters
Sex					
Male	96.1	72.6	59.2	70.0	45.9
Female	3.9	27.4	40.8	30.0	54.1
Age					
Early 20's	0	18.6	28.9	14.8	10.2
Late 20's	2.0	14.3	14.8	10.8	10.7
30's	21.6	34.5	23.9	28.0	26.7
40's	37.3	21.5	16.2	25.2	20.9
50's	23.5	6.8	9.2	16.0	15.4
Over 60	15.7	4.2	7.0	5.2	16.1
Education					
Elementary	19.6	22.5	48.6	76.8	57.0
Secondary	39.2	49.5	47.2	22.4	33.8
Higher	39.2	28.0	4.2	0.4	8.5
Monthly income of respondent					
Less than $83	4.0	17.0	33.1	36.4	25.6
$83 to $139	5.9	31.9	38.0	32.0	31.3
$140 to $278	47.0	43.0	18.3	24.0	32.2
$279 or more	35.2	4.3	0.7	1.2	4.7
Monthly income of respondent's family					
Less than $83	0	3.0	9.9	10.0	5.9
$83 to $139	2.0	15.3	26.1	25.6	20.1
$140 to $278	43.1	60.0	33.8	46.4	40.7
$279 or more	45.1	16.3	12.7	6.4	15.9
Number of employees where respondent works					
1 to 9	7.8	11.4	27.5	16.8	4.9
10 to 99	33.3	27.7	31.7	45.6	10.6
100 to 999	27.5	21.2	12.7	20.0	5.9
Over 1,000	31.4	38.4	23.2	13.2	8.1
Union membership					
Member	15.7	51.1	33.1	34.0	39.6
Nonmember	51.0	20.5	20.4	24.0	23.7
Nonunionized	33.3	28.4	46.5	42.0	36.6
Total†	(51)	(307)	(142)	(250)	(2,472)

* Since the response "unknown" is excluded from the above table, the total figure in each column does not reach 100 percent.
† Numbers in parentheses indicate total respondents.

bership of managerial workers came out, as was expected, the lowest at 15.7 percent (the sampling error being ±10.1 percent), while that of white-collar workers was the highest at 51.1 percent (with ±5.8 percent sampling error). This finding is backed up by other surveys including the 1968 Tokyo survey which found an overall low degree of union membership (see Table 4). It would be dangerous, however, to assume from this finding that a metropolis like Tokyo is characterized by massive nonunionization. According to the 1967 Tokyo survey, which included both male and female eligible voters, rates of union membership were 47.1 percent among white-collar workers, 27.4 percent among sales and services workers, and 27.3 percent among field workers, and thus the average union membership of the four categories was 34.4 percent.[5] The findings of the 1967 Tokyo survey are closer to those of the 1968 national survey than to those of the 1968 Tokyo survey.

Second, the size of employers for white-collar workers is larger than that of either field workers or workers in sales and services. While employers who have over 1,000 employees include both national and local government organizations, the size of the employer has no relationship to the conservative or progressive ideology and party preference of white-collar workers, but those workers in sales and services and field workers who are employed by big organizations, both public and private, are distinctly more progressive than those of small employers.

Third, a worker's educational background is relevant only to the analysis of his objective attributes and cannot be correlated with his voting behavior or party preference. Educational attainments decrease noticeably in the order of managerial workers, white-collar workers, and field workers. The Japanese white-collar workers share an attribute with the general public in that about 70 percent of the specialists, technicians, and clerical workers have no more than a secondary education, which contributes to a stronger class consciousness than their counterparts in other countries.

Fourth, a laborer's income has recently been found to be an important variable affecting his voting behavior, party preference, and political ideology. The income of a white-collar worker and a worker in sales and services is correlated with their ideology. Conversely, field workers strongly share the feeling of their common living opportunities, and income differentials do not affect their ideology. According to both national and Tokyo surveys, income levels decrease in the order of managerial workers, white-collar workers, sales and services workers, and field workers, and the white-collar group has a big edge over field workers. While both the workers in sales and services and field workers form a low income bracket, the former, youngest among the three labor categories, have more income at their disposal than the latter.

Fifth, age is no longer correlatable with voting behavior or ideology. The correlation persists, however, between age and political and social consciousness, with the younger generation more progressive and more modern. Indeed, the finding that 40 percent of the workers in sales and services and 30 percent of the white-collar workers in the 1968 national survey, 50 percent of the former and 40 percent of the latter in the 1968 Tokyo survey, and even larger percentages in the 1967 Tokyo survey are in their twenties seems to partly account for the progressive political and social tendencies of those two labor groups.

Voting Behavior and Party Preference*

According to the 1968 national survey (see Table 5), managerial workers and white-collar workers had higher voting rates than the sales and services workers and field workers in the July 1968 election for the House of Councillors. Since World War II, white-collar workers, more than any other category of labor, have been voting the JSP. As contrasted with the white-collar workers' strong preference for the JSP, managerial workers have noticeably been voting the LDP and the Democratic Socialist Party (the DSP), while the workers in sales and services have been more or less dividing their support between the LDP and the JSP. Their preference for the JSP has been significantly lower than field workers' who have voted the JSP to a statistically significant degree with reliability being 95 percent. Even if their

* According to the *Jiji* press poll, administered in June 1970, to 1,250 respondents 20 years of age and over, randomly sampled on a nationwide basis, 33 percent of the respondents supported the LDP, 14 percent of them the JSP, 4 percent the FPP, and 3 percent the DSP. The same poll finds that 37 percent of the respondents support the Satō administration whereas 33 percent of them do not. *Jiji* yearbook of 1971, p. 212. Likewise, according to the *Asahi* press poll, conducted in September 1970 on 6,000 randomly sampled eligible voters on a nationwide basis, 50 percent of the respondents supported the LDP, 23 percent the JSP, 5 percent the FPP, 7 percent the DSP, and 3 percent the JCP. *Asahi*, October 8, 1970.

Table 5. Party preference and voting behavior from the 1968 national survey (in percentage)

Voting behavior and party preference	Mana- gerial workers	White- collar workers	Workers in sales and services	Field workers	Average, eligible voters
Voting record					
Voters	88.2	86.6	80.3	78.4	82.9
Nonvoters	11.8	13.4	19.7	21.6	17.1
Total	(51)*	(307)	(142)	(250)	(2,472)
Party preference					
LDP	37.3	21.5	26.8	18.0	39.4
JSP	9.8	39.7	27.5	32.8	20.5
FPP	3.9	4.6	7.7	11.2	5.3
DSP	19.6	3.6	2.8	5.6	3.3
JCP	0	3.3	2.8	2.0	2.0
No preference	19.6	21.5	23.2	24.4	21.6
Total	(51)	(307)	(142)	(250)	(2,472)
Parties (voters only) in prefectural constituency					
LDP	44.4	28.2	39.5	25.5	48.2
JSP	20.0	48.1	39.5	40.8	27.0
FPP	2.2	5.3	9.6	13.3	5.2
DSP	17.8	3.8	2.6	4.6	4.6
JCP	0	6.0	4.4	5.6	4.0
Miscellaneous and independent	4.4	4.1	0	3.6	3.6
Unknown	11.1	4.5	4.4	6.6	7.5
Total	(45)	(266)	(114)	(196)	(2,050)
Parties (voters only) in national constituency					
LDP	51.1	30.8	36.0	24.5	48.2
JSP	15.6	39.1	31.6	34.7	22.1
FPP	2.2	6.4	13.2	16.8	9.0
DSP	11.1	4.5	5.3	6.6	4.1
JCP	0	6.4	6.1	4.6	3.5
Miscellaneous and independent	6.7	7.1	4.4	6.6	4.9
Unknown	13.3	5.6	3.5	6.1	8.1
Total	(45)	(206)	(114)	(196)	(2,050)

* Numbers in parentheses indicate total respondents.

support for two other progressive parties, the DSP and the JCP, is taken into account, the conservative tendency of the workers in sales and services has remained conspicuous.

The sales and services workers, with their increased numbers, showed conservative tendencies and voted for the LDP candidates, particularly those running from the nationwide constituency in the election for the House of Councillors. At the same time, their votes for the candidates of the Fair Play Party (the FPP) running from the nationwide constituency increased to 13.2 percent. The field workers cast 13.3 percent of their votes to the FPP candidates from the local constituency and 16.8 percent from the nationwide constituency. The field workers' votes for the FPP would increase from 13.3 percent to 14.8 percent in the local constituency and from 16.8 percent to 19.3 percent in the nationwide constituency, had their votes to the five parties (the LDP, JSP, FPP, DSP, and JCP) totaled 100 percent, thereby disregarding their votes to miscellaneous and independent candidates as well as unidentifiable votes. Put simply, approximately 20 percent (to be more precise, 26 percent or 14 percent because of ±6 percent sampling error) of the field workers voted the FPP candidates running from the nationwide constituency in the House of Councillors election.

Party preferences of labor in Tokyo (Table 6) roughly coincide with those of labor in Japan except for the stronger conservative ideology among the Tokyo sales and services workers. Workers in

Table 6. Party preference from the 1968 Tokyo survey on international consciousness (in percentage)

Party	Managerial workers	White-collar workers	Workers in sales and services	Field workers	Average, eligible voters
LDP	47.1	16.7	38.8	17.6	32.0
JSP	17.6	34.3	16.4	33.6	24.9
FPP	0	3.7	3.0	11.8	5.3
DSP	14.7	6.5	4.5	5.9	5.1
JCP	0	7.4	1.5	5.9	3.3
No preference or unknown	20.6	31.5	35.8	25.2	29.2
Total*	(34)	(108)	(67)	(119)	(902)

* Numbers in parentheses indicate total respondents.

sales and services give many more votes to the LDP than either white-collar workers or field workers, and they give very little support to the progressive parties including the JSP, DSP, and JCP. This finding with 95 percent reliability can be accounted for in part by the infrequency of union membership and high monthly income of sales and services workers in Tokyo.

Table 7. Various media influencing voting behavior

Determining factor	Mana-gerial workers	White-collar workers	Employees in sales and services	Field workers	Average, eligible voters
Prefectural constituency					
Legalized election campaigns	53.3	38.3	27.2	33.2	35.4
Personal communication	8.9	18.4	22.8	19.4	22.8
Mass communication	8.9	11.7	10.5	13.3	12.6
Recommendation by organizations	6.7	21.1	26.3	21.9	13.6
Other means	15.6	9.0	11.4	11.2	9.9
Unknown	6.7	1.5	1.8	1.0	1.9
Job-related	8.8	25.2	22.8	19.9	8.5
Nationwide constituency					
Legalized election campaigns	48.9	31.6	26.3	33.2	35.0
Personal communication	13.2	19.9	24.6	15.3	22.1
Mass communication	8.9	12.8	15.8	13.8	14.4
Recommendation by organizations	11.1	27.4	21.9	24.0	16.9
Other means	15.6	7.5	9.6	12.2	10.3
Unknown	2.2	0.8	1.8	1.5	1.2
Job-related	8.9	27.4	20.2	18.4	8.4

Table 7 shows the results of the poll on what most influenced a respondent to choose a candidate for the House of Councillors. The following figures inside the parentheses indicate the average percentages of responses given by eligible voters in all prefectural constituencies in Japan. First, the election campaign methods provided for by law (35.4) with the breakdown of government publicity on behalf of the candidates (18.0), live debates (2.0), televised debates (2.4), public speech meetings by an individual candidate (1.9), on-the-street speeches (1.4), newspaper advertisements by the candidates (5.2), radio publicity of a candidate's background and political opinions (4.4), postcards sent by candidates (1.0), flyers and billboards (2.4), and repeated calls by campaign workers (0.5). Publicity given by the government on behalf of the candidates was the most effective source of information and also influenced more than any other means the voting behavior of the largest number of voters in all of the four categories of employees. Second, the category of personal communication (22.8) which is broken down into family discussions (14.1), discussions with neighbors (1.3), on-the-job discussions (3.0), solicitations by friends or relatives (3.1), solicitations by superiors or other influential people (0.2), and solicitations by election workers (1.0). Third, the category of mass communication (12.6) consisting of press election reports (8.2), televised election reports (3.7), and radio election reports (0.6). Fourth, solicitation by various organizations (13.6) is composed of rather heterogeneous subcategories of solicitations by labor unions (5.5), solicitations by job-related organizations such as the association of trade unions and stores (1.2), and solicitations by other kinds of organizations such as religious and cultural groups (3.8). On-the-job discussions and solicitation by labor unions are singled out as particularly relevant to the present study of labor and are shown in Table 7.

A very low rate of managerial workers regard on-the-job discussions and solicitation by labor unions as the most effective source of information. The majority of them, instead, obtained much of their information from the campaign methods provided for by law. While respondents in the three categories of labor acknowledged solicitation by various organizations as their main source of information, the white-collar workers had the largest percentage of respondents who were most influenced in choosing their candidates, particularly those candidates who ran from the nationwide constituency, by on-the-job discussions and solicitation by labor organizations. Thus, the job atmosphere of white-collar workers in contemporary Japan seems to promote their voting for progressive parties. Workers in sales and services are generally found somewhere between white-collar workers and field workers, but their reliance upon personal communications in voting for a candidate from the nationwide constituency is significantly higher (with 95 percent statistical reliability) than that of field workers.

Table 8 shows the respondents' reasons for selecting certain candi-

Table 8. Various factors and issues considered in voting

Factors and issues	Managerial workers	White-collar workers	Employees in sales and services	Field workers	Average, eligible voters
Factors					
Local interests	0	1.9	2.6	0.5	3.7
Business interests	11.1	1.9	2.6	0.5	4.1
Position of labor	15.6	25.9	21.9	27.6	14.1
Living conditions	2.2	7.5	5.3	7.7	8.0
Policies and viewpoints	31.1	21.8	16.7	16.8	20.4
Recommendation by organization and unions	2.2	13.9	8.8	12.2	9.2
Agreement with a candidate's opinion	22.2	13.9	17.5	15.8	18.1
Familiarity with a candidate through mass media	4.4	5.6	11.4	8.7	8.4
Others and unknown	11.1	7.5	13.2	10.2	13.9
Issues					
National security	28.9	30.8	22.8	19.4	17.7
Vietnam war	2.2	1.9	1.8	0.5	1.5
Return of Okinawa	4.4	0.8	0	2.0	1.2
Commodity prices	24.4	33.8	35.1	43.4	37.6
Political reforms	11.1	7.9	10.5	9.7	8.4
Education	8.9	5.6	2.6	2.6	3.7
Unknown	0	1.9	4.4	2.0	2.3
No issues	20.0	17.3	22.8	20.4	27.5
International issues	35.5	33.5	24.6	21.9	20.4
Domestic issues	44.4	49.2	52.6	57.7	49.7
Total*	(45)	(266)	(114)	(196)	(2,050)

* Numbers in parentheses indicate total respondents.

dates running from the nationwide constituency and the issues they considered for 1968 upper house election. Similar but less clear characteristics are found on the prefectural level in the same election. Several points are particularly noticeable in Table 8: (1) The managerial workers form a separate category more than any other group in that they choose their candidates on the grounds of the candidates' business interests, ideology, principles, and party affiliation. (2) Approximately one-fourth of the respondents in each of the three labor categories choose the candidate who claims to take the position of laborer. Many Japanese white-collar workers, in spite of their higher education and higher monthly income than both workers in sales and services and field workers, appear to choose their candidates for the same reasons as the latter two, an indication of their strong class consciousness. (3) Among the three categories of labor: (a) the sales and services workers have the lowest rate of respondents whose voting behavior is most influenced by solicitations of various organizations and unions; (b) the white-collar workers have the highest rate of respondents who choose their candidates on the basis of ideology and principle; and (c) the white-collar workers have the smallest percentage of respondents who choose candidates through mass media. With respect to findings (b) and (c), managerial workers are much closer to white-collar workers than to either workers in sales and services or field workers.

The findings on issues (see the lower half of Table 8) closely resemble the above. Each respondent chose from the list of six issues, ranging from national security to education, those issues which he considered before voting.* Although how much their voting was influenced by the issues studied is unknown, relatively high numbers of managerial and white-collar workers and relatively low numbers of sales and services and field workers consider international issues to be major in the election. Furthermore, field workers are most sensitive to prices of commodities. As far as the effect of mass media on voting behavior is concerned, sales and services and field workers seem to be the most influenced. The other surveys' finding, however, that the higher the level of one's education, the greater one's contact with the mass media (particularly printed media like newspapers and magazines), is buttressed by the high degree of contact with mass media of managerial and white-collar workers, both of whom have higher education than the other two categories of employees. As Table 9 shows, in response to the question "From what sources do you primarily obtain knowledge on political issues and present

* The *Jiji* press poll administered to 1,250 respondents in December 1969 finds that the following issues generate most interest at a general election: Okinawa (8 percent), United States–Japan Security Treaty (23 percent), commodity prices (35 percent), colleges (8 percent), agricultural policies (7 percent), housing (6 percent), others (1 percent), and none or unclear (14 percent). *Jiji* yearbook of 1971, p. 212.

Table 9. Various sources of information concerning politics from the 1968 national survey (in percentage)

Source	Managerial workers	White-collar workers	Employees in sales and services	Field workers	Average, eligible voters
Mass media	196.0	190.9	162.7	149.6	157.1
Newspapers	84.3	85.7	73.9	68.0	69.8
Television	72.5	67.4	66.2	65.6	66.9
Radio	15.7	16.6	12.7	8.0	10.7
Magazines	23.5	21.2	9.9	8.0	9.7
Discussion with others	9.8	11.7	14.1	13.2	11.3
Party organization bulletins	0	7.8	3.5	4.8	3.0
Other means	3.9	2.3	1.4	0.8	1.6
None	0	0.3	3.5	7.6	5.1
Unknown	0	0.7	2.8	1.2	2.8
Total responses*	209.8	212.7	181.7	168.4	173.1
Total respondents†	(51)	(307)	(142)	(250)	(2,472)

* Due to multiple answers the sum total exceeded 100 percent.
† Numbers in parentheses indicate total respondents.

conditions in Japan?" both managerial workers and white-collar workers reveal a wide source of information-gathering and also a heavy reliance on mass media for their political knowledge. They especially use newspapers and magazines more than either workers in sales and services or field workers.

Finally, according to Table 10, while strong labor consciousness is found among the three labor groups, about half of the Japanese white-collar workers answered affirmatively to the question, "Do you consider yourself to be part of 'We the labor' as used by the progressives?" Thus, the middle-class concept has found acceptance only among the managerial class, and many white-collar workers consider themselves to be laborers, especially in the narrow sense of what the progressives would call "labor."

A further analysis of the responses to the question "Do you support a conservative or progressive administration?" reveals that the highest number of supporters of a progressive administration comes from the white-collar workers, resulting not so much from a decrease of conservative-party supporters among the white-collar class as from

Table 10. Political and social consciousness from the 1968 national survey (in percentage)

Category of self-identity or political viewpoint	Managerial workers	White-collar workers	Workers in sales and services	Field workers	Average, eligible voters
Class consciousness					
Progressive labor	25.5	48.5	41.5	54.0	29.6
Labor	25.5	23.8	32.4	28.4	25.6
Middle class	41.2	15.6	11.3	8.8	21.0
Capitalist	0	1.6	2.8	0	2.6
Other classes or unknown	7.8	9.4	12.0	8.8	21.2
Administration supported					
Conservative	39.2	22.5	23.2	15.6	33.7
Progressive	15.7	43.0	31.7	36.8	23.8
Neither or unknown	45.1	34.5	45.1	47.6	42.6
View on U.S.–Japan Security Treaty					
Long-term automatic extension	17.7	14.0	16.2	10.4	14.2
Revision and continuation	41.2	30.6	22.5	23.2	26.0
Revision and abolition	29.4	23.5	16.9	20.8	17.3
Abrogation	7.8	17.6	18.3	16.0	10.7
Unknown	3.9	14.3	26.1	29.6	31.8
Total*	(51)	(307)	(142)	(250)	(2,472)

* Numbers in parentheses indicate total respondents.

the shift of many undecided white-collar workers to support for the progressives. This progressive shift among white-collar workers becomes even more noticeable in analyzing their opinions on the United States–Japan Security Treaty. As Table 10 shows, 41.1 percent of them favor revision or even abolition of the treaty, and, when those white-collar workers who favor the DSP's view of continuing the treaty with some changes are added to it, this figure soars to 71.7 percent, the highest among the four categories of employees.

Conclusion

The present study of labor in Tokyo and Japan has reconfirmed, if not newly discovered, several previous findings.

First, it seems that the government census overestimates the size of the employee category, particularly the field workers. If it does, then the size of the white-collar workers should increase relative to other categories of labor, and a study thereof would become important in interpreting and predicting Japanese politics. Likewise, workers in sales and services, though smaller than the white-collar group, will increase in importance relative to the field workers.

Second, in terms of voting behavior, party preference, and other forms of political consciousness, the managerial workers are extremely conservative whereas the white-collar workers are still progressive. Also, sales and services workers are relatively more conservative than either the white-collar workers or the field workers.

Until around 1964 the progressive tendencies of the white-collar workers were often accounted for by their high level of education and relatively young age.* But since that time age is no longer considered correlatable with voting behavior. Indeed, the argument that youth had become more conservative is completely untenable.† Furthermore, in the absence of a correlation between educational attainment and voting behavior, causes of the persisting white-collar progressiveness must be sought elsewhere. The present study suggests the following reasons: (1) The permeation of labor consciousness among the white-collar workers; (2) a high degree of union membership, which supports contention (1); and (3) contentions (1) and (2) contribute to a great reliance by white-collar workers on on-the-job communications and solicitations by the labor unions as a major factor in voting. Since many factors are involved in establishing a labor consciousness, the reasons why the Japanese white-collar workers have stronger feelings in that direction than their counterparts in many other countries are still unclear.

Although education level can no longer be correlated with progressive or conservative tendencies in voting behavior, it is still significant with relation to the degree of political knowledge and interest. Indeed, both managerial and white-collar workers are found to possess much higher degrees of political knowledge and interest than the workers in sales and services or field workers.

---

* Jōji Watanuki, "Patterns of Politics in Present-day Japan," in Seymour M. Lipset and Stein Rokkan, eds., *Party Systems and Voter Alignments* (New York: The Free Press, 1967), pp. 447–466, was written in the fall of 1963 on that assumption.
† Watanuki, "Daitoshi jūmin no seijiishiki."

Third, differences between managerial workers and white-collar workers in terms of voting and other political behavior are yet to be clarified. For example, does a white-collar worker change his political attitude when he moves up to a managerial position within an organization?

Furthermore, white-collar workers show a high degree of consistency between their political and social consciousness on the one hand and their party preference on the other, but it is not clear whether the former is an independent variable (a cause) and the latter is a dependent variable (a result) or vice versa.

A proposed research project for the future would consist of a detailed analysis of these labor groups at the level of enterprises and labor unions, starting with the white-collar class. It would be conducted on the basis of the findings and problem areas revealed in the present study.

Notes to Selection 5

1. Author's polls: A poll of July 1966 conducted on eligible male voters of the eighth election district in Itabashi ward, Tokyo, will be hereafter referred to as the 1966 Itabashi survey. Also, a poll of March 1968 administered to voters of both sexes in all districts in Tokyo (excluding Izushichitō islands) will be referred to as the 1968 Tokyo survey (on international consciousness).

Joint polls: A poll of April 1967 conducted shortly after the sixth unified local election on eligible male and female voters in all districts of Tokyo will be referred to as the 1967 Tokyo survey. A poll given to eligible voters of both sexes in Japan right after the July 1968 election for the House of Councillors will be referred to as the 1968 national survey.

2. Jōji Watanuki, "Daitoshi jūmin no seijiishiki" [Political consciousness of big-city dwellers], *Nihon rōdō kyōkai zasshi* [Journal of the Japan Labor Association], January 1967, pp. 11–23.

3. The validity of raising such a question was touched on in my article based on the 1966 Itabashi survey. Ibid., p. 23.

4. Jōji Watanuki, "Seijiishiki to senkyokōdō no jittai: Tokyotomin no seijiishiki to tōhyōkōdō" [Conditions of political consciousness and voting behavior of the resident of Tokyo], *Senkyochōsa kenkyūkiyō* [Annal of

election surveys] (Tokyo, 1967), vol. 3; Ichiro Miyake, Tomio Kinoshita, and Juichi Aiba, *Kotonaru reberu no senkyo ni okeru tōhyōkōdō no kenkyū* [Study of voting behavior at different levels of elections] (Tokyo, 1967).

  5. Watanuki, "Seijiishiki to senkyokōdō no jittai," p. 33.

Consciousness of Human Rights and Problems of Equality*

NOBUYOSHI ASHIBE

An individual's consciousness of human rights is determined by numerous interwoven variables that are much more complex than those that influence his consciousness of other constitutional issues such as the governing structure. The measurement of human-rights consciousness, the most difficult of all constitutional issues, requires the gathering of relevant data, construction of cross tabulations, and comprehensive analyses thereof. It should be kept in mind that the present study deals with limited areas of human-rights consciousness and that the data used are far from complete.

The Questionnaire

The following are questionnaire items and answers used in connection with the present public-opinion survey.

Item 3. To what extent do you think organizations engaged in political activities should be freely recognized?
1. Any and all political organizations should be recognized.
2. Organizations which allow violent and destructive activities should not be recognized.
3. All organizations should be recognized, but their activities should be strictly controlled.
4. I do not know.

Item 4. Which of the following strikes do you approve of?
1. I approve of any strike.
2. I approve of any strike except by policemen or firemen.

* This selection is taken from "Jinken ishiki to byōdō mondai" in Naoki Kobayashi, ed., *Nihonjin no kempō ishiki* [Constitutional consciousness of the Japanese] (Tokyo: Tokyo University Press, 1968), pp. 94–112. Translated and reprinted with permission of the author.

3. In addition to those by policemen and firemen, I do not approve of strikes by those who are engaged in public utilities.

4. Since strikes are not desirable, I do not approve of any strike.

5. I do not know.

Item 5. What would you do if a policeman wanted to search your house?

1. I would freely admit the policeman.

2. I would admit him after carefully listening to his reason.

3. I would request the presentation of a writ.

4. I cannot say one way or the other.

Item 6. What would you do if problems should arise concerning lending or leasing money, house, or property?

1. I would consult the police.

2. I would request the advice of someone influential (boss, party leader, or the official of an organization).

3. I would seek assistance from relatives or friends.

4. I would consult a lawyer.

5. I would take my claim to court.

6. I would give up and let things go.

7. I do not know.

Item 7. What is your impression of the present police force?

1. I think the police, as friends of the citizenry, are very reliable.

2. I think the police are performing their duties for the citizen.

3. I am somewhat afraid of the police.

4. I resent the police because they restrict demonstrations too severely.

5. I cannot say one way or the other.

Item 8. In the light of the constitutional guarantee of "the minimum standards of wholesome and cultured living," do you think that the present level of guarantee of the people's livelihood is sufficient?

1. Since even the livelihood of the poor people has not been guaranteed, I think it is totally insufficient.

2. I think the present level of guarantee corresponds to the strength of the nation and is the best the government can do.

3. Since social welfare makes a man lazy, there is no need to assist people's livelihood.

4. I have not taken any interest in it (I do not know).

Item 9. What do you think of the recent condition in the Diet where confrontations between the ruling and opposition parties have been violent?

1. The will of the majority party should always be followed. It is not proper for the opposition parties to resort to force.

2. The majority party should be given first priority but should not force through a decision without listening to the opposition parties.

3. A certain degree of forceful resistance should be allowed to opposition parties whose opinions are not respected.
4. Since the present majority party is despotic, all kinds of resistance should be allowed.
5. I cannot say one way or the other (I do not know).

Item 10. When you vote in an election for the members of the Diet, which of the following bases do you rely upon?

1. I vote on the basis of a candidate.
2. I vote on the basis of a political party.
3. I follow the opinion of influential and respected persons.
4. I vote for a candidate requested by somebody.
5. I have never voted.
6. I do not know.

Item 11. We would like to ask you about equality. Do you think that in your area unreasonable discriminations are still practiced because of family status, sex, and personal status, or do you think everyone is equally treated?

1. There still remains much unreasonable discrimination.
2. Equality prevails most of the time except for some discrimination in marriage and employment.
3. There is hardly any discrimination.
4. I do not know.

Item 12. According to an existing law, all children should be equal in inheriting property. Do you think the eldest son should be treated differently from the rest of the children, or do you think all children should be treated equal?

1. All children should be treated equal.
2. The eldest son (or a child who lives with a parent) should be given preferred treatment.
3. Various discriminations are necessary in cases of the daughter-in-law or adopted children.
4. I do not know.

Consciousness of Freedom

Freedom of Political Associations. To analyze the consciousness of intellectual freedom,* our 1966 poll asked only the question, "To what extent do you think organizations engaged in political activities

* Intellectual freedom refers primarily to those freedoms stipulated in Articles 19, 20, 21, and 23 of the Japanese Constitution which state, in part: "Freedom of thought and conscience shall not be violated" (Article 19); "Freedom of religion is guaranteed to all" (Article 20); "Freedom of assembly and association as well as speech, press, and all other forms of expression are guaranteed" (Article 21); and "Academic freedom is guaranteed" (Article 23).

should be freely recognized?" In contrast, our 1965 poll had asked the following questions: To what extent should free speech be allowed? Are public criticisms of trials good or bad? To what extent should mass demonstration marches be permitted? Do you approve of amending the Constitution to restrict human rights in order to maintain public welfare? It would be very difficult to draw any meaningful conclusions on the consciousness of political freedom from the 1966 poll only. The difficulty increases because the expression "violent and destructive activities" contained in answer 2 to item 3 in the 1966 questionnaire evoked a wide range of meanings in the minds of the respondents. The findings in the 1966 poll will be compared with those from the previous year and other statistics.

First, it is questionable whether answer 2, which as high as 41 percent of the respondents chose, should be interpreted as a totally negative attitude to freedom of association. In the opinion of Hirohisa Ueno, wide approval of the control of "violent and destructive activities" might give the government an excuse to regulate all anti-institutional political activities. By combining the 41 percent of the respondents who chose answer 2 and the 30 percent who preferred the "strict control" in answer 3, Ueno concludes that "those who approve of restrictions upon the freedom of association exceed 70 percent of the Japanese . . . and the people's consciousness thereof is still weak. . . . The government can easily, through its maneuvering of mass media, steer public opinion so that the public might allow the government to suppress anti-institutional political associations." [1] But answers 2 and 3 are not necessarily of the same kind.

"Strict control" of violent and destructive activities is preferred by 30 percent of the respondents, manifesting a wide range of attributes. Granted that the public consciousness of political freedom is still weak, the 41 percent of the respondents who approve of the control of "violent and destructive activities" should not be interpreted as manifesting a totally negative attitude to the freedom of association. In terms of occupation, a very large number of students and white-collar workers chose answer 2, but only a small number of them chose answer 3. In terms of age, 48 percent of the respondents in their 20's, 44 percent in their 30's, and 43 percent in their 40's chose answer 2 while 28 percent of the respondents of these age groups chose answer 3. But the number of respondents who selected answer 2 decreases a great deal (to 38 percent) among the 50-year-olds while those who selected answer 3 increases to 38 percent, a tendency seen in other realms of human-rights consciousness as well. Educational background particularly makes a great deal of difference in one's consciousness of human rights.* Ratios (in percentage) between answers 2 and 3 are: 51 to 21 among prewar college graduates; 43 to 35 among prewar high-school and technical-school graduates; 44 to 32 among prewar high-school graduates; 31 to 32 among prewar elementary-school graduates; 57 to 13 among postwar college graduates; 51 to 32 among junior-college graduates; 52 to 29 among postwar senior-high-school graduates; 31 to 33 among postwar junior-high-school graduates. Thus, one's attitude toward organized political activities and one's educational attainment are generally inversely proportional.

The respondents who chose answer 2 undoubtedly present many problems. First, as Ueno fears, there seem to be many among them who approve of the restriction of any organization engaged in anti-institutional political activities. In terms of party preference, 21 percent of the supporters of the JCP, 44 percent of the JSP supporters, 36 percent of the FPP supporters, 49 percent of the DSP supporters, and 40 percent of the LDP supporters preferred answer 2. Likewise, 36 percent of those respondents who declined to identify their party preference and 42 percent of those who had no party preference also selected answer 2. In terms of income, ratios (in percentage) between answers 2 and 3 are: 30 to 34 for respondents with a yearly income of less than $833; 40 to 30 for those whose yearly income is between $833 and $1,667; 45 to 29 for those between $1,667 and $2,778; 47 to 29 for those between $2,778 and $5,556; and 46 to 28 for those above $5,556. All income brackets except that of less than $833 scored 40 percent or more in their choice of answer 2. (Indeed, the higher the income, the higher the percentage of selecting

* The pre-1945 school system was structured as follows: elementary school (6 years of compulsory attendance), middle school (usually 5 years), high school (3 years), and university (3 years). In addition to these academic schools, there were vocational schools: technical middle school (usually 1 to 5 years for ages 13 through 17) and technical high school (normally 1 to 5 years for ages 16 through 20). The post-1945 school system is elementary school (6 years), junior high school (3 years), senior high school (3 years), and college and university (4 years) or junior college (2 years). Compulsory attendance has been extended to 9 years.

answer 2.) Thus, some of the respondents who chose answer 2 may very well favor restriction of leftist groups and their activities.

Related to this is the second problem that the percentage of respondents who chose answer 2 may contain a large degree of qualitative weakness, as pointed out in the 1965 poll on intellectual freedom.[2] For example, the high degree of correlation usually seen between the consciousness of equality and freedom is a characteristic of human-rights consciousness, but whatever ideological differences may exist between respondents of answers 2 and 3 on the question of freedom (item 3) disappear when the results of the question on equality (item 11) are cross tabulated (see Figure 1). Likewise, the

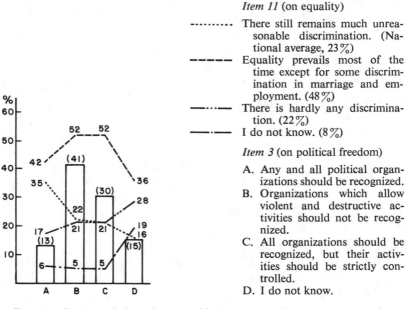

Item 11 (on equality)

--------- There still remains much unreasonable discrimination. (National average, 23%)

– – – – – Equality prevails most of the time except for some discrimination in marriage and employment. (48%)

—·· — There is hardly any discrimination. (22%)

—·— I do not know. (8%)

Item 3 (on political freedom)

A. Any and all political organizations should be recognized.

B. Organizations which allow violent and destructive activities should not be recognized.

C. All organizations should be recognized, but their activities should be strictly controlled.

D. I do not know.

Figure 1. Cross tabulation of results of items 3 and 11 from the questionnaire

findings in Figure 2 (item 9 cross tabulated with item 3) seem to show another instance of the absence of correlation between consciousness of freedom and opinion on the opposition parties' right to dissent. Nevertheless, a respondent's occupation, education, and age do make a great deal of difference in his attitude toward political organizations (item 3) and other human-rights issues.

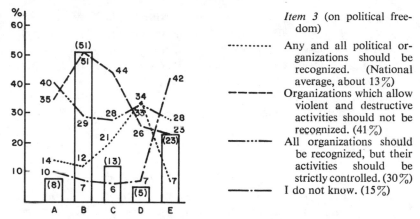

Item 3 (on political freedom)

··········· Any and all political organizations should be recognized. (National average, about 13%)

------ Organizations which allow violent and destructive activities should not be recognized. (41%)

----··--- All organizations should be recognized, but their activities should be strictly controlled. (30%)

---·--- I do not know. (15%)

Item 9 (on opposition-party dissent)

A. The will of the majority party should always be followed. It is not proper for the opposition parties to resort to force.

B. The majority party should be given first priority but should not force through a decision without listening to the opposition parties.

C. A certain degree of forceful resistance should be allowed to opposition parties whose opinions are not respected.

D. Since the present majority party is despotic, all kinds of resistance should be allowed.

E. I cannot say one way or the other (I do not know).

Figure 2. Cross tabulation of results of items 3 and 9 from the questionnaire

*Consciousness of Physical Freedom.** The degree of a person's human-rights consciousness depends a great deal on the relevancy of such human rights to that person's own interests.[3] The finding that as many as 58 percent of the respondents chose answer 3 (the request for presentation of a formal search warrant) in response to

---

* Physical freedom is an aggregate of those freedoms that are guaranteed by the provisions of Articles 31 through 39 in the Constitution. Those provisions are as follows:

Article 31. No person shall be deprived of life or liberty, nor shall any other criminal penalty be imposed, except according to procedure established by law.

Article 32. No person shall be denied the right of access to the courts.

Article 33. No person shall be apprehended except upon warrant issued by a competent judicial officer which specifies the offense with which the person is charged, unless he is apprehended while the offense is being committed.

Article 34. No person shall be arrested or detained without being at once informed of the charges against him or without the immediate privilege of counsel; nor shall he be detained without adequate cause; and upon demand

item 5 dealing with a police search of their house may indicate a high degree of relevancy of the question to the respondents themselves, but it may be more accurate to assume that many respondents accept a priori answer 3 out of the limited number of alternatives. Indeed, it would be impossible to make any generalizations on awareness of physical freedom merely on the basis of the available data on item 5.

The public-opinion poll on protection of human rights (*jinkenyōgo nikansuru seronchōsa*) conducted by the Publicity Room of the Prime Minister's Secretariat in October 1966 provides a good reference. The poll questionnaire included the following: Is a policeman infringing on a suspect's human rights when he puts his hand in the pockets of the suspect with the intention of searching for a concealed weapon? Is a teacher violating a human right when he hits an unruly student in order to discipline him? Are villagers impinging upon a human right when they agree among themselves not to associate with a selfish neighbor who does not cooperate in a community project? Are neighbors violating a human right of a person whose marriage engagement is broken due to rumors, founded or unfounded, spread by them? Is a person's human right infringed upon when he suffers damage caused by smog and bad odor in an industrial area?

---

of any person such cause must be immediately shown in open court in his presence and in presence of his counsel.

Article 35. The right of all persons to be secure in their homes, papers, and effects against entries, searches, and seizures shall not be impaired except upon warrant issued for adequate cause and particularly describing the place to be searched and things to be seized, or except as provided by Article 33. 2. Each search or seizure shall be made upon separate warrant issued by a competent judicial officer.

Article 36. The infliction of torture by any public officer and cruel punishments are absolutely forbidden.

Article 37. In all criminal cases the accused shall enjoy the right to a speedy and public trial by an impartial tribunal. 2. He shall be permitted full opportunity to examine all witnesses, and he shall have the right of compulsory process for obtaining witnesses on his behalf at public expense. 3. At all times the accused shall have the assistance of competent counsel who shall, if the accused is unable to secure the same by his own efforts, be assigned to his use by the state.

Article 38. No person shall be compelled to testify against himself. 2. Confession made under compulsion, torture, or threat, or after prolonged arrest or detention shall not be admitted in evidence. 3. No person shall be convicted or punished in cases where the only proof against him is his own confession.

Article 39. No person shall be held criminally liable for an act which was lawful at the time it was committed, or of which he has been acquitted, nor shall he be placed in double jeopardy.

Table 1. Consciousness of physical freedom as found in government surveys (in percentage)

Subject of poll question	Ministry of Justice survey (1959)				Publicity Room survey (1966)		
	Strongly opposed	Occasionally approved	Approved	Unknown	Infringement on human rights	No infringement	Cannot say one way or the other
Rough police treatment of suspected criminals	49	36	8	7			
Stop and frisk					21	47	32
Physical punishment in schools	52	38	2	8	33	31	36
Trading of human beings	86	9	2	3			
Parents' interference in marriage	28	57	8	7			
Neighbors' interference in marriage					52	19	29
Village ostracism	47	21	3	29	39	27	34
Pollution					44	22	34

A comparison in Table 1 of the findings in the government poll with a similar poll conducted by the Civil Liberties Bureau (*Jinkenyōgo-kyoku*) of the Ministry of Justice in January 1959 reveals that public consciousness of physical freedom is not necessarily high. It would not be a gross mistake, therefore, to assume that the respondents' choice of answer 3 in item 5 in our poll is largely an a priori one.

As would be expected, the higher the overall human-rights consciousness the greater the chance of choosing answer 3 (request for a formal warrant) and conversely, the lower such consciousness the higher the chance of choosing answer 2 (admission of the policeman after carefully listening to his reason for a house search). For instance, in the cross tabulation of items 4 and 5, the propensity for choosing answer 3 decreases from those respondents who are sympathetic with the right to strike (those who choose answers 1 or 2 in item 4) to those who are unsympathetic with or indifferent to it (those who answer 3, 4, or 5) at the rate of 68–68–64–53–40 percent. Conversely, the propensity for choosing answer 2 increases from the former to the latter at the rate of 28–29–33–41–51 percent. These two curves are even more evident in the relationship between educational background and the respondents' attitudes toward police search. The propensity for choosing answer 3 is very high among the prewar and postwar college graduates (79 and 77 percent, respectively) and decreases from the prewar senior-high-school and technical-school graduates to the prewar junior-high-school graduates (68 to 66 percent), and from the junior-college graduates to the postwar senior-high-school graduates (70 to 66 percent). Both the prewar elementary-school and postwar junior-high-school graduates chose answer 2 more often than answer 3 with the incidence of selecting answers 2 and 3 being 48 to 44 percent among the former and 51 to 43 percent among the latter. Furthermore, the ratios of selecting between answers 2 and 3 are 41 to 52 percent among the females and 32 to 64 percent among the males, thereby indicating a lower human-rights consciousness among women. (The government poll shown in Table 1 found similar differences of consciousness between men and women.) Whether or not the high degree of constitutional knowledge usually seen among respondents having high educational backgrounds can be correlated with the high degree of their human-rights consciousness as much as statistical figures seem to show has yet to be studied.

Human Rights and the Police. According to the analysis of item 7 on physical freedom, only 10 percent of the respondents were found to be either "afraid" or "resentful" of the police, whereas 66 percent of them had a favorable impression (saw them as "reliable" or "satisfactorily performing their duties"). This finding to some extent can be correlated with other human-rights consciousness. For example, as many as 39 percent of those respondents who would "freely admit" the police feel that they are "reliable" and 33 percent of them believe them to be "satisfactorily performing their duties." Conversely, only 12 percent of the respondents who would admit them for a search after "carefully listening to the reason" and 8 percent of those who would request a formal warrant think them to be "reliable," and 54 percent of the former and 59 percent of the latter think them to be satisfactorily performing their duties. Furthermore, 8 percent of those who would request a warrant "resent" the police as compared with only 2 percent of those who would "freely admit" them.

Item 6 was designed to examine the public consciousness of rights as manifested in daily life. As many as 64 percent of the respondents desired to have their rights protected through legal means since 42 percent of them would "consult their lawyers" and 22 percent of them would "take their claims to court." Educational backgrounds made considerable differences in attitudes toward item 6, and the number of respondents who would "consult with attorneys" decreases in the order of prewar college graduates (70 percent), prewar high-school and technical-school graduates (59 percent), prewar junior-high-school graduates (48 percent), prewar elementary-school graduates (27 percent); and the number also decreases in the order of postwar college graduates (63 percent), junior-college graduates (63 percent), postwar senior-high school graduates (45 percent), and junior-high-school graduates (31 percent). Thus, an inverse relationship exists between educational level and the propensity of relying on such methods as consultation with the police, the good offices of influential people, and help from relatives.

Many respondents, however, seem to have answered item 6 a priori, and the above findings are not sufficient to measure the public consciousness of rights. The government's public-opinion survey on the protection of human rights reported that 54 percent of the respondents thought many Japanese would keep silent and tolerate infringement on their rights, while 23 percent answered that few would, and 23 percent had no opinion. Also, a large number of respondents with high degrees of human-rights consciousness, when measured in terms of their age, sex, education, occupation, and residence, also concurred that many people would keep silent and tolerate such infringement. (For instance, 62 percent of the prewar senior-high-school and technical-school graduates, the postwar college graduates, and the white-collar workers, respectively.) Although Takeyoshi Kawashima argues that "it is only a matter of time for the Japanese to acknowledge a relationship between individuals just as legal and clearly defined in accordance with standards of law as the one between individuals and the government," [4] it appears that such acknowledgment will still take many years.

Consciousness of Social Rights*

Attitudes toward Labor Strikes. Public-opinion polls often find
that the people are not necessarily sympathetic with the right of
labor to strike, and our 1965 poll found this not to have basically
changed in spite of the long-range prediction of Naoki Kobayashi
that an increasing number of people will approve of the right to
strike.[5] According to the findings in our 1966 poll, as many as 30
percent of the respondents deny the right to strike in any kind of
work and 23 percent deny striking in a public utility, thus rendering
53 percent of the respondents reluctant toward labor strikes for one
reason or another. Even if the respondents in favor of any strike (10
percent) are combined with those who approve it except for policemen and firemen (22 percent), only 32 percent of the respondents
recognize the right to strike.

  The government's public-opinion survey on the protection of human rights revealed that, when asked whether or not it is unavoidable
and permissible to disregard other people's interests or cause some
trouble to them in order to protect human rights, approximately 15
percent of the respondents thought it unavoidable and permissible,
65 percent thought it impermissible, and 20 percent had no opinion.
When asked whether there are many or few people in Japan who do
not mind disregarding other people's interests or causing some trouble
in order to insist on their own rights, 43 percent of the respondents
answered that there are many, 25 percent held that there are few,
and 32 percent had no opinion. To the question of whether a worker,
employed on the condition that he will not engage himself in any
union activities, should be regarded as having his rights infringed
upon when he is dismissed because he started union activities, 29
percent of the respondents thought he should be dismissed, 39 percent did not think he should, and 41 percent held no opinion. Find-

  * Social rights include, among other things, the following constitutional
rights: "All people shall have the right to maintain the minimum standards of
wholesome and cultured living," and "In all areas of life, the state shall use its
endeavors for the promotion and extension of social welfare and security, and
of public health" (Article 25, Sections 1 and 2). "All people shall have the
right to receive an equal education correspondent to their ability, as provided
by law" (Article 26). "The right of workers to organize and to bargain and
act collectively is guaranteed" (Article 28).

ings in the government's poll appear to reveal attitudes very similar to those found in our 1966 poll on the right to strike.

Many of the respondents who approved of labor strikes except by policemen and firemen were students, professional technicians, clerical workers, or manual laborers in their 20's and 30's with yearly incomes between $833 and $2,778 and postwar college degrees as well as being supporters of the JCP or JSP. The consciousness of the right to strike differs considerably on several points from that of other human rights. First, relatively few respondents at any level of educational background with the exception of postwar college graduates positively approved of the right to strike (see Figure 3). Par-

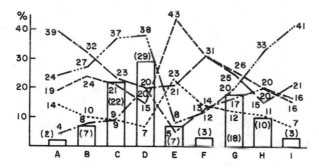

Item 4 (right to strike)

‑‑‑‑‑‑‑‑‑ I approve of any strike. (National average, 10%)
‑‑‑‑‑‑ I approve of any strike except by policemen or firemen. (22%)
‑‑‑‑‑ In addition to those by policemen and firemen, I do not approve of strikes
   by those who are engaged in public utilities. (23%)
‑‑‑‑·‑‑ Since a strike is not desirable, I do not approve of any strike. (30%)
‑‑‑·‑‑ I do not know. (15%)

Educational background

A   Prewar college graduates
B. Prewar high-school and technical-school graduates
C. Prewar junior-high-school graduates
D. Prewar elementary-school graduates
E. Postwar college graduates
F. Junior-college graduates
G. Postwar senior-high-school graduates
H. Postwar junior-high-school graduates
I. Others

Figure 3. Cross tabulation of results of item 4 from the questionnaire with respondents' educational background

ticularly, many managerial workers, despite their high consciousness of freedom, and a high rate of the respondents over 40 opposed the right to strike. Second, the consciousness of the right to strike is not clearly related to that of other human rights. For example, according to Figure 4, only 43 percent of the respondents who complained

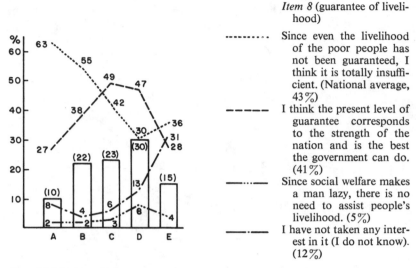

Item 8 (guarantee of livelihood)

.... Since even the livelihood of the poor people has not been guaranteed, I think it is totally insufficient. (National average, 43%)

– – – – I think the present level of guarantee corresponds to the strength of the nation and is the best the government can do. (41%)

—·····— Since social welfare makes a man lazy, there is no need to assist people's livelihood. (5%)

—·—·— I have not taken any interest in it (I do not know). (12%)

Item 4 (right to strike)

A. I approve of any strike.
B. I approve of any strike except by policemen or firemen.
C. In addition to those by policemen and firemen, I do not approve of strikes by those who are engaged in public utilities.
D. Since a strike is not desirable, I do not approve of any strike.
E. I do not know.

Figure 4. Cross tabulation of results of items 4 and 8 from the questionnaire

about an insufficient guarantee of livelihood upheld the right to strike, while 44 percent of them denied it, although some correlation does exist between the consciousness of the right to livelihood and that of the right to strike. A total of 27 percent of the respondents who regarded the present level of the government's guarantee of the people's livelihood as being in proportion to the present Japanese strength were also for the strike while 62 percent of them were against it. Meanwhile 17 percent of the respondents who thought it unnecessary to have the government guarantee the people's livelihood were for the strike whereas 69 percent of them were against it. According to the cross tabulation of item 4 with consciousness of a future social system for Japan, however, 23 percent of those who favor communism (1.3 percent of all respondents) and 40 percent of those who desire a socialist democracy (24 percent of all respondents) opposed the right to strike. Incidentally, ratios between the advocates and opponents of the right to strike were 60 to 31 percent among the proponents of modified capitalism (45 percent of all respondents), and 59 to 21 percent among the supporters of existing capitalism (11 percent of all respondents). The number of respondents without any opinion greatly increased. Furthermore, as high as 45 percent of the respondents who considered the present Constitution adequate (36 percent of all respondents) opposed the right to strike, as compared with 49 percent of those who approved it. Thus, the consciousness of the right to strike strongly reflects the class interests of respondents.

Right to Livelihood and Guarantee Thereof. Our 1965 poll had tried to find the degree of consciousness of the right to livelihood by asking the respondents whether or not they were enjoying "wholesome and cultured living" as guaranteed by the Constitution. But that phrase seems to have evoked different meanings in the minds of many respondents, and consequently no adequate findings resulted. Item 8 in the 1966 poll was apparently better phrased, and the following two characteristics were found.

First, the consciousness of the right to livelihood seems to be influenced not only by variables such as the respondent's age, sex, educational background, occupation, family income, party preference, and place of residence, but also by the size, social security, housing, welfare benefits, income taxes, and conditions of health of the respondent's family. Moreover, the prevailing public opinion at the time (in this case, soon after a national poll on the government's policies, particularly on commodity prices) appears to affect the consciousness of the right to livelihood. These causal relationships cannot adequately be analyzed on the basis of the findings on item 8 in our 1966 poll alone; consequently the results of other polls, as far as they are relevant to the analysis of the aggregate data of item 8, will be incorporated.

According to a poll conducted in the middle of August 1966 by the Japan Public-Opinion Poll (Nihon Seron Chōsakai)[6] and circulated by the *Kyōdō Press* through nationwide mass media, the support for the Satō administration had declined to 34 percent, reflecting criticism of rising prices (with opposition to his administration being 27 percent and support for the LDP being 47 percent). Only 8 percent of the respondents answered their living conditions were "better," whereas 49 percent of them felt that their living conditions were the "same" and 40 percent thought them "worse." The ratio of choosing the three answers was 10:51:35 percent (in the order of better, the same, and worse living conditions) among the supporters of the Satō administration, and 7:41:50 percent among critics. Indeed, 48 percent of the respondents preferred, as a government measure to ease their cost of living, the "stabilization of prices." Furthermore, when asked what policy they wanted the government to undertake after the forthcoming general election, a majority (51 percent) of the respondents chose stabilization of prices, followed by reduced taxes (8.7 percent), better social security and welfare (7.2 percent), and increased income (6.7 percent).

A public-opinion survey on people's living conditions (*kokuminseikatsu nikansuru seronchōsa*), a collection of a large bulk of research material made public by the government in June 1967, also showed that ratios of respondents who thought their living conditions to be better, the same, or worse were 7:50:42 percent in 1966, and 8:60:30 percent in 1967. A large plurality (42 percent in 1966) of the respondents cited "insufficient income and high prices" as the cause of dissatisfaction with their living conditions, whereas only 13 percent of them complained about inadequate housing. Thus, these public-opinion polls support the high percentage (43 percent) of the respondents in our 1966 poll who complained of entirely insufficient living conditions.

The same government poll found that as many as 41 percent of the respondents wanted the government to put its long-range policy priority on "improvement of roads, sewage, parks, housing, and social security" rather than reduced taxes; 25 percent preferred the tax reduction, with the remaining 34 percent having other or no answers. According to the 1966 poll, however, reduced prices were desired as the government's immediate policy by 55 percent of the respondents, followed by improved social security (20 percent), reduced taxes (17 percent), better politics (14 percent), and better housing (12 percent).[7] The 1967 poll showed the following changes in the respondents' preferences: reduced prices (56 percent), reduced taxes (26 percent), better politics (19 percent), improved social security (17 percent), better housing (15 percent). Thus, when a man feels that the general distrust of politics and rising prices have made his living increasingly difficult, the higher that man's consciousness of human rights, the more likely he would be to feel that the government's guarantee of the people's livelihood had been "totally inadequate" and he would be more likely to concentrate his attention on reduced prices and other issues that closely related to his daily interests. Conversely, if an issue is not closely related to his daily interests and even if his consciousness on the right to livelihood is not particularly low, the more difficult his living becomes, the more likely he would be to feel that "the present level of guarantee is the best the government can do." This state of mind, which a relatively low degree of human-rights consciousness alone cannot account for, seems to be the reason that 41 percent of the respondents chose the answer that the present level of guarantee is the best the government can do, and that 4 percent denied "any need for aid," with 12 percent having "neither interest in nor any knowledge about it."

Second, the more progressive a man is on other human rights, the more likely he is to answer that the government's guarantee of the people's livelihood is "totally inadequate." For instance, the cross tabulation of item 4 with item 8 (Figure 4) shows a high degree of correlation between a respondent's attitude toward the right to strike and that of the government's guarantee of livelihood. Likewise, in terms of a future social system, 70 percent of the proponents of communism and 54 percent of the supporters of socialist democracy held that the "present level of the guarantee is inadequate," whereas 12 percent of the former and 33 percent of the latter were of the opinion that "the present level of the guarantee is the best the government can do." Of those respondents who desired a welfare state for Japan, 46 percent accepted the present level of the guarantee while 44 percent were dissatisfied. Interestingly enough, the ratio between acceptance and dissatisfaction was reversed to 51:21 percent among the supporters of capitalism. Only 2 percent of the respondents who felt the present level of guarantee of livelihood to be "insufficient," however, inclined to communism and 30 percent to socialist democracy. A seeming inconsistency was found widely among the proponents of a welfare state in that 46 percent of them regarded the present level of guarantee as being insufficient but, at the same time, 34 percent felt no "need for the government to support people's livelihood." (Of the advocates of socialist democracy and of capitalism 26 and 20 percent respectively denied the need for such a government guarantee.) All of our findings seem indicative of the low level which social rights, centering around the rights to strike and to livelihood, occupy in the public consciousness.

Moreover, judging from the cross tabulation of family income with item 8 (Table 2), respondents in low-income brackets do not

Table 2. Cross tabulation of family income of respondents with results of item 8 on the constitutional guarantee of livelihood

| | Answers to item 8 | | | | | |
Family income	No answer	Totally insufficient	Best the government can do	No need for guarantee	Don't know	Totals
No answer	1.9	36.6	37.1	2.3	22.1	5.4
Less than $833	0.1	45.8	33.8	5.4	14.9	12.7
$834–$1,667	0.7	42.8	39.0	5.6	11.9	31.5
$1,668–$2,778	0.2	42.7	44.2	3.6	9.3	32.6
$2,779–$5,556	0.6	42.0	42.8	4.7	9.8	14.4
Over $5,557	0.3	42.0	41.9	3.1	12.7	3.4
Totals	0.5	42.7	40.6	4.5	11.7	100.0

show any peculiar type of human-rights consciousness, particularly with respect to the guarantee of livelihood. Nevertheless, as Hirohisa Ueno has pointed out: "The people in the rural areas do not seem to be aware of the fact that government support for livelihood is based upon the constitutional right to livelihood, and that their low incomes and hard living tend to make them less sympathetic with the recipients of welfare aid and even keep others from receiving it." [8] Herein lies a subtle problem of the consciousness of the right to livelihood.

Consciousness of Politics and Equality

Attitude toward Politics and Elections. The findings on items 9 and 10 on the consciousness of politics and elections confirm much of what might seem to be common sense. First, in item 9, 51 percent of the respondents held that "the majority party should be given first priority but should not force through a decision without listening to the opposition parties." Since 13 percent of the respondents agreed that "the opposition parties are justified in showing some resistance" with another 5 percent of them approving "all kinds of resistance" by opposition parties, a total of 70 percent of the respondents were not only critical of the manner in which the LDP had been running the Diet, but also were pressing for serious review of the repeatedly forced votes in the Diet by the LDP. Age and income apparently did not affect opinions on item 9. Also as many as 58 percent of the LDP supporters answered that "the majority party should not force through bills without hearing opinions of the opposition parties," while only 12 percent thought that the opposition parties should always follow the decision of the majority party. It is regrettable, however, that somewhere between 30 and 40 percent of the less educated, in particular, the prewar elementary and postwar junior-high-school graduates, and female respondents had no opinion.

Although the important question of whether or not the political consciousness as found in the opinions on the majority and opposition parties is closely related to all other human-rights consciousness has not been tested, the finding in the cross tabulation of item 9 with item 3 (Figure 2) that only 30 percent of the respondents who were more or less critical of the manner in which the LDP runs the Diet believed that political freedom "should be strictly controlled" seems to indicate no high correlation between political consciousness and human-rights consciousness. The same seems to be true concerning voting behavior and human-rights consciousness. The findings on item 10 are somewhat unexpected when compared with other polls, in that as many as 60 percent of the respondents voted on the basis of candidates, whereas 32 percent voted on the basis of political parties.[9] Furthermore, ratios (in percentage) between candidate-oriented voters and party-oriented voters were 59:36 among males; 59:34 in non-agricultural areas; 55:31 among respondents in their 20's; 56:39 in their 30's; and 64:31 in their 40's. Party preference of the respondents divided candidate-oriented and party-oriented voters almost equally (46 percent for the former and 51 percent for the latter among JSP supporters, 51:44 among DSP supporters, and 47:46 among FPP supporters). While respondents in all groups were more candidate-oriented than party-oriented, voters' educational backgrounds were

significant: 46 percent of the prewar college graduates, 41 percent
of the prewar high-school and technical-school graduates, 33 percent
of the prewar junior-high-school graduates, 26 percent of the prewar
elementary-school graduates, 46 percent of the postwar college graduates, 39 percent of the junior-college graduates, 33 percent of the
postwar senior-high-school graduates, and 28 percent of the postwar
junior-high-school graduates were party-oriented.

Granted that detailed study would be required to answer the
question of how the difference between these two types of electoral
behavior is reflected in human-rights consciousness, a cross tabulation
between electoral behavior (item 10) and equal inheritance* (item
12) revealed no substantial difference: 46 percent of the candidate-
oriented voters favored equality of all children, 43 percent chose the
answer that "the eldest son should be given preferred treatment,"
and 7 percent answered that a daughter-in-law or an adopted child
should be discriminated against, whereas 41 percent of the party-
oriented voters chose the answer that "the eldest son should be
given preferred treatment," 8 percent felt a daughter-in-law or an
adopted child should be discriminated against, and 48 percent answered that all children are equal. Thus, despite the peculiar nature
of issues involving inheritance, a distinction between candidate-
oriented and party-oriented voters does not seem to be reflected in
their consciousness of freedom and social rights.

Consciousness of Equality in Social Life.† The consciousness of
equality is somewhat different from that of other human rights.
Referring to unreasonable social discrimination, Naoki Kobayashi
suspects that "Item 11 is not adequately phrased even if differences
in the respondents' living environments and occupations are dis-
counted" and doubts whether "responses thereto can reveal the consciousness of equality and critical spirit thereof." [10] Cross tabulations,
however, between item 11 and other items from the questionnaire
do contain some pertinent findings.

* Article 24, Section 2, of the Constitution reads: "With regard to choice
of spouse, property rights, inheritance, choice of domicile, divorce, and other
matters pertaining to marriage and the family, laws shall be enacted from the
standpoint of individual dignity and the essential equality of the sexes."

† Article 14, Section 1, of the Constitution reads: "All of the people are
equal under the law and there shall be no discrimination in political, economic,
or social relations because of race, creed, sex, social status, or family origin."

First, the question of which one of the first two answers to item 11 reflects more faithfully a respondent's constitutional consciousness cannot be answered with certainty, inasmuch as the meaning of phrases like "much" in answer 1 and "most of the time except for" in answer 2 varies subtly in the minds of different respondents. Nonetheless, cross tabulations with other items suggest that the respondents who feel the persistence of "unreasonable discrimination" possess a higher degree of human-rights consciousness than those who feel that "equality prevails most of the time." More comprehensive analyses of cross tabulation with other items, of which Figure 5 (the cross

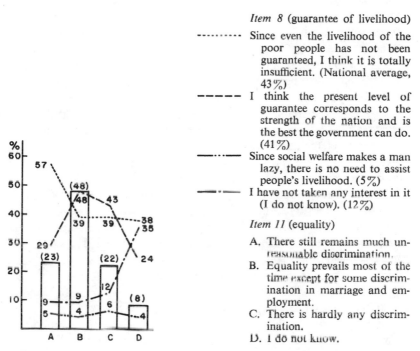

Item 8 (guarantee of livelihood)

-------- Since even the livelihood of the poor people has not been guaranteed, I think it is totally insufficient. (National average, 43%)

------ I think the present level of guarantee corresponds to the strength of the nation and is the best the government can do. (41%)

—··— Since social welfare makes a man lazy, there is no need to assist people's livelihood. (5%)

—·— I have not taken any interest in it (I do not know). (12%)

Item 11 (equality)

A. There still remains much unreasonable discrimination.
B. Equality prevails most of the time except for some discrimination in marriage and employment.
C. There is hardly any discrimination.
D. I do not know.

Figure 5. Cross tabulation of results of items 8 and 11 from the questionnaire

tabulation of item 11 with item 8) is a typical example, would lead us to believe that those who gave answer 1 reveal human-rights consciousness that is not only higher in degree but also better in quality than those who chose answer 2. Likewise, in the cross tabulation of item 11 with item 3 (Figure 1), a relatively high degree of permissiveness toward organizations engaged in political activities was found among the respondents who acknowledged unreasonable social discriminations.

Second, the findings in item 11 are distinctive to the consciousness of equality as opposed to the other types of consciousness previously discussed. The respondents in their 30's and 40's recorded the highest rate (24 percent) of all age groups in acknowledging the existence of "much unreasonable discrimination" while showing the lowest incidence (approximately 19 percent) in choosing the answer that "there is hardly any discrimination." The respondents in their 20's come very close to those in their 50's. In terms of respondents' educational backgrounds, 27 percent of the prewar college graduates and 30 percent of the postwar college graduates felt that much social discrimination exists, but there was a slight gradual increase (20–22–24 percent) from the postwar junior-college graduates to the junior-high-school graduates, with nearly equal rates among the prewar junior-high and elementary-school graduates. Furthermore, the junior-college graduates claimed the highest rate (61 percent), with both the prewar elementary-school graduates and postwar college graduates sharing the lowest rate (43 percent), for the response that "equality prevails most of the time except for some discrimination in marriage and employment." It seems that respondents with less education tended to feel more strongly the persistence of unreasonable discrimination in their social life. Next, in terms of occupation, those engaged in family businesses (agriculture or fishing) formed the fourth largest group following students, specialized technicians, and labor in complaining about much social discrimination. Even these meager data indicate the peculiar nature of the consciousness of social equality and the problems associated with it.

Third, no significant correlation is found between respondents' views of the Emperor and the imperial family and their views of equality except that an exceptionally large number of respondents who felt rebellious toward the Emperor also sensed much unreasonable discrimination.

Equality in Inheritance. One's sense of equality in inheritance seems to indicate that the issue of equal inheritance (see cross tabulation of item 11 with item 12 in Figure 6) is more complex than other

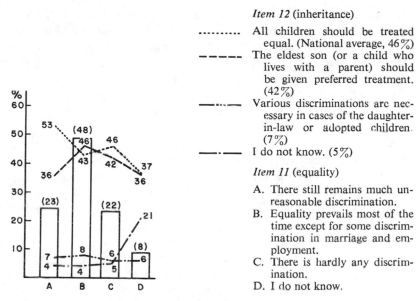

Item 12 (inheritance)

.... All children should be treated equal. (National average, 46%)

– – – – – The eldest son (or a child who lives with a parent) should be given preferred treatment. (42%)

— •••— Various discriminations are necessary in cases of the daughter-in-law or adopted children. (7%)

— • — I do not know. (5%)

Item 11 (equality)

A. There still remains much unreasonable discrimination.

B. Equality prevails most of the time except for some discrimination in marriage and employment.

C. There is hardly any discrimination.

D. I do not know.

Figure 6. Cross tabulation of items 11 and 12 from the questionnaire

issues of equality. The peculiarity of this issue is examined by asking the question of why the respondents who answered that "the eldest son should be given preferred treatment" increased from 26 percent in 1965 to 42 percent in 1966 while the answer "all children are equal" decreased from 54 percent to 46 percent. One reason for such an increase is probably the rephrasing of the answer from "different treatments are necessary" in the 1965 questionnaire, an answer which drew 9 percent of the respondents, to "a daughter-in-law and adopted children should be discriminated against" in the 1966 poll. Another and more important reason, however, may be that answer 2 to item 12 in the 1966 questionnaire, which read that "the eldest son (or a child who lives with a parent) should be given preferred treatment," gained a considerable increase from the feeling that whoever lives with parents and supports them should be given just as much of a preferred treatment as an eldest son.

Thus interpreted, however, the fact still remains that the respondents who argued a need for discrimination of one sort or another were found largely among those who showed low degrees of consciousness in other human-rights issues. For instance, only 9 percent of the respondents who supported the JCP agreed that the eldest son should be given preferential treatment whereas 36 percent of the JSP supporters and 51 percent of the LDP supporters shared that opinion; almost opposite ratios were given to the answer that "all children are equal." Likewise, 37 percent of the respondents in non-agricultural areas and 52 percent in agricultural areas selected to treat the eldest son better than the rest of the children.

The peculiar nature of the consciousness of equal inheritance is also supported by examining other variables. A respondent's occupation is found to be a relevant factor. In terms of a respondent's educational background, only 19 percent of the postwar college graduates agreed to the eldest-son preferred treatment whereas 74 percent of them selected the answer that "all children are equal." In contrast, more than 30 percent of the respondents of all other educational levels, particularly those who were educated under the prewar system, with the prewar junior-high and elementary-school graduates recording 47 percent and 54 percent, respectively, chose answer 2. Age analysis is even more revealing in that ratios (in percentage) between "equal treatment" and "preferred treatment" were 61:28 among the respondents in their 20's, and 49:38 in their 30's, but starting with the respondents of 40 and over, they were reversed to 40:47 among those in their 40's, 39:48 in their 50's, and 29:57 in their 60's and over. Thus, the respondents in their 20's and 30's who received a postwar education seemed to possess a strong consciousness on the issue of equal inheritance, although such consciousness may very well be the result of their a priori knowledge of equality. The respondents over 40 who received a prewar education tended to accept discrimination in property inheritance for various reasons such as traditional family sense, need of supporting parents, the necessity of agricultural management among farmers, and their personal experience and social mores in contemporary life. The acceptance of unequal inheritance may be one of the Japanese characteristics which will not easily be changed during the next several generations. Public consciousness of equal inheritance needs to be clarified by scientifically examining the question of why the need for such discrimination is felt and how this issue is related to other human-rights consciousness.

Conclusion

According to Harold J. Laski, "Any Bill of Rights depends for its efficacy on the determination of the people that it shall be maintained, and it is just as strong, and no more, than the popular will to freedom." [11] The present poll has proven that the "popular will to freedom" in Japan is far below a satisfactory level. A few reflections on this subject follow.

First, it is necessary to re-examine the question of what is meant by human-rights consciousness, the sense of human rights, or what Laski calls "the popular will to freedom." Merely finding that one has a high degree of knowledge of the Constitution or that many respondents in a public-opinion poll choose proper answers concerning human-rights issues will not immediately attest to a strong consciousness or the effectiveness of the Bill of Rights. A proof of strong human-rights consciousness is found not in a priori knowledge thereof, but in the extent to which the constitutional guarantee of human rights has been rooted and realized in specific aspects of day-to-day living. Therefore, an analysis of human-rights consciousness cannot bear much fruit unless some control of a priori knowledge of human rights is introduced and attempts are made from many perspectives to measure the public reaction to concrete issues.

Second, an accurate knowledge of human rights as embodied in the Constitution is a prerequisite of putting into practice the "determination of the people" that human rights "shall be maintained." In this sense, the degree of human-rights consciousness one possesses can be said to be in proportion to the amount of one's knowledge pertaining to it, although the latter is not identical with mathematical figures in a poll. The mathematical measurement of consciousness is undoubtedly influenced by various factors including subtleties of phrasing in a questionnaire[12] and the number of alternative answers available. Casual observers tend to interpret statistical findings arbitrarily, through the spectacles of their own ideology, and to disregard complex interrelationships among the variables that are not easily subject to statistical treatment. Herein lies the most difficult problem in probing human-rights consciousness.

Notes to Selection 6

1. Hirohisa Ueno, "Okayamashimin no kempōishiki" [Constitutional consciousness of Okayama residents], *Okayama daigaku kyōyōbu kiyō*, no. 3 (1967), p. 18.

2. Naoki Kobayashi, "Minshukempō ni kansuru seronchōsa" [Public opinion on the democratic constitution], *Hōritsu Jihō*, vol. 38, no. 6 (1966), p. 13; Nobuyoshi Ashibe and Takatoku Sumino, "Minshukempō ni kansuru seronchōsa: Chūgoku chihō" [Public opinion on the democratic constitution: Chūgoku district], *Hōritsu Jihō*, vol. 38, no. 6 (1966), p. 45; Teruya Abe, "Kinkichihō niokeru kempōishiki" [Constitutional consciousness in the Kinki district], *Hōgaku Ronsō*, vol. 79, no. 5 (1967), p. 45.

3. Naoki Kobayashi, *Nihonkoku kempō no mondai jōkyō* [The problem of the Japanese constitution] (Tokyo, 1964), pp. 88–89. Chapters 2, 3, and 4 are very informative on this subject.

4. Takeyoshi Kawashima, *Nihonjin no hōishiki* [Japanese consciousness of the law] (Tokyo, 1967), p. 203.

5. N. Kobayashi, "Minshukempō ni kansuru seronchōsa," pp. 15–16. See also N. Kobayashi, ed., *Nihonjin no kempōishiki* [Constitutional consciousness of the Japanese] (Tokyo, 1968), chap. 1, sec. 1.

6. The Japan Public-Opinion Poll is an organization of the *Kyōdō Press* and 35 other affiliated agencies. Three thousand men and women over 20 were interviewed by nationally stratified random sampling.

7. Since each respondent could choose more than one answer, the total responses exceeded 100 percent.

8. Hirohisa Ueno, "Fukushikokka nikansuru ishiki" [Consciousness of the welfare state], in *Gendai fukushikokkaron hihan* [Criticism on the modern welfare state] (Tokyo, 1967), p. 253.

9. For example, according to the public-opinion survey concerning women's voting in 23 wards in Tokyo conducted by the Public Opinion Science Association at the request of the Research Department of the Housewives Federation in February 1967, in which 600 were interviewed by random sampling, 64 percent chose political party as a criterion of their voting behavior and 34 percent chose the candidate, thus almost reversing our survey results. The reason for this contradictory finding is unknown.

10. N. Kobayashi, "Seitōshijibetsu ni miru kempōishiki" [Constitutional consciousness measured in terms of party preference], *Gendai no me*, October 1967, pp. 138–139. Also N. Kobayashi, ed., *Nihonjin no kempōishiki*, chap. 3, sec. 3.

11. Harold J. Laski, *Liberty in the Modern State* (New York: Harper and Brothers, 1939), p. 51.

12. Shigeyoshi Nishihira, "Seron karamita tennōsei to daikyūjō" [The imperial system and Article 9 seen from public opinion], in *Jiyū*, vol. 4, no. 5 (1962), p. 56, points out that "generally speaking, you can sometimes predict a respondent's answer by changing a questionnaire's phrasing."

PART III

**POLICY-MAKING AT
THE LOCAL LEVEL**

Editor's Introduction

Article 92 of the 1947 Constitution strengthened the principle of local autonomy within the unitary system framework of Japan's governmental structure. The Local Autonomy Law of 1947 put this constitutional principle into practice by granting extensive policy-making powers to local governmental units and forbidding the exercise of concurrent powers by national agencies.

The highest level of local governmental unit* consists of one district (Hokkaido), one metropolis (Tokyo), two urban prefectures (Kyoto and Osaka), and forty-two rural prefectures. Each prefecture or its equivalent is subdivided into cities (561), towns (2,007), and villages (808). Tokyo constitutes a special, self-governing district, with wards (23), cities (17), towns (15), and villages (9). A prefecture or its equivalent has a popularly elected governor and a unicameral legislature. Likewise, a city, towns, or village is governed by a popularly elected mayor and a single-house assembly. At each level, from the prefecture down, the checks-and-balances principle applies in that the chief executive may dissolve his assembly or the latter may remove him by a vote of no-confidence.

In practice, the principle of local self-government has been vitiated greatly by several factors. First, local officials tend to apply and administer whatever policies have already been established by national agencies. Second, when they do make decisions, local officials tend to look to the national government in Tokyo for policy-making guidance and turn out a carbon copy of the latter's model. Third, most local governments are in financial trouble, and national subsidies and grants-in-aid cover 20 percent or more of their basic revenues. This

* This does not include the Ryūkyū and Daitō islands, which were classified as a rural prefecture after 1972.

financial dependency has served to increase the national government's control over and influence on the local governments.

Ritsuo Akimoto, in Selection 7, analyzes a community power structure and its decision-making process, a grossly neglected research area. In Japan, the power of local government is extremely limited and informal leaders often affect decision-making processes; according to Akimoto, decision-makers can be identified by their reputation among those informed on local politics and by their participation in actual decision-making processes. Akimoto finds that the economic elites fill the upper echelons of the power structure in K. City, a one-company city. He attributes this to the increased role of business through its sharing in the city's revenue burdens in the wake of industrialization and urbanization in the locality. His other studies also indicate that various relationships exist between the economic elite and local leadership, although a study by Yasumasa Kuroda conducted in a predominantly agricultural community near Tokyo does not find a similar type of power-elite structure.* Thus it appears that industrialization and urbanization in Japan have been affecting, to greater or lesser degrees, policy-making at the local level.

* *Community Power Structure and Political Change in Reed Town, Tokyo* (forthcoming).

Leadership and Power Structure in Local Politics*

RITSUO AKIMOTO

This study deals with the question of how the leadership has changed in a selected local community as a result of rapid industrialization after 1955. An examination of the power structure in a local community[1] involves locating the community's power holders and analyzing their interrelationships and decision-making processes. The focus is on the power relationships of the local leadership that emerge in resolving local issues.

Local leadership in the present study comprised three groups of people: (1) those who enjoyed reputations among the politically informed in the community; (2) those who held positions in local organizations, especially public office; (3) those regarded as being influential in resolving specific local issues. K. City in Aichi prefecture† experienced rapid industrialization after World War II. The following five groups of leaders were found there, with each group relatively homogeneous in terms of social attributes and roles: (1) 35 upper-middle-class rural leaders who held public office; (2) 36 urban leaders, many of whom were self-employed in medium or small enterprises; (3) 17 progressive leaders; (4) 7 city-executive officials; (5) 13 company executives affiliated with the influential T. Automobile Manufacturing Corporation. Each of these 108 local leaders was then requested to select from among themselves the ten persons he considered to have the strongest influence in the admin-

---

* This selection is taken from "Chiiki shakai no kenryoku kōzō to rīdā no kōsei" in *Shakaigaku hyōron* (Waseda University Review of Sociology), vol. 16, no. 4 (1966), pp. 11–19. Translated and reprinted with permission of the author.

† Aichi prefecture, with Nagoya as its capital city, is located roughly 180 miles southwest of Tokyo.

istration of K. City. Table 1 shows the ranking of the "top influentials" thus selected.

Among the 31 "top influentials" the first three were selected by very large numbers of local leaders. In particular, the chairman of the T. Corporation–affiliated companies received the largest number of votes. The so-called "economic elite" associated with the T. Corporation and city executives also received large numbers of votes. Since K. City was supported after World War II by the T. Corporation–affiliated companies, which came to exert a strong influence in the city administration, it is natural that the company executives should receive so many votes. Approximately 95 percent or 99 out of 104 local leaders acknowledged the substantial influence of the T.-affiliated companies on city politics. Furthermore, this finding was confirmed by the company executives themselves.

Table 1. Ranking and attributes of the "top influentials"

Rank	Votes received	Native or moved into K. City	Occupation	Present position in city government	Past positions in city government	Major public positions
1	99	Moved in	Chairman, T.-affiliated companies	City councillor; honorary citizen		Advisor, chamber of commerce
2	84	Moved in	Mayor	Mayor	Vice-mayor; Mayor	
3	84	Native	President, T. Transport Co.	City councillor; member, prefecture assembly		Permanent member, chamber of commerce
4	71	Native	Unemployed	City councillor; honorary citizen	Townchief; member, prefecture assembly and House of Representatives	
5	63	Moved in	Executive director, N. Ceramic Pipe Co.	City councillor; director, board of education		Chairman, chamber of commerce
6	61	Native	Official, Y. Industrial Co.	Chairman, city assembly	Member, city assembly	
7	50	Native	Tile manufacturer	Vice-mayor	Member, city assembly; vice-mayor	
8	42	Moved in	President, N. Power Co.			Permanent member, chamber of commerce
9	36	Moved in	President, N. Ceramic Pipe Co.	City councillor		Chairman, economic affairs discussion group

Table 1. (continued)

Rank	Votes received	Native or moved into K. City	Occupation	Present position in city government	Past positions in city government	Major public positions
10	33	Native	Chief, general affairs dept., city government			Director, recreation assoc.
11	29	Native	Soybean paste maker	Member, city assembly (5 terms)	Chairman, city assembly	Permanent member, chamber of commerce
12	28	Moved in	President, T. Steel Co.	City councillor	Member, city assembly	Chairman, federation of agriculture co-op.
13	26	Native	Agriculture	City councillor		Director, grocery co-op.
14	25	Native	Grocery owner	Member, city assembly (4 terms)	Member, city assembly	Vice-chairman, chamber of commerce
15	24	Moved in	President, T. Auto Body Manufacturing Co.			
16	22	Native	Pawnshop owner	Member, city assembly (4 terms)	Chairman, city assembly	Director, agriculture co-op.
17	20	Native	Agriculture	Member, agricultural commission	Village chief	Chairman, gymnastics league of elementary and junior high schools
18	15	Native	Director, board of education, city government			

Table 1. (*continued*)

Rank	Votes received	Native or moved into K. City	Occupation	Present position in city government	Past positions in city government	Major public positions
19	14	Native	Interior decoration sales	Member, city assembly (4 terms)	Member, city assembly	Director, regional alumni
20	11	Native	Agriculture	Member, city assembly (5 terms)	Chairman, city assembly	
21	11	Native	President, O. Trading Co.		Member, public security commission	Vice-chairman, chamber of commerce
22	10	Native	Treasurer, city government		Vice-mayor	
23	9	Moved in	Director, K. Livelihood co-op.	City councillor	Member, prefecture assembly	
24	9	Moved in	President, N. Steel Co.	City councillor	Member, equity commission; city assembly	Executive secretary, chamber of commerce
25	8	Native	Agriculture	Member, agricultural commission		Director, agriculture co-op.
26	8	Native	Wine manufacturer	Chairman, election control commission		Permanent member, chamber of commerce
27	8	Native	Hog raiser, greengrocery owner	Member, city assembly (3 terms)	Member, village and city assemblies	
28	7	Native	Soybean paste maker	Member, city assembly (3 terms)	Member, village and city assemblies	

Table 1. (continued)

Rank	Votes received	Native or moved into K. City	Occupation	Present position in city government	Past positions in city government	Major public positions
29	6	Moved in	President, I. Industrial Co.			
30	6	Moved in	Director, T. Weaving Machinery Manufacturing Co.			Chairman, Rotary Club
31	6	Native	Executive director, T. Weaving Machinery Manufacturing Co.			Permanent member, chamber of commerce

After 1955 the T.-affiliated companies began to wield strong influence in city politics. Neither the political nor economic system in prewar Japan necessitated the participation of business in local politics. The T.-affiliated companies did not then occupy a central position in the economy of K. City. Consequently, they had neither been interested nor intervened in city politics before 1955.

Generally speaking, the 1950 tax reform initiated by the Shoup Mission, an American economic advisory body to the Japanese government, brought about many radical changes in the relationship between business and local politics. The Shoup tax reform strengthened the financial basis of local governments. Municipal taxes were to be composed of municipal residents' taxes (individual and corporate), municipality property taxes, utility taxes, and automobile taxes. K. City greatly increased its tax revenue at the expense of prosperous T.-affiliated companies. After 1955, the corporation tax, city-planning tax, and utility tax paid by the T.-affiliated companies made up more than 45 percent of the total revenue for K. City. The more tax the T.-affiliated companies paid, the more they began to take an interest and assume an active role in city politics.[2]

Issues decided	*Votes received*
Acquisition of land for factory expansion	44
Enactment of city ordinance to acquire land for factory	4
Improvement of industrial roads near company's factory	31
Company ownership of city roads on factory premises	5
Land improvement for housing (including redistricting of residential areas)	6
Installation and improvement of water, sewage, and gas facilities for industry	6
Promotion of employment	2
Construction of hospitals (and free land leasing by city)	15
Creation of industrial high school (and of the curriculum of automobile engineering)	3
Installation of lighting facility at a city-run baseball stadium	2
Construction of labor hall	1
Decisions on city personnel	2
Promotion of merger with town and village	1

The policies in the accompanying list were selected by local leaders as having been decided under the influence of the companies. (The figures include the selection of more than one answer by some respondents.) They seem to reflect the well-calculated and self-serving interests of big business, which has penetrated deeply into the government of K. City where it has played the major role in industrialization. As long as local governmental units increase their tax revenue from business in order to cope with financial difficulty, business involvement in local politics will continuously increase. Concurrently the local leaders will gradually be removed from the center of the local power structure. Ties between the city executives and the companies have increased, and local administration has been carried out by the business management in the name of the local government. The fact that K. City's executives received large numbers of votes (see Table 1) is not unusual; this commonly occurs in Japan's local governmental units. Figure 1 is a sociogram of mutual relationships

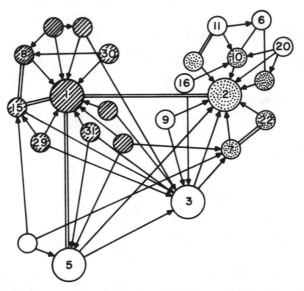

Figure 1. Sociogram of mutual relationships between the T.-affiliated companies and city executive officials. The number inside each circle indicates the rank of the top influential as shown in Table 1. ◕ indicates T.-affiliated companies' management. ◉ indicates city officeholders.

between the management of the T.-affiliated companies and the city executives.

Each of the local leaders was called upon to select from among themselves the three persons with whom he felt he had the closest mutual relationship in city politics. The chairman of the T.-affiliated companies and the mayor named each other. The chairman of the T.-affiliated companies and the chairman of the chamber of commerce, a leader in local economic circles, also selected each other. Furthermore, relatively strong ties were found not only among these three men (see Figure 2), but also among all the economic leaders,

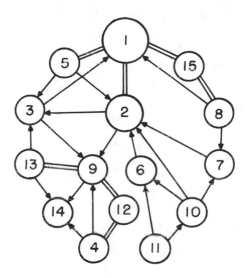

Figure 2. Sociogram of first fifteen of the "top influentials." The number inside each circle shows the rank of the top influential as shown in Table 1.

clustering around the company and city executives. Rural leaders and former middle-class urban leaders, in the absence of much close co-operation among themselves, interacted with the city executives and economic leaders in a disunited manner.

For example, rural leaders' choices were concentrated on the vice-mayor and the chairman of the city assembly, both of whom came from rural areas, but there was no close working relationship between those two men. This may indicate that rural leaders are preoccupied with their own interests so strongly as to exclude any close interactions with other rural or urban leaders, with the result that each rural leader comes in contact with city officials only when dictated by his own interests. Furthermore, the vice-mayor, as well as the mayor, works closely with the companies' management, and the chairman of the city assembly also is strongly supported by one company official. Consequently, these companies and city executives can, if necessary,

Table 2. Attributes and areas of influence of "key influentials"

Rank	Rank of selection			Score	Areas of influence			Occupation	Major public positions (present)
	1	2	3		All	Partial	Unknown		
1	69	20	3	250	83	7	2	Chairman, T.-affiliated companies	Advisor, chamber of commerce
2	18	21	11	107	39	9	2	Mayor	City councillor
3	2	22	22	72	32	12	2	President, T. Transport Co.	Member, prefecture assembly; city councillor
4	9	15	10	67	24	8	2	Unemployed	City councillor
5	3	5	7	26	12	2	1	Executive director, N. Ceramic Pipe Co.	Chairman, chamber of commerce; city councillor
6	0	5	12	22	8	7	2	Official, Y. Industrial Co.	Chairman, city assembly
7	0	3	8	14	7	3	1	Chief, general affairs dept., city government	
8	1	2	5	12	7	1	0	President, N. Ceramic Pipe Co.	City councillor; chairman, economic affairs discussion group
9	0	2	5	9	4	1	2	Vice-mayor	
10	0	2	3	7	4	1	0	President, N. Power Co.	Permanent member, chamber of commerce; ex-chairman, Rotary Club
11	1	0	3	6	3	1	0	Agriculture	City councillor; chairman, federation of agriculture co-op.
12	0	0	5	5	1	3	1	Agriculture	Member, agricultural commission; director, agriculture co-op.

oblige other local leaders to cooperate with them in making city policies. For instance, with the full cooperation of local leaders, a T.-affiliated company completed the acquisition of land for new factories within an extremely short period of time. Thus, the power structure in K. City is clustered around city executives and economic leaders, particularly those of T.-affiliated companies.

Next, each local leader was called upon to select from among the "top influentials" three persons with the strongest influence in the

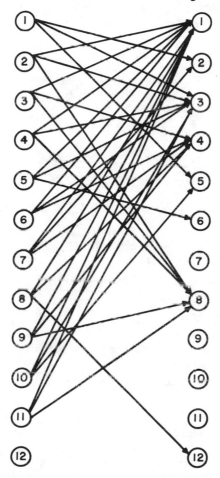

Figure 3. Selection of policy-makers by the "key influentials." The numbers inside the circles indicate the rank of the key influential as shown in Table 2.

decision-making of the city policies; the individuals thus selected are referred to as "key influentials" (see Table 2). The "key influentials" [3] consisted of the local economic leaders and city executive officials, with the chairman of the T.-affiliated companies at the apex. As is shown in Figure 3, all twelve of the "key influentials" selected each other and formed a very tight inner group. Choice was heavily concentrated on the upper "key influentials," and, particularly noteworthy, the chairman of the T.-affiliated companies by far exceeded the mayor, thereby suggesting an extremely strong company influence on the city's policy-making. Figure 4 shows only the first choice selection among the "key influentials."

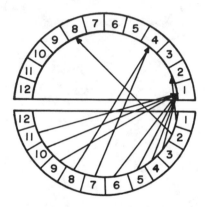

Figure 4. The first choice of policy-makers among the "key influentials."

Thus the T.-affiliated companies, through their deep involvement in city politics, have also affected the city's economic structure by various subcontracts with and absorption of local small enterprises. The city executives will continue to increase their ties with the companies, and the other local leaders will be further divided among themselves and increase their dependence on the companies. At the same time, the political realignment of K. City will be expedited from below when local residents turn to the economic leaders for political leadership.

The power structure in K. City is certainly typical of many local industrial cities where big businesses participate in local politics, but it cannot be made a model for all other industrial cities in Japan. In E. City in Fukushima prefecture, political power is structured in a centripetal manner clustering around a business, and yet economic factors affect decision-making more directly than in K. City. A business in another industrial city indirectly controls the city executive, whereas the power relationship is bipolarized between the business and local leaders.[4] When a single company carries overwhelming weight in a local community, rapid development of the company promotes local industrialization and urbanization, but subsequent changes in the local structure bring about a substantial change in group formation as well as the reorganization of local power relationships. When a large business becomes involved in local politics, there exists the danger of weakening the established local leadership and readily opening the way to a new type of political power centered around the business organization. Meanwhile, in the midst of rapid industrialization, urbanization, and changes in the local power structure, residents are unable to create new organizations of their own and remain merely as recipients of policies. A problem lies in the fact that today's rapid changes in the local power structure continue to destroy various factors which have previously retained the traditional ruling structure and unilaterally forced the reorganization of local politics.

To attempt to analyze local politics and the power structure therein poses the problem that there is no sufficiently refined frame of reference. The present study reveals in the severest manner some methodological problems and, at the same time, attempts to provide a framework with which to analyze a local power structure.

Notes to Selection 7

1. The term "local community" has several meanings. To the extent that a power structure is closely related to the administrative process, particularly the policy-making process, administrative units of villages, towns, and cities will be the object of the present study. This does not mean, however, that the actual power structure of a local community always corresponds to or confines itself to these administrative units.

2. Shigeru Katsumura, "Chiiki rīdā no kōsei to seisakukettei" [The formation of regional leadership and policy-making], *Shakai kagaku tōkyu*, no. 29 (1965), pp. 400–403.

3. The term "key influentials" designates sociometric leaders selected from among local leaders, although it also refers to "top influentials" in the dimension particularly related to policy-making.

4. Ritsuo Akimoto, "Chiikishakai niokeru kenryokubaitai to rīdā no kōsei" [The intermediary of power and the formation of leadership in a regional society], *Shakai kagaku tōkyu,* no. 29 (1965), p. 347. For other examples, see Ritsuo Akimoto, "Sangyōshakai niokeru kenryokukōzō" [The power structure in an industrial city], *Shakai kagaku tōkyu,* no. 24 (1964), pp. 55–94.

PART IV

THE MAKING OF FOREIGN POLICY

Editor's Introduction

Article 73 of the Constitution confers upon the cabinet the power to "manage foreign affairs and . . . conclude treaties" with the Diet's approval. In practice, leadership in foreign policy has been concentrated in the prime minister's office, although intraparty and interfactional rivalry within the ruling party sometimes make the prime minister's strong personal leadership difficult. Party deliberation on foreign affairs starts among the ruling-party leaders before a proposal is submitted to the Diet. Once an official party stand is worked out through bargaining and compromise, the strict party line almost always is followed by party members. Committee hearings on foreign affairs normally involve the budget and finance as well as foreign affairs committees of both houses. When the ideological stands of the LDP and the JSP and other opposition parties are irreconcilably different, pitched battles rather than the parliamentary process of negotiation and compromise are often the result. For instance, the ruling party in 1964–1965 favored the signing of a treaty establishing normal diplomatic relations with South Korea and also in 1960 and 1970 supported the security treaty with the United States. On both occasions, however, the JSP campaigned vigorously against the treaties with the help of leftist groups outside the Diet. When a foreign-policy issue involves the adjustment of relations with communist or neutral countries, the opposition parties soften their tactics considerably.

As part of the Japanese bureaucracy, the Ministry of Foreign Affairs has been an integral part of policy-making machinery in working out technical details of foreign policy and administering policy outputs. Because a major emphasis of Japan's foreign policy has been on foreign trade, the Finance Ministry and the Ministry of International Trade and Industry also are involved in policy-making. The ties of organized business with the ruling party are as extensive on foreign-policy matters, particularly foreign trade, as on domestic issues, although the extent of business interest groups' influence or control over the ruling party's policies varies from issue to issue. In contrast, the effective influence of labor on foreign policy is extremely limited. The General Council of Trade Unions of Japan along with the leftist student organizations have been opposed to the United States–Japan Security Treaty, as well as to the presence of American military bases in Japan, and they have advocated neutralism and closer relations with Communist China and the U.S.S.R.

The public normally is more indifferent to and uninformed about foreign-policy issues than domestic problems. If public opinion has any influence on decision-makers it is largely attributable to three factors: (1) public opinion creates the general mood in which decision-makers operate; (2) opinion polls on specific foreign-affairs issues may have some impact on policy-makers; and (3) public opinions as articulated by various friendship societies (e.g., the Japan-China Friendship Society), trade promotion groups, and prominent individuals, as well as mass media, tend to increase any potential influence. It appears, however, that public opinion normally leaves decision-makers with a much wider latitude in foreign-policy areas than in domestic fields.

Foreign policy has been a major concern of all postwar administrations. The American occupation greatly influenced the course of Japan's foreign policy even after it ended in April 1952. The successive LDP administrations have followed the policy of a close relationship with the United States and its Western allies. The United States was primarily responsible for the conclusion of the 1951 San Francisco Peace Treaty, which restored peace with forty-eight of Japan's former belligerents. The United States has not only become a major trade partner but is also committed to Japan's national defense through the 1951 Security Treaty and the 1960 Security Pact, extended in 1970, which authorize the American military bases in Japan. About 260,000 American military men were stationed in Japan at the end of 1952, but their number decreased to 38,500 in October 1970. Both the United States and Japanese governments agreed in December 1970 that by the end of the 1971 fiscal year the U.S. forces stationed in Japan proper would be reduced to 27,000 residual troops at the Iwakuni and Yokota bases, but that they reserve the right to reactivate the Japanese bases in case of emergency in the Far East. Close ties between the two countries have also been manifested in the increasing tendency to cast concurring votes at the United Nations. Furthermore, the return of Okinawa to Japan in 1972 is regarded as an additional achievement of Japan's conservative government. Indeed, the opposition parties have long been critical of Japan's close relations with the United States.

Ever since Japan's admission to the United Nations in 1956, the conservative administrations have proclaimed their intention of relying on that organization as the major instrument through which to settle any international disputes involving Japan. In practice, though, Japan's participation in only a nominal number of conferences and activities has rendered her relatively obscure in the world arena. The LDP administrations have also claimed to adopt a policy of close cooperation with the nations in the so-called Afro-Asian bloc. In this respect, concluding reparations agreements with former enemies in Southeast Asia has certainly prepared the road for better and closer relations; Saburō Matsumoto, however, in Selection 8, argues that, as far as voting at the United Nations between 1956 and 1962 is concerned, Japan was increasingly isolating itself from other Afro-Asian bloc nations.

With regard to Japan's relations with communist countries, the 1956 executive agreement with the U.S.S.R. restored peace and established official diplomatic relations, although subsequent negotiations have failed to solve many basic issues including the return of four small northern islands and fisheries. For many years Japan did not recognize the government of the People's Republic of China, but recently changes have been taking place, as is exemplified by Japan's support for Communist China's admission to the UN and the 1972 joint declaration which restored normal diplomatic relations between the two Asian powers. The LDP has always given first priority in foreign policy to foreign trade and has been remarkably successful. In fact, its policy of separation of economics and politics allowed Japan to promote trade with many communist countries. The balance of trade has been favorable for Japan, although the country faces many problems ranging from tariffs and discriminatory markets abroad to increasing trade competition.

The Preamble and the provision of Article 9 of the 1947 Constitution renounce rearmament. But in 1950, in the wake of the outbreak of the Korean War, the Yoshida administration, acting on the

Table 1. Military strength in the vicinity of Japan as of 1970, as estimated by the Japanese Defense Agency (*Asahi*, October 20, 1970)

Nation	ARMY		NAVY		AIR FORCE
	Units	Soldiers	Warships	Tonnage	Aircraft
U.S.S.R.	17 divisions	240,000	500 (including 20 nuclear and 50 conventional submarines), 250 aircraft	500,000	2,000
Communist China	118 divisions	2,450,000	340 (including 33 regular submarines)	200,000	2,800
North Korea	22 divisions, 5 brigades	370,000	120 (including 4 submarines)	14,000	580
South Korea	19 divisions, 2 brigades	570,000	80 (Marine Corps)	70,000 (30,000 men)	200
Nationalist China	22 divisions, 1 brigade, 2 regiments	387,500	210 (Marine Corps, 2 divisions)	130,000 (36,000 men)	413
U.S.A.	2 divisions	65,000	150 (including 10–12 conventional and over 3 nuclear submarines), 550 aircraft, 51,000 engineers	550,000	400
Japan	13 divisions	179,000	210	125,000	450

instruction of General Douglas MacArthur, created the 75,000-man Police Reserve. Although the professed objective of the Police Reserve was to supplement the existing police force in maintaining domestic peace and order, the group, after several reorganizations, gradually took on the appearance of a de facto military force. For many years the government was reluctant to build the nation's military strength beyond a minimal level, but the Self-Defense Force is definitely expanding. According to the 1970 defense white paper (*Bōei hakusho*), by the end of 1971, the Ground Self-Defense Force was expected to reach an authorized strength of 180,000 uniformed personnel plus a reserve of 39,000; the Maritime Defense Force was expected to have an approximately 200-ship fleet (about 142,000 tons) and 220 aircraft, and the Air Defense Force will have approximately 880 aircraft (see Table 1).

Each step in the expansion of the Self-Defense Force (SDF) has been accompanied by bitter disputes involving Article 9 of the Constitution and the alleged danger of military alliance with the United States. The government's contention that the Constitution does not prohibit a self-defense force as opposed to offensive weapons and armed forces has been side-stepped by the Supreme Court as a nonjusticiable "political question." Also, the Defense Agency has been completely subordinated to the civilian-government cabinet in order to alleviate the charge of revived militarism. The findings of Hideo Wada's opinion polls reveal many interesting attitudes of the Japanese on the question of national defense. Wada's perspective and his interpretations of the unconstitutionality of the SDF and the undesirability of amending Article 9 are common among leading intellectuals. He finds that the government's efforts to convince the people of the need for the Self-Defense Force seem to be bearing some fruit. But he also finds that an unexpectedly large percentage of respondents feel the Self-Defense Force is needed not so much against foreign aggressors as for the civic services they perform, especially in case of natural disaster.

Japan's Voting Behavior in the United Nations*

SABURŌ MATSUMOTO

After Nobusuke Kishi assumed the premiership from Tanzan Ishibashi, in February 1957, he initiated three foreign policies which were followed by Kishi's successor Hayato Ikeda: (1) the use of the United Nations as the main instrument of Japanese diplomacy; (2) cooperation with the free nations; and (3) the promotion of Japan's national interests as part of the Afro-Asian bloc (AA bloc). From the beginning, these three policies aroused doubt and attracted criticism. It was argued that the policy of cooperation with the free nations might be contradictory to the policy of promoting Japanese interests as part of the AA bloc, particularly in light of the fact that India and the United Arab Republic, the two major AA bloc countries that strongly advocate neutrality, differ greatly from the United States and pro-American countries in terms of foreign policy. The actual implementation by the Japanese government of two seemingly incompatible foreign policies has received much attention.

The present study attempted to probe the situation by analyzing Japan's voting behavior in the United Nations. A total of 143 roll calls were selected from seven general assemblies between the eleventh assembly of December 1956, which witnessed Japan's admission to the UN, and the seventeenth in 1962: 14 roll calls in the eleventh, 22 in in the twelfth, 19 in the thirteenth, 19 in the fourteenth, 27 in the fifteenth, 27 in the sixteenth, and 15 in the seventeenth. In selecting only the General Assembly roll calls the following considerations were

* This selection is taken from "Kokuren niokeru nihon no tōhyō taido: kaku burokku tono dōchōdo no tōkei kara" in *Nempō: Seijigaku* (The Annals of the Japanese Political Science Association) (Tokyo, 1964), pp. 67–81. Translated and reprinted with permission of the author.

taken: (1) Among the six major UN organizations (the General Assembly, the Security Council, the Economic and Social Council, the Trusteeship Council, the International Court of Justice, and the Secretariat), the General Assembly is the only organization where all member nations participate. Also, only the General Assembly decides policies in all areas of UN activities. (2) The General Assembly is composed of the general meeting and seven major committees. The selected roll calls were those in the general meetings which were concerned with political issues, and those in three committees, the First Committee (which deals with political and security matters), the Special Political Committee, and the Fourth Committee (which handles trusteeships and non–self-autonomous regions). (3) Voting at the General Assembly takes the form of roll call, show of hands, or without-objection. Since important proposals are, as a rule, decided by roll calls, only roll-call votes were selected. Thomas Hovet, Jr., in *The Bloc Politics in the United Nations*,* states that approximately 700 votings took place in general meetings and the seven major committees in each of the first thirteen general assemblies and that roughly 20 percent of them were by roll call. (4) The question of whether all or some of the roll calls should be analyzed was solved by adopting the following procedures: First, wherever the voting of each committee overlapped that of the general meeting, the latter was used; second, in view of the fact that votes are sometimes taken paragraph by paragraph rather than a single voting on the whole proposal, votes taken on the most important paragraphs in a bill were used; and third, votes on less significant matters such as procedural questions or near unanimous votes were omitted.

The 143 roll calls thus selected were then classified in the following categories, on the basis of issues on which the votes were taken: 45 roll calls on the peaceful solution of international conflicts like the Korean War and the Hungarian incident; 29 on colonial issues like the one in Algeria; 25 on the issue of nuclear weapons and disarmament; 14 on human rights in the broad sense, including the apartheid policy† in the Republic of South Africa; and 30 on other issues such

* Thomas Hovet, Jr., *The Bloc Politics in the United Nations* (Cambridge: Harvard University Press, 1960).
† The apartheid policy is a stringent segregation measure taken by the government of the Republic of South Africa. A law requires black persons 16 years of age and older to carry identification cards and punishes a violater thereof with hard labor. Also interracial marriage is subject to eight years of impris-

as the admission of Communist China and South Korea into the United Nations.

Japan's Voting Behavior

One way of determining Japan's position in the United Nations is to analyze Japan's support of proposals made by other countries and their support of Japanese proposals.[1]

$$\text{Propensity to support} = \frac{\text{yes} + \frac{1}{2}\text{ abstention}}{\text{yes} + \text{no} + \text{abstention}} \times 100$$

Out of 32 proposals submitted separately or jointly by the U.S.A. bloc, Japan supported 29, opposed none, and abstained on 3 (once on a colonial issue and twice on the issue of nuclear weapons and disarmament), with a resultant 95 percent support. She voted for only 1 communist-bloc–sponsored proposal (on the issue of expanding the general committee), while voting against 13 of their proposals and abstaining on 2 colonial issues. Thus, the propensity of Japanese support of communist proposals was only 14 percent. With regard to proposals made by the India-U.A.R. bloc, Japan voted for 21 (with 58 percent propensity to support) and against 13 (4 on international conflicts, 4 on colonial issues, 2 on human rights, and 3 on the question of admitting Communist China into the UN). She abstained from voting on 14 out of 48 India-U.A.R. bloc proposals. Conversely, the support rendered to 17 Japanese proposals by each of these blocs was 79 percent for the U.S.A. bloc, 29 percent for the Communist bloc, and 68 percent for the India-U.A.R. bloc.

Another method of analyzing Japan's position in the UN is to examine the incidence of concurring votes among the 109 UN-member states and Japan on the 143 roll calls.

The incidence of the concurring votes =

$$\frac{\text{concurring votes} + \frac{1}{2}\text{ neutral votes}}{\text{concurring votes} + \frac{1}{2}\text{ dissenting votes} + \text{neutral votes}} \times 100$$

Application of this formula to a few selected countries gives the following results: With the U.S.A., the U.S.S.R., India, and the U.A.R., the

---

onment. Each year the United Nations General Assembly debates the issue and passes a resolution condemning this racial discrimination.

incidence was 81 percent, 34 percent, 56 percent, and 49 percent, respectively.

Japan's position can be clarified further by analyzing the incidence of concurrence of Japan's votes with those of either the United States, the leader in the so-called free world, or those of India, a major country in the AA bloc, whenever those two countries cast opposing votes. In 114 cases in which the U.S.A. and India cast split votes, Japan sided with the former 75 times and with the latter 26 times. Thus, Japan cast her vote with the United States three times as often as she did with India.

These analyses of voting behavior, when combined, depict Japan as often being pro-American and anti-Russian and somewhere in-between in her relationship with India and the U.A.R. A comparison of concurrence and disagreement between Japan and other UN-member states, however, leaves many problems unsolved, because voting behavior varies from one kind of issue to another and also from year to year. Since blocs have been formed among UN states, Japan's position should be analyzed through her relationships not only with other individual countries but also with blocs of countries, particularly the AA bloc.

Tendency toward Bloc Voting

As of the seventeenth General Assembly in 1962, the United Nations had 110 member countries, the breakdown being 54 Asian and African countries, 22 Central and South American countries, 15 West European countries, 11 communist countries, and 8 U.S.A. bloc countries (the U.S.A., Great Britain, Canada, Australia, New Zealand, the Republic of South Africa, Nationalist China, and Israel) (see Table 1). The AA bloc, largest of the UN blocs, had 53 countries, nearly half of the entire UN membership. The AA bloc, only 11 countries of which were original signatories to the UN charter, was in a very low position in the United Nations (see Table 2). The 1946 gentlemen's agreement concluded in London assigned only one nonpermanent Security Council seat to the Near and Middle East and no seat to the Southeast Asian and African countries.

By 1950 the AA bloc membership had increased from 11 to 17, but its position in the UN remained very weak. Issues involving relations between East and West were always decided in favor of the

Table 1. The growth of United Nations membership*

	General assemblies							
Blocs†	1 (1946)	11 (1956)	12 (1957)	13 (1958)	14 (1959)	15 (1960)	16 (1961)	17 (1962)
Afro-Asia (the AA bloc)	11	28	29	29	29	46	50	54
Southeast Asia (including Japan)	2	12	13	13	13	13	13	13
Near and Middle East	7	13	13	12	12	13	14	15
Africa	2	3	3	4	4	20	23	26
Central and South America	20	20	20	20	20	20	20	22
Western Europe	7	15	15	15	15	15	15	15
Communist bloc	6	10	10	10	10	10	11	11
Others‡ (including United States)	7	8	8	8	8	8	8	8
Total	51	81	82	82	82	99	104	110

* As of the 25th General Assembly in 1970, the UN had 127 member states with the following breakdown: 72 AA bloc countries (18 Asian, 13 Near and Middle Eastern, and 41 African countries), 26 American countries, 17 West European countries, 10 communist-bloc nations, and 2 Oceanian countries.

† The above classification closely conforms to the one made by the United Nations Bureau of the Ministry of Foreign Affairs.

‡ The Republic of China, Israel, and the Republic of South Africa, all of which geographically belong to the Afro-Asian bloc, are grouped together with the U.S.A., England, Canada, Australia, and New Zealand.

West by about 40 votes to 6 plus extra votes in the General Assembly. The Western hegemony once caused a Russian delegate to complain that "the United Nations is an organ where the United States imposes her will upon others."

The outbreak of the Korean War in June 1950 precipitated the AA bloc's internal unity, resolute policies, and concerted activities. After the 5th General Assembly in 1950, when the Arab countries, which had been conducting their own organized activities, formed the center of the bloc, joined by such neutral countries as India and Burma, the unity of the AA bloc was strengthened through the deliberation of such issues as the independence of Morocco, Tunisia, and Algeria, the removal of armed forces from the Suez, and the unification of Germany. The AA bloc began to convene regularly after

Table 2. Strength of various United Nations blocs

Blocs	General assemblies						
	11 (1956)	12 (1957)	13 (1958)	14 (1959)	15 (1960)	16 (1961)	17 (1962)
Pro-Western countries	52 (12)*	53 (13)	52 (12)	52 (12)	50 (11)	50 (11)	50 (9)
Communist countries	10	10	10	10	11	12	12
Positive neutralists	12 (11)	12 (11)	13 (12)	13 (12)	18 (17)	21 (20)	24 (23)
Moderate neutralists	7 (5)	7 (5)	7 (5)	7 (5)	20 (18)	21 (19)	24 (22)

* Numbers inside parentheses indicate number of AA bloc countries.

the 10th General Assembly of 1955, and its 29 members, meeting in Bandung, Indonesia, in April 1955, clearly demonstrated to the rest of the world their unity. Despite the conspicuous activities of the AA bloc, the U.S.A. kept its predominance in the United Nations between 1951 and 1955, partly because the U.S.S.R. vetoed the admission of new UN members and partly because the United States always secured 20 votes from the Central and South American countries. After the 10th General Assembly of December 1955, however, when 16 countries were admitted at once, the AA bloc membership rose to 28, with Ceylon and five other countries joining in 1955 and Japan and four other countries in 1956. Thus that bloc exceeded one-third of all UN member states.

The rapid growth of the bloc brought about a substantial change in power relationships within the United Nations. On colonial and disarmament issues that had contributed to the unity of the bloc, there arose a possibility that the AA bloc might be able to obtain roughly half of all General Assembly votes, provided ten communist countries cast concurrent votes. Likewise, on important issues that required a two-thirds-majority vote, the AA bloc, with the concurring votes of its neutral countries and ten communist countries, could obtain one-third of the total votes. Therefore, it became necessary for the Western countries to moderate as much as possible the content of their proposals that required two-thirds-majority votes so that the AA bloc would not oppose them. Thus, the 10th and 11th general assemblies (in 1955 and 1956) witnessed the beginning of the break-down of Western hegemony in the UN. The rapid growth of the AA bloc, particularly its neutral countries, and their stiff stand on the Hungarian incident and colonial issues caused the Western countries to form their own bloc.

The independence and resultant admission into the UN of numerous African countries expanded the AA bloc again from 29 to 50 countries by the end of 1961. Western hegemony broke down completely when the AA bloc membership increased to 54 countries at the 17th General Assembly of 1962, inasmuch as the bloc then contained almost half of the 104 UN members and controlled the majority of the General Assembly whenever the moderate and neutral subblocs and the communist bloc voted with it. A close look at Figure 1 and Table

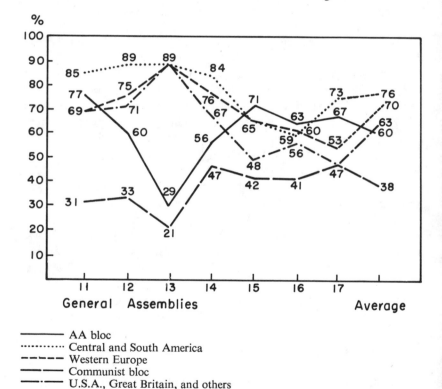

——————— AA bloc
············· Central and South America
— — — — Western Europe
——·—— Communist bloc
——·—— U.S.A., Great Britain, and others

Figure 1. Propensity of each bloc to vote with the majority of the General Assembly

Table 3. Propensity of each bloc to vote with the majority of the General Assembly (in percentage)

Bloc	18th General Assembly	Average
AA	100	64
Central and South America	77	76
Western Europe	60	69
Communist	65	41
U.S.A., Great Britain, and others	44	61

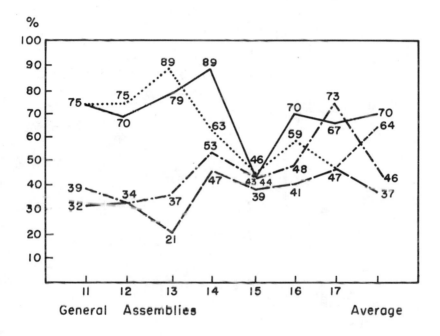

General Assemblies   Average

——————— Japan
············ U.S.A.
——— —— U.S.S.R.
——·—— India

Figure 2. Propensity of Japan, the U.S.A., the U.S.S.R., and India to vote with the majority of the General Assembly. For the 18th General Assembly, Japan's propensity was 53 percent, making her overall average 69 percent.

Table 4. Propensity of some selected countries to vote with the majority in the UN

Issues	Country	General Assembly												Average	Average of the five most recent general assemblies
		11	12	13	14	15	16	17	18	20	21	22	23		
Involving East-West relations	Japan	100	94	100	100	76	100	100	100	79	67	100	100	91	85
	U.S.A.	100	94	100	100	74	100	100	100	57	67	100	100	88	76
	Argentina	100	88	100	100	82	100	100	100	64	67	100	100	90	79
	India	58	38	38	25	38	25	63	50	79	50	25	25	42	52
	U.S.S.R.	0	13	0	0	32	6	0	0	36	33	0	0	14	21
Involving North-South relations*	Japan	44	71	86	93	56	65	75	70	55	55	71	57	64	37
	U.S.A.	50	64	86	79	78	65	50	40	25	23	21	21	50	27
	Argentina	75	71	86	79	86	63	81	75	75	77	93	79	77	79
	India	56	50	71	71	50	65	88	100	75	86	93	75	74	86
	U.S.S.R.	50	36	57	79	44	63	69	100	80	82	100	100	71	91

* North-South issues refer to colonial problems and human rights as well as those between developed and developing nations.

Table 5. Propensity of Japan to vote with the majority of the UN (in percentage)

Issues	Average (15th–18th assemblies)
Peaceful solution	89
Colonial issues	31
Nuclear disarmament	83
Races, human rights	50
Other issues	69

3 on the propensities of different blocs in voting with the majority in the UN and Figure 2 on the propensity of the U.S.A., the U.S.S.R., Japan, and India in concurring with the UN majority reveals the increasing tendency for the AA bloc to cast concurring votes with the

Table 6. The degree to which Japan voted with a two-thirds majority, 1956 through 1963

General Assembly	Percentage
11th (1956)	77
12th	88
13th	100
14th	100
15th	82
16th	90
17th	92
18th (1963)	90
Average	90

UN majority and the tendency for the U.S. and the Western bloc to vote with the minority, because the United States and the U.S.S.R. recorded only 47 percent respectively in joining the majority group at the 17th General Assembly (see also Tables 4, 5, and 6).

Breakdown of the AA Bloc

After 1955 the UN members increasingly voted in blocs. But the AA bloc, which had been giving impetus to the formation of other blocs, began to break down. The admission of Japan into the UN in December 1956 marked the beginning of the breakdown by transforming the character of the bloc when such pro-Western countries as the Philippines, Pakistan, Thailand, and Turkey left the neutral group centered around India. The AA bloc then had two centers of power, India and Japan. Those pro-Western countries having bilateral treaties with the United States, along with Jordan and I ʹoya, both of which had often taken pro-Western stands on the solution of East-West disputes, began to form a subbloc with Japan at its center.

A second weakening of the AA bloc was occasioned by the admission of sixteen African countries in 1960, further expanding the AA bloc. Eleven of them were former French colonies and most of them adopted moderate neutralism after the 16th General Assembly of 1961, thus weakening the mainstream of the bloc which advocated positive neutralism. Some ten African countries took a moderate neutralist stand at the Brazzaville Conference in December 1960 and the Casablanca Conference in May 1961, whereas several other African countries, part of the AA bloc mainstream led by India and the U.A.R., advocated positive neutralism at the Monrovia Conference in January 1961. As a result of these internal transformations, the AA bloc then had three major subblocs, all containing elements for both unity and disunity.

The Afro-Asian bloc is a geographical organization encompassing Asia and Africa, but geographical ties alone cannot hold together that vast territory with a population of over eighteen billion. It is an undisputed fact that the AA bloc is, to a greater or lesser extent, a community of states sharing brotherly consciousness, the same destiny, and common concern about their less advanced position in the world.

Table 7. Propensity of the Philippines, Thailand, Pakistan, and Argentina to concur with the U.S.A. or the U.A.R.

| Countries | General assemblies | | | | | | |
	11th	12th	13th	14th	15th	16th	17th
Philippines	68	88	95	74	81	72	60
	(61)*	(47)	(47)	(68)	(33)	(50)	(70)
Thailand	64	76	97	84	80	67	68
	(64)	(60)	(45)	(50)	(35)	(52)	(61)
Pakistan	69	73	89	71	65	50	38
	(62)	(55)	(53)	(71)	(50)	(76)	(92)
Argentina	86	86	95	82	84	81	73
	(43)	(36)	(47)	(55)	(26)	(38)	(57)

* The numbers inside parentheses show propensity to agree with the U.A.R.

For example, some pro-Western AA bloc countries (the Philippines and Thailand) and the Central and South American countries have recently inclined to positive neutralism on the North-South issues (see Table 7).

Unity and Disunity within the AA Bloc

The elements of unity and disunity within the AA bloc can be examined by analyzing issues brought before the UN. Since a common front against colonialism was the most powerful factor leading to the formation of the AA bloc, the incidence of Japan's concurrence with the AA bloc on colonial issues was highest between the 11th and 14th general assemblies (1956–1959), while the incidence of agreement with the American bloc for the same period was only 56 percent (see Figure 3). But a change of Japanese administration from Kishi to

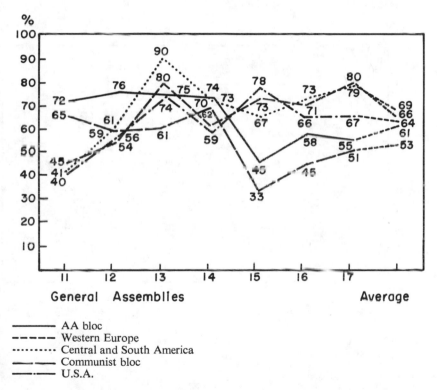

―――――― AA bloc
― ― ― ― Western Europe
·········· Central and South America
―・―・― Communist bloc
――・―― U.S.A.

Figure 3. Propensity of Japan to vote with various blocs on colonial issues

Ikeda and the personal appearance of Khrushchev at the 15th General
Assembly of 1960 contributed to the change in Japan's voting be-
havior at the UN. On issues involving East-West conflict, the pro-
Western members of the AA bloc including Japan have been com-
pletely isolated from the rest of the bloc. The incidence of Japan's
concurrence with the AA bloc on colonial problems after the 15th
General Assembly decreased to 53 percent, while her voting with the
American bloc increased to 69 percent.

This trend was manifested even more clearly with regard to human
rights issues, in that Japan always voted with the AA bloc between
1956 and 1959, while concurring with the American bloc only 66
percent of the time, but from 1960 to 1962 the propensities of Japan's
concurrence with the two blocs were reversed to 75 percent with the
American bloc as opposed to 43 percent with the AA bloc (see Figure
4). Indeed, after the 15th General Assembly, neither the colonial nor

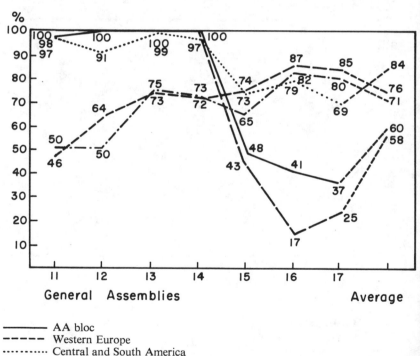

Figure 4. Propensity of Japan to vote with various blocs on human rights issues

human rights issues were unifying elements between Japan and the rest of the AA bloc.

In the 17th General Assembly in 1962, however, the AA bloc was again united with respect to colonial and human rights issues, reflecting the tendency for the pro-Western AA bloc members, except for Japan and a few other countries, to have inclined once again toward positive neutralism on North-South issues (see Figure 5 and Table 8). But, as far as Japan was concerned, nuclear weapons and disarmament seemed to be the only unifying issues. It was on these issues that Japan often presented her own views in the General Assembly and consistently scored relatively high degrees of concurrence with the AA bloc. According to Figure 6, the average propensity (82 percent) of Japan's

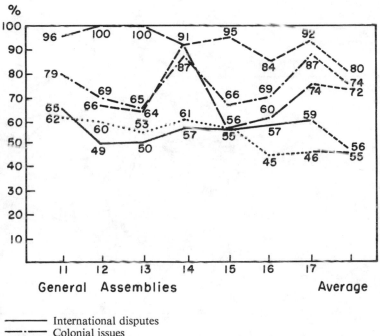

International disputes
Colonial issues
Nuclear weapons and disarmament
Human rights issues
Other issues

Figure 5. Degree of unity among the members of the AA bloc on various issues. The formula used is:

$$\text{Degree of unity} = \frac{\text{Votes cast by majority in bloc}}{\text{Total votes cast in bloc}} \times 100$$

Table 8. Analysis of 160 votes cast between the 11th and 18th general assemblies showing propensity of the AA bloc to unite (in percentage)

Bloc or subbloc	International disputes	Colonial problems	Nuclear weapons and disarmament	Human rights	Other* issues	Average
Entire AA bloc	55	77	81	75	58	69
Military alliance faction	91	70	75	79	86	79
Nonmilitary alliance faction (Belgrade Conference members)	79	87	92	82	85	86
Radical neutralists (Casablanca Conference members)	90	95	90	94	95	93

* For example, admission of Communist China and South Korea.

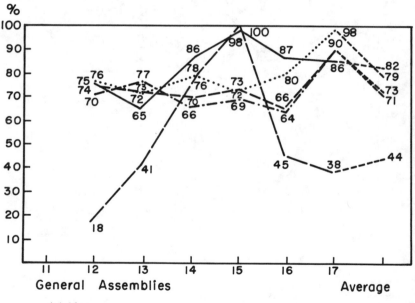

Figure 6. Propensity of Japan to vote with various blocs on nuclear weapons and disarmament issues

voting with the AA bloc on issues of nuclear weapons and disarmament was considerably higher than either her voting with the American bloc (71 percent) or the West European bloc (73 percent).

The question of peaceful solution of international disputes and other issues arising from East-West relations also tended to disrupt the unity of the AA bloc, a reflection of the different political backgrounds

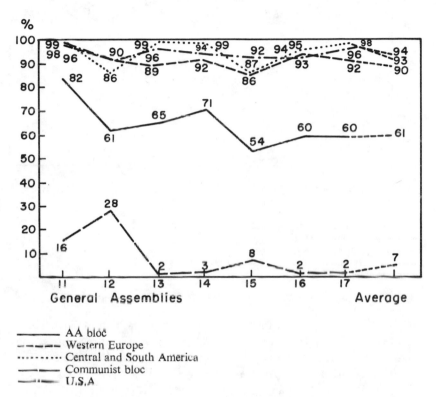

—————— AA bloc
— —— —— Western Europe
·········· Central and South America
——·—— Communist bloc
——·⸱—— U.S.A

Figure 7. Propensity of Japan to vote with various blocs on international disputes

of member countries. As Figure 7 shows, the incidence of Japan's concurrence with the AA bloc on international disputes (61 percent) was considerably lower than her concurrences (more than 90 percent) with Central and South America, the West European countries, or the American bloc. The only lower concurrence was that with the communist bloc. Furthermore, Figure 8 shows the same trend on other issues involving East-West relationships, with the average propensity

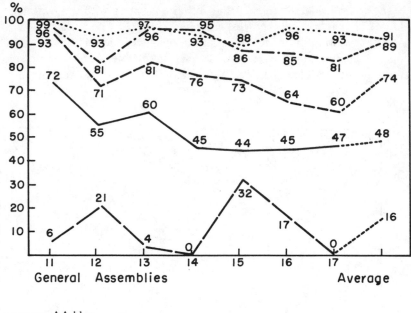

```
        AA bloc
------  Western Europe
........  Central and South America
—·—·—   Communist bloc
—·—     U.S.A.
```

Figure 8. Propensity of Japan to vote with various blocs on other issues

of Japan's concurrence with the American bloc as high as 98 percent as compared with 48 percent with the AA bloc. On these issues, the AA bloc is divided roughly into three subblocs: pro-Western, positive neutralist, and moderate neutralist. According to Tables 9 and 10, the propensities of Japan's concurrent voting with each of the three subblocs were 88 percent, 40 percent, and 65 percent respectively on issues of international conflict and 82 percent, 22 percent, and 51 percent respectively on other East-West issues. The pro-Western and positive neutralist subblocs represent opposite ends of the spectrum with the moderate neutralist bloc in-between. Indeed, the pro-Western subbloc including Japan often voted with the Western bloc countries.

Table 9. Incidence of concurrence in the voting of Japan and other blocs (11th–17th general assemblies)

Blocs	Issues					
	International disputes	Colonial issues	Nuclear weapons and disarmament	Human rights	Other issues	Total
Afro-Asia	61% (396-158-504)*	6?% (573-225-766)	82% (551-5-300)	60% (242-137-145)	48% (307-339-367)	62% (2,069-862-2,082)
Pro-Western	83% (224-2-69)	73% (226-37-172)	80% (161-3-98)	72% (76-18-37)	82% (234-17-77)	79% (900-72-453)
Positive neutralists	40% (37-124-267)	57% (219-124-315)	81% (217-1-133)	57% (95-63-61)	22% (28-261-120)	51% (596-573-896)
Moderate neutralists	65% (135-32-168)	56% (128-37-279)	85% (173-1-69)	54% (71-56-47)	51% (66-61-170)	62% (573-217-733)
Central and South America	94% (512-17-39)	69% (419-104-312)	79% (307-19-166)	84% (177-8-64)	91% (496-16-74)	82% (1,911-164-655)
Western Europe	91% (387-2-77)	56% (500-90-253)	73% (210-37-125)	76% (117-13-73)	74% (282-65-98)	76% (1,296-207-626)
Communist bloc	7% (1-253-39)	53% (142-111-206)	44% (62-95-99)	58% (65-43-36)	16% (30-236-36)	35% (300-738-416)
Others (United States)	94% (198-2-24)	64% (150-56-137)	71% (107-25-61)	71% (56-13-32)	89% (185-6-39)	77% (696-102-293)

* The three numbers in parentheses indicate concurrence, disagreement, and abstentions in this order.

Table 10. Propensity of each AA subbloc to concur with Japan, 11th (1956)–18th (1963) general assemblies (in percentage)

Blocs	Inter-national disputes	Colonial issues	Nuclear disarma-ment	Human rights	Others	Average
			Issues			
AA bloc (57)*	62	60	81	65	54	63
Military alliance faction (6)	95	75	78	76	88	82
Brazzaville Conference members (12)	76	51	87	55	65	64
Belgrade Conference members (23)	46	59	80	65	36	56

* Numbers in parentheses indicate number of countries in bloc or subbloc.

Conclusion

India's position changed at the 17th General Assembly in 1962. As Figure 9 and Table 11 show, India formerly was one of the leading forces in the AA bloc and, along with other positive neutralist countries like the U.A.R. and Indonesia, concurred with Japan in the neighborhood of 50 percent. But in 1962, India's concurrence with Japan increased to 70 percent and her concurrence with the United States also rose from 30 percent to 50 percent, mainly because she often abstained from voting instead of casting opposition votes. Consequently, the instances of India's siding with the majority in the AA bloc drastically dropped whereas instances of her siding with the majority in the UN General Assembly rose significantly (see Figures 2 and 9). Therefore, India's role in the AA bloc's mainstream of positive neutralism was greatly reduced.

Japan, furthermore, was moving away from the rest of the AA bloc, exemplified by the fact that her propensity for concurrent votes with the bloc dropped by as much as 15 percent after the 15th General Assembly. Conversely, her concurrence with the American and West European blocs rose, although by only a few percentage points, between the 11th and 14th general assemblies and after the 15th General Assembly. Furthermore, Japan began to disagree not only

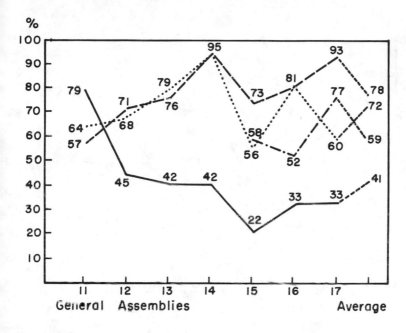

Japan
India
U.A.R.
Central Africa

Figure 9. Propensity of Japan, India, Central Africa, and the U.A.R. to vote with the majority of the AA bloc

with the positive neutralist countries, but also with the pro-Western countries within the AA bloc (see Figure 10).

Issues of colonial and human rights primarily accounted for Japan's isolation within the bloc, as already seen. In the 74 roll calls in which

Table 11. Propensity of Japan, India, Central Africa, and the U.A.R. to vote with the majority of the AA bloc (in percentage)

Country or area	18th General Assembly	Average
Japan	50	44
India	94	77
U.A.R.	81	77
Central Africa	93	65

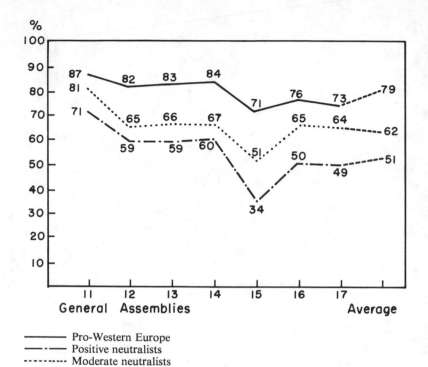

——————— Pro-Western Europe
——·—— Positive neutralists
·········· Moderate neutralists

Figure 10. Yearly trends of Japan's propensity to vote with various subblocs in the AA bloc

Japan participated between the 11th and 14th general assemblies, she was never in the minority in the AA bloc, whereas in her 69 roll calls between the 15th and 17th general assemblies she often found herself either in complete isolation or in the company of only a few countries (three times in the 15th, twice in the 16th, and four times in the 17th). Japan's isolation on colonial and human rights issues indicates that there is still room for the Japanese government to review their foreign policy at the UN. Insofar as Japan's voting behavior in the United Nations reveals, Japan has apparently not put into practice her foreign policy principle of the promotion of Japan's national interests as part of the Afro-Asian bloc.

Note to Selection 8

1. Of the 143 roll calls, Japan cast 77 affirmative and 35 negative votes. Her 31 abstentions were higher than the U.S.S.R. (13) and the U.S.A. (22) but lower than the U.A.R. (40) and India (40).

Consciousness of Peace and National Security*

HIDEO WADA

Domestic and International Situations at the Time of the 1966 Public-Opinion Poll

Tensions existing in the state of affairs in 1965 at home and abroad involving the so-called "peace and war" provision in the Japanese Constitution (Article 9)† increased in 1966, the sixth year of the ten-year United States–Japan Security Treaty.‡ The Vietnam War was escalated with both sides being increasingly pulled into the quicksand from which there was no escape. As anti–Vietnam War campaigns

* This selection is taken from "Heiwa no ishiki to anzen hoshō" in Naoki Kobayashi, ed., *Nihonjin no kempō ishiki* [Constitutional consciousness of the Japanese] (Tokyo: Tokyo University Press, 1968), pp. 113–128. Translated and reprinted with permission of the author.

† Article 9 reads as follows: (1) "aspiring sincerely to an international peace based on justice and order, the Japanese people forever renounce war as a sovereign right of the nation and the threat or use of force as a means of settling international disputes," and (2) "in order to accomplish the aim of the preceding paragraph, land, sea, and air forces, as well as other war potentials, will never be maintained. The right of belligerency of the state will not be recognized."

‡ The treaty was first concluded by the Yoshida administration in 1951. As a provisional measure, it allowed the U.S. to maintain its armed forces in and around Japan, presumably for Japanese national defense, but without obliging the U.S. to defend Japan. It also permitted the U.S. to "put down large-scale riots and disturbances" in Japan upon the request of the Japanese government and to use its bases for maintaining peace in the Far East. In 1960 the Kishi administration forced through the Diet a new security pact bill, which would give greater discretionary power to Japan, committing the U.S. to defend Japan and requiring Japanese consent before using American bases in Japan for military operations outside Japan or introducing nuclear weapons into Japan. It would also deny the use of American forces in case of internal riots. In June 1970, the 1960 Security Pact was extended against much opposition both inside and outside of the Diet.

gained momentum in both America and Japan and Communist China succeeded in the testing of atomic bombs, the issue of national defense came to receive close attention in Japan. References by a vice-minister of Foreign Affairs to the issue of the "nuclear umbrella" [1] increased public tension, and the appearance of American atomic submarines at the ports of Sasebo and Yokosuka became daily routine. The Eniwa case, used in the 1966 poll, assumed an importance similar to the Mitsuya Strategy Research at the time of the 1965 opinion poll.* Furthermore, the effects of the expanding Cultural Revolution in Communist China were being felt in the 1966 poll as well. Parliamentary democracy was still far from being perfect in Japan as the government was attempting to institute the single-member electoral district and also opposed any amendment to the political-contribution regulation law. These domestic and international situations were cer-

---

† The Eniwa case (Sapporo District Court, March 29, 1967; 9 *Kakyū keishū* [Inferior Court Report] 3 at p. 359) involved two defendant farmers who in 1962 cut the telephone cables installed where the Self-Defense Force practiced. On the strength of the provision of the Self-Defense Force Law making it a crime to destroy "defense installations and equipment," the prosecutor's office brought a suit against the two. Defense attorneys contended that the action was to protect their livelihood inasmuch as the noise of the SDF's practicing had been disturbing their cows, causing reduced milk production, and that the Self-Defense Force and the law thereof were in violation of the Preamble and Article 9 of the Constitution as well as the principle of peace therein. The Sapporo District Court acquitted them and ruled that the cutting of cables should not be regarded as the destruction of "defense installations and equipment." The court did not pass a judgment on the constitutionality issue, saying it was irrelevant to the disposition of the criminal charge against the defendants. Since the prosecutor's office decided not to appeal, the decision was finalized. This case was given wide publicity by the mass media and was widely debated by both proponents and opponents of the Self-Defense Force.

The Mitsuya Strategy Research took place in 1963 when middle-rank officers of the Self-Defense Force were engaged in planning national defense strategy on the assumption that Communist China and North Korea would attack South Korea and that their invasion would have an impact on Japan. Their strategy plans called not only for military operations but also for emergency legislation and restriction of civil liberties. In 1965, a JSP member of the Ways and Means Committee of the House of Councillors exposed what he had found out about the strategy simulation and pressed the government to submit a detailed account. Although opposition party criticism died down when a Ways and Means subcommittee investigated the matter, the public was disturbed by the secret manner in which the Self-Defense Force had taken upon itself such military strategies when the constitutionality of the force itself was not fully settled. Meanwhile, the Self-Defense Force reprimanded its vice-minister and other officials for allowing its top-secret military matters to leak out to the public.

tainly not conducive to the removal of public misgivings surrounding Article 9 of the Constitution. The Eniwa ruling and the issue of the return of Okinawa to Japan certainly did affect the development of public thought on Article 9 of the Constitution.

The Questionnaire

The following are questionnaire items and answers used in connection with the present public-opinion survey.

Item 13. Do you think that the present Self-Defense Force is in violation of the Constitution?
1. I think it is unconstitutional.
2. I do not think it is unconstitutional.
3. I cannot say if it is constitutional or unconstitutional.
4. I do not know.

Item 14. Do you think that the Self-Defense Force is necessary?
1. I think it is necessary.
2. I do not think it is necessary.
3. I do not know.

Item 15. If you answered in the previous question (Item 14) that the Self-Defense Force is necessary, please answer this question: Which one of the following reasons do you think is the major reason for having the Self-Defense Force?
1. To defend against foreign aggression.
2. To maintain domestic peace and order.
3. To assist the public in case of disasters.
4. To cooperate with the United States.
5. To defend the free world.
6. Other reasons.

Item 16. If you answered in Item 14 that the Self-Defense Force is necessary, do you think we should possess nuclear weapons?
1. We should not possess nuclear weapons.
2. We should possess nuclear weapons.
3. I do not know.

Item 17. The Constitution (in Article 9) states that, "land, sea, and air forces, as well as other war potentials, will never be maintained." Do you approve of amending Article 9 to have full-scale armament?
1. I approve of it.
2. I oppose it.
3. I cannot say whether or not I approve of it.
4. I do not know.

Item 18. If you chose answer 2 in Item 17, which one of the following is a major reason?
1. Strengthened armed forces have the danger of reviving militarism.
2. The possession of armed forces will increase the danger of inviting a war.
3. Japanese armed forces will be subjected to foreign countries through security treaties with them.
4. Having useless armed forces will waste taxpayers' money.
5. The present size of the Self-Defense Force is sufficient to defend the country.
6. Other ambiguous reasons.

Item 19. Under the present international conditions, which of the following methods do you think is the best to protect Japan?
1. The U.S.–Japan Security Treaty should be strengthened (and nuclear weapons should be introduced into Japan).
2. Japan should gradually strengthen her own defense system while maintaining the Security Treaty.
3. The U.S. bases should be removed, and the American forces should be allowed to station in Japan only in case of an emergency.
4. The treaty with the U.S. should be discontinued and replaced by our own military forces. We should also maintain neutrality.
5. The ideal of unarmed neutrality should be maintained, and non-aggression treaties should be concluded with both the East and West.
6. We should shift our cooperation away from the United States to the communist bloc.
7. Other reasons.
8. I do not know.

Item 20. Under the present international conditions, which country (or countries) do you think pose(s) the threat of launching aggressions and attacks against Japan?
1. Communist China
2. Soviet Union
3. North Korea
4. South Korea
5. Although aggression from the communist bloc is unlikely, there is a danger of counterattacks from it as long as there are American military bases in Japan.
6. The danger of aggression or attack is inconceivable.
7. The U.S. should be considered to have already launched a sort of aggression against Japan.
8. Other answers.
9. I do not know.

Item 21. The following opinions exist concerning Okinawa. Which one do you agree with?
1. Okinawa should be immediately returned to Japan.
2. The transfer of Okinawa to Japan should be started whenever possible.
3. Okinawa should be granted independence.
4. The status quo should be maintained (because there is no other way).
5. The island should be transferred to the U.N. trusteeship.
6. Okinawa should be incorporated into a U.S. territory.
7. I do not know.

Item 22. We would like to ask you about the Eniwa case. What kind of case is it?
1. It is a case which has been criticized as a coup d'état conspiracy by the Self-Defense Force.
2. It is a case in which dispatch of the Self-Defense Force abroad was debated in the Diet.
3. It is a case in which farmers were charged with a violation of the Self-Defense Force Law in Hokkaido, the northernmost island.
4. It is a case in which the guarantee of livelihood was debated.
5. It is a case which has been criticized as a Star-Chamber trial.
6. I have never heard of it.

Item 23. In which direction do you think the Japanese social system should be moving in the future?
1. Communism.
2. Socialist democracy.
3. Capitalism adopting welfare-state policies.
4. The present form of capitalism should be maintained.
5. I do not know.

Item 24. Do you think that the present constitution is, as a whole, suitable to Japan?
1. Suitable.
2. Not suitable.
3. I cannot say if it is suitable or not.
4. I do not know.

Issue of the Self-Defense Force

Despite heated controversy over the constitutionality of the Self-Defense Force (SDF) as revealed in the Eniwa case, our 1966 poll confirmed a general anticipation that the expansion of the SDF would increasingly become a *fait accompli*. Both the respondents who denied the constitutionality of the SDF and those who upheld it decreased from 25 percent in 1965 to 15 percent in 1966 and from 30 percent to 22 percent respectively. But the number of respondents who could not take sides increased from 23 percent to 38 percent, thereby suggesting that many of them have, in fact, been drawn to the side of the power holders who have consistently upheld the SDF's constitutionality. Meanwhile, those who deny its constitutionality will continue to decrease and be further isolated. Likewise, although there was no change in the size (13 percent) of the proponents of amending Article 9, its opponents decreased from 52 percent in 1965 to 31 percent in 1966, whereas the number of respondents who could not take sides increased from 26 percent to 36 percent, again raising the concern that they might eventually coalesce with the power holders.* Since the Constitution leaves to each individual citizen the sovereign right to pass final judgment, the finding that as many as 36 percent of the respondents did not have definite opinions on amending Article 9 is disconcerting.

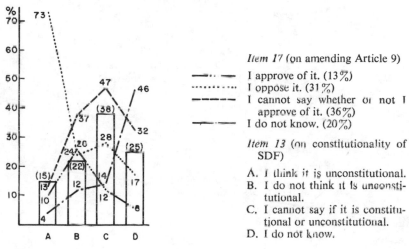

Item 17 (on amending Article 9)

—··— I approve of it. (13%)
············ I oppose it. (31%)
————— I cannot say whether or not I approve of it. (36%)
—·—·— I do not know. (20%)

Item 13 (on constitutionality of SDF)

A. I think it is unconstitutional.
B. I do not think it is unconstitutional.
C. I cannot say if it is constitutional or unconstitutional.
D. I do not know.

Figure 1. Cross tabulation of results of items 13 and 17 from the questionnaire

The cross tabulation of items 13 and 17 (Figure 1) shows a close relationship between the respondents' attitudes on the SDF's constitutionality and the feasibility of amending Article 9. Of the re-

* According to the *Asahi* press poll taken in June 1970, 27 percent of its respondents were in favor of amending Article 9 and 55 percent were opposed. *Asahi,* June 23, 1970.

spondents who denied the SDF's constitutionality 73 percent were opposed to any attempt to amend the constitutional provision, whereas 26 percent of the respondents upholding its constitutionality, the highest rate of all answers, were in favor. Logically speaking, the respondents upholding the SDF's constitutionality should have denied any need for such an amendment because the SDF does exist under the present constitution. They probably would like to amend in such a manner, however, as to completely remove any doubt from the issue. In any case the number of respondents upholding the SDF's constitutionality while favoring a constitutional amendment increased from 23 percent in 1965 to 26 percent in 1966.

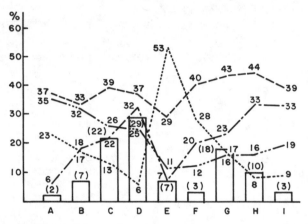

Item 13 (on constitutionality of SDF)

··········· I think it is unconstitutional. (15%)
——··—— I do not think it is unconstitutional. (22%)
— — — — I cannot say if it is constitutional or unconstitutional. (38%)
——·—— I do not know. (25%)

Educational background

A. Prewar college graduates
B. Prewar high-school and technical-school graduates
C. Prewar junior-high-school graduates
D. Prewar elementary-school graduates
E. Postwar college graduates
F. Junior-college graduates
G. Postwar senior-high-school graduates
H. Postwar junior-high-school graduates
I. Others

Figure 2. Cross tabulation of respondents' education with results of item 13 from the questionnaire

Figure 2 clearly reveals that the higher the education, particularly familiarity with the new Constitution, the greater the chance of denying the SDF's constitutionality. As high as 53 percent of the postwar college graduates held the SDF unconstitutional, whereas 28 percent of the junior-college graduates, 23 percent of the prewar college graduates, 17 percent of the prewar and postwar high-school graduates, and 6 percent of the prewar elementary-school graduates were of that opinion. Conversely, 11 percent of the college graduates, 12 percent of the junior-college graduates, 16 percent of the postwar junior-high-school and senior-high-school graduates, 25 percent of the prewar elementary-school graduates, 26 percent of the prewar junior-high-school graduates, 32 percent of the prewar high-school graduates, and 35 percent of the prewar college graduates upheld its constitutionality. Thus, the opponents of the SDF exceeded the proponents thereof by only 1 percent among the postwar senior-high-school graduates. Furthermore, according to Figure 2, the legal, particularly constitutional, education offered in postwar colleges has not only sharpened the constitutional consciousness, vital for the development of constitutional democracy in Japan, but also apparently accounts for the high rate of postwar college graduates who denied the SDF's constitutionality. (Hence, it is regrettable that as many as 32 percent of the prewar elementary-school graduates and 33 percent of the postwar junior-high-school graduates should have had no opinions on the issue.)

With regard to the party preference of respondents and their views on the SDF's constitutionality, 78 percent of the JCP supporters, 28 percent of the JSP supporters, and 23 percent of the FPP supporters held the SDF unconstitutional, while 5 percent, 14 percent, and 20 percent respectively upheld its constitutionality.[2] Conversely, ratios between constitutionality and unconstitutionality were 22 percent to 20 percent among the DSP supporters, 16 percent to 13 percent among the respondents with no party preference, and 33 percent to 5 percent among the LDP supporters. Also, the number of respondents who could not take sides increased, except for 10 percent of the JCP supporters, to as high as 34 percent through 41 percent among the supporters of the JSP, FPP, DSP, and LDP, as well as among respondents with no party preference or no desire to express such preference. In the light of the allegedly liberal stance of the JSP, it is somewhat surprising that only 28 percent of their supporters, as compared with 78 percent of the JCP supporters, should have denied the SDF's constitutionality. Furthermore, those who denied the constitutionality exceeded their opponents among the DSP supporters (22 percent to 20 percent), whereas among the FPP supporters the latter exceeds the former (20 percent to 23 percent). Thus, the DSP, which claims to be a progressive party, seems to have become the second most conservative party.

Views on the Self-Defense Force

The responses to item 14 in the 1966 poll reveal that the number of respondents who acknowledged the need for the SDF increased from 60 percent in 1965 to 71 percent in 1966, showing an increment of more than 10 percent within a year. (Especially the fact that "as many as 58 percent of the JSP supporters feel the need for the SDF, and only 27 percent of them think otherwise"[3] presents a problem to the JSP, which claims to be a progressive party.) The number of those respondents who strongly denied the need for the SDF decreased from 16 percent to 13 percent in 1966 and respondents who had no opinion were relatively few (15 percent). (In 1965, 20 percent of the respondents could not say one way or the other while 5 percent had no opinion.) This finding is no more suggestive of the immediate revival of the former Imperial Armed Forces than the findings on item 15 but is indicative of the tendency for the SDF to become increasingly a *fait accompli.*[4]

The respondents gave three reasons for the need for the SDF in the following order of importance: nonmilitary services to the people; activities in maintaining domestic peace and order; and activities in preventing military aggression from abroad. The order of importance attached is very puzzling because Article 3 of the Self-Defense Force Law lists the prevention of foreign aggression as the first duty of the SDF and the "maintaining of domestic peace and order" as its secondary duty. Except for Article 83, which provides for the "dispatch of the SDF in case of a disaster," no provision in the law requires the SDF to perform the kind of nonmilitary services to the public which are regarded by many respondents as the primary reason for the SDF's existence. In this respect it should be noted that the legal ground for the use of the SDF in the 1964 Olympics was the provision of a miscellaneous rule, Article 100(3), Chapter 8, of the SDF Law, which allows the use of the SDF in "assisting athletic meets." Thus, it is ironic that the primary duty of "preventing foreign aggression" should be attached only a tertiary importance and, conversely, the indirect line of SDF's duty in case of disasters, the primary importance. The order of importance attached by respondents coincides with the legally prescribed order of importance only with regard to the secondary duty of "maintaining domestic peace and order." In any case, the finding that regardless of a respondent's party preference the "prevention of foreign aggression" scored lower than both the SDF's public services and maintenance of domestic peace and order should be fully taken into account in any attempt to analyze the public image of the SDF.

The government's third defense plan estimated the SDF's expenditure to exceed 5.5 billion dollars.* The "irreconcilability between the military state and the welfare state" is bound to emerge because the expanded military budget will adversely affect the nation's economy and the guarantee of people's livelihood. With regard to Figure 3 (the cross tabulation of items 8 and 14 [see Selection 6 for item 8]), which relates the guarantee of livelihood to the need for the SDF, 80 percent of those respondents who felt a need for the SDF while answering that "the present level of guarantee of the people's livelihood is the best the government can do" seemed to accept the concept of a balance between the welfare state and the military state, or between "guns and butter." [5] Conversely, 65 percent of the respondents who felt the present level of guarantee inadequate while advocating the SDF did not seem to realize the difficulty of achieving both the welfare state and the military state. (They should be reminded that in the United States the "war against poverty" was shelved by President Lyndon Johnson due to increasing military expenditures for the Vietnam War.)

The finding on item 16 that an overwhelming majority of those who recognize the need for the SDF oppose Japan's possession of nuclear weapons obviously corresponds with the previous finding which ascribes the primary role of the SDF to public service instead of the prevention of foreign aggression. Moreover, the case against the possession of nuclear weapons probably has much in common

* For many years Japan was spending only about 7 percent of its annual budget for the SDF. For the fourth five-year defense plan, which started in 1972, the Japanese Defense Agency announced an appropriation of 15 billion dollars, the seventh largest defense expenditure in the world.

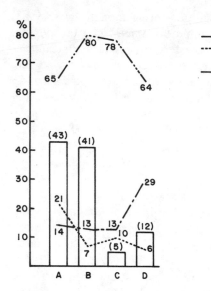

Item 14 (need for SDF)

——···— I think it is necessary. (71%)
---------- I do not think it is necessary.
                    (13%)
——·— I do not know. (15%)

Item 8 (guarantee of livelihood)

A. Since even the livelihood of
   the poor people has not been
   guaranteed, I think it is totally
   insufficient. (National average, 43%)
B. I think the present level of
   guarantee corresponds to the
   strength of the nation and is
   the best the government can
   do. (41%)
C. Since social welfare makes a
   man lazy, there is no need to
   assist people's livelihood. (5%)
D. I have not taken any interest
   in it (I do not know). (12%)

Figure 3. Cross tabulation of items 8 and 14 from the questionnaire

with the case against the "introduction into Japan of American nuclear weapons," both reflecting the widely felt fear of being driven into another war and the growing de facto recognition of the SDF.

Item 18 helped to clarify this point. Many respondents, in opposition to having full-scale armed forces by amending Article 9, chose the very realistic reason that having armed forces might "involve us in another war" rather than ideological reasons of the revival of militarism or Japanese dependency on the United States through the mutual security treaty. As far as logic is concerned, those who viewed the present level of the SDF as "sufficient" should belong not to the protectionist group of the present Constitution but to the advocates of amendment through reinterpretation of Article 9 so as to allow the expansion of the SDF.

The Issue of National Defense

With the intensification of the Vietnam War and the further establishment of the SDF, what did the public think of the national security? One of the main objectives of the 1966 poll was to examine closely the respondents' perception of imaginary enemies and reasons for any potential aggression against Japan.

We made a slight change in phrasing in the 1966 questionnaire: Proponents of a strengthened United States–Japan Security Treaty decreased from 9 percent in 1965 to 2 percent in 1966, probably due to the addition of the phrase "the introduction into Japan of nuclear weapons." On the other hand, respondents who favored the "continuation of the present Security Treaty" (which corresponded to the phrase "the Security Treaty without a modification" in the 1965 questionnaire) increased from 18 percent to 22 percent. Proponents of unarmed neutrality and the conclusion of nonaggression pacts with both the East and the West dropped substantially from 30 percent to 20 percent whereas respondents without any opinion rose from 22 percent to 31 percent. These changes usually have been interpreted as indicative of an increase in the group who favored the status quo of the security-treaty system; but the supporters for either the existing security treaty (22 percent) or reinforcement thereof (2 percent) when added together do not reach one-third of all the respondents and are exceeded by the opposition groups which include proponents of unarmed neutrality (20 percent), neutrality through strengthened Japanese (not American) forces (11 percent), and cooperation with the communist bloc (1 percent). Thus, contrary to the government's claim, maintaining the present treaty neither represents the people's wishes nor receives more support than the case for neutrality without any security treaty, granted that the term "neutrality" includes wide latitudes of complex and different implications and that the number of proponents of neutrality considerably decreased from 48 percent in 1965.

According to Figure 4, which relates the issue of the necessity of the SDF to the question of Japanese national defense, 54 percent of the respondents who denied the need for the SDF favored neutrality and the conclusion of nonaggression pacts with both the East and West. Many problems surrounding the United States–Japan Security Treaty seem to manifest themselves in the finding that only 29 percent of the respondents who recognized the necessity of the SDF upheld the continuation of the security treaty, while 11 percent of them favored the stationing of U.S. forces in Japan only in time of emergency.* When the question of national defense is examined in terms

* The *Asahi* poll came up with the following findings with regard to the question of national security: No need for either U.S. forces or the SDF (15 percent), greatly strengthened SDF and no U.S. forces (22 percent), in-

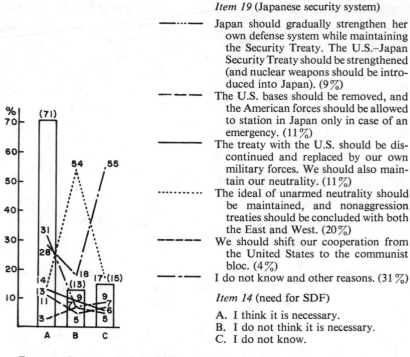

Item 19 (Japanese security system)

————··—— Japan should gradually strengthen her own defense system while maintaining the Security Treaty. The U.S.–Japan Security Treaty should be strengthened (and nuclear weapons should be introduced into Japan). (9%)

—— —— —— The U.S. bases should be removed, and the American forces should be allowed to station in Japan only in case of an emergency. (11%)

—————— The treaty with the U.S. should be discontinued and replaced by our own military forces. We should also maintain our neutrality. (11%)

··········· The ideal of unarmed neutrality should be maintained, and nonaggression treaties should be concluded with both the East and West. (20%)

—— —— — We should shift our cooperation from the United States to the communist bloc. (4%)

——— ·—— I do not know and other reasons. (31%)

Item 14 (need for SDF)

A. I think it is necessary.
B. I do not think it is necessary.
C. I do not know.

Figure 4. Cross tabulation of items 14 and 19 from the questionnaire

of respondents' party preference, 35 percent of the LDP supporters, the highest rate of all parties, chose the continuation of the security treaty, whereas the proponents of unarmed neutrality were considerably suprapartisan, consisting of 42 percent of the JCP supporters, 36 percent of the JSP supporters, 30 percent of the DSP supporters, and 25 percent of the FPP supporters.

To ask whether or not there is a "danger of attack against Japan under the present international conditions" might seem slightly shocking; nonetheless, when armaments and national defense are at issue, the public supposition of imaginary aggressors is probably unavoidable, and an inquiry into the reasons why offensive countries are considered to be what they are can be very important.

---

creased SDF and strengthened Japanese position in U.S.–Japan cooperation (26 percent), maintaining the status quo of the SDF and U.S. forces in Japan (22 percent), and other answers (4 percent). *Asahi,* June 23, 1970.

Putting aside for a moment the implication of respondents without any opinion (35 percent) on the overall analysis, attention should be focused on the finding that as high as 33 percent of the respondents felt that aggression from the communist bloc was unlikely but that there was a danger of counterattack as long as American bases existed in Japan, whereas an unexpectedly small rate (11 percent) of the respondents feared the "danger of aggression and attack from the communist bloc" (Communist China, the U.S.S.R., and North Korea). This almost matched the 10 percent of the respondents who could hardly imagine aggression or attack from any country. Thus, it appears that the chance of aggression and attack (to be more precise, counterattack) from the communist bloc depends on the existence of military bases in Japan. Indeed, as many as 33 percent of the respondents answered that since aggressions from the communist bloc were unlikely, had the American bases been removed, there would be no danger of counterattack. Herein lies the gravity of having American military bases in Japan and why that aspect is such a central part of the current issue of national defense.* Hanson Baldwin, a well-known American strategist (obviously not speaking for the U.S. government), once argued that the overseas American military bases were established to draw enemy attacks, like a magnet. A serious review should be given to the role that the American bases scattered throughout Japan, particularly for bombers and fighters, have been playing in the anticommunist strategy as was exposed in the Mitsuya Strategy Analysis. The finding that fear of communist counterattack was felt several times as much as the danger of unilateral aggression from Communist China or the U.S.S.R. seems to point to the existence of strong and healthy adherence to the peace-oriented Japanese Constitution and neutralism.†

* According to the *Asahi* poll, the respondents' attitudes toward the U.S.-Japan Security Treaty in the 1970's were as follows: extension for another 10 years or so (4 percent), automatic extension (16 percent), stationing of U.S. forces only in case of emergency (8 percent), gradual abrogation (42 percent), immediate abrogation (9 percent), and other or no answers (21 percent). *Asahi*, June 23, 1970.

† The *Asahi* poll found that 37 percent of its respondents regarded the U.S.-Japan Security Treaty as being beneficial to Japan while 14 percent thought it otherwise for the following various reasons: the treaty would be used only to the advantage of the U.S. (2 percent); Japan has no say in the treaty (1 percent); the treaty may endanger Japan's interests (2 percent); the treaty is not beneficial to the Japanese people (2 percent); the American bases

According to Figure 5, 37 percent of the respondents based their opposition to acquiring nuclear weapons on the fear that they might increase the chance of communist counterattack induced by American bases in Japan, while another 13 percent of them opposed on the

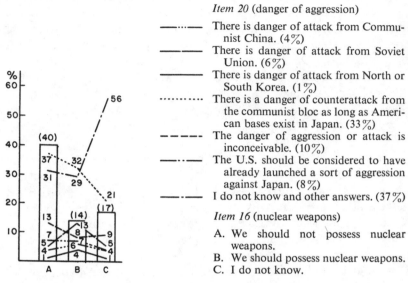

Item 20 (danger of aggression)

———·····— There is danger of attack from Communist China. (4%)

————— There is danger of attack from Soviet Union. (6%)

————— There is danger of attack from North or South Korea. (1%)

·············· There is a danger of counterattack from the communist bloc as long as American bases exist in Japan. (33%)

————— The danger of aggression or attack is inconceivable. (10%)

——··—— The U.S. should be considered to have already launched a sort of aggression against Japan. (8%)

——·—— I do not know and other answers. (37%)

Item 16 (nuclear weapons)

A. We should not possess nuclear weapons.
B. We should possess nuclear weapons.
C. I do not know.

Figure 5. Cross tabulation of items 16 and 20 from the questionnaire

ground that any attacks were inconceivable. Meanwhile, 32 percent of the respondents who favored nuclear weapons for defense should there be communist counterattack on American bases, seemed still to want the American bases in Japan forming the "nuclear umbrella" for the Japanese defense system. As far as the finding in Figure 5 indicates, Japan's possession of nuclear weapons would be more likely to drive her into war than to contribute to defense.

Under the present international conditions, the relationship between the selection of a national security system and imaginary enemies is very subtle but undoubtedly important. According to Figure 6, 50 percent of the advocates of unarmed neutrality were afraid

---

in Japan cause too much public harm (1 percent); the treaty is detrimental to peace diplomacy (1 percent); the treaty is likely to create domestic riots in Japan (less than 0.5 percent); other or no special reasons (2 percent); and wouldn't give a reason (6 percent). *Asahi,* June 23, 1970.

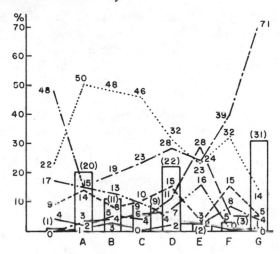

Item 20 (danger of aggression)

———···— There is danger of attack from Communist China. (4%)
——— There is danger of attack from Soviet Union. (6%)
▬▬▬ There is danger of attack from North or South Korea. (1%)
········· There is a danger of counterattack from the communist bloc as long as
        American bases exist in Japan. (33%)
— — — — The danger of aggression or attack is inconceivable. (10%)
——·— The U.S. should be considered to have already launched a sort of aggression
        against Japan. (8%)
——·— I do not know and other answers. (37%)

Item 19 (security system)

A. We should shift our cooperation away from the United States to the communist
   bloc.
B. The ideal of unarmed neutrality should be maintained, and nonaggression
   treaties should be concluded with both the East and West.
C. The treaty with the U.S. should be discontinued and replaced by our own military
   forces. We should also maintain neutrality.
D. The U.S. bases should be removed, and the American forces should be allowed
   to station in Japan only in case of an emergency.
E. Japan should gradually strengthen her own defense system while maintaining the
   Security Treaty.
F. The U.S.-Japan Security Treaty should be strengthened (and nuclear weapons
   should be introduced into Japan).
G. I do not know and other reasons.

Figure 6. Cross tabulation of items 19 and 20 from the questionnaire

of communist counterattack due to American bases. Furthermore, among the proponents of a strengthened security treaty, the evaluation of American bases differed: 28 percent feared aggression from the U.S.S.R., as if to confirm Japan's fear of the U.S.S.R., despite the foreign policy of Communist China and improved relationships among the U.S.A., the U.S.S.R., and Japan (as exemplified by the opening of air service between Tokyo and Moscow); 16 percent feared Communist China; and 23 percent based their fear of Communist counterattack on American bases in Japan. Of the respondents who favored cooperation with the communist bloc, 48 percent even believed that there was evidence to prove American aggression on Japan. Generally speaking, one's selection of a security system was related to one's feeling on imaginary enemies through one's attitude toward communism, and American bases in Japan and the treaty authorizing them are often subtly and inevitably tied to communist aggression and counterattack.

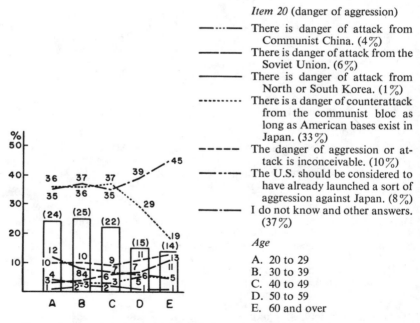

Item 20 (danger of aggression)

———···— There is danger of attack from Communist China. (4%)

——— There is danger of attack from the Soviet Union. (6%)

——— There is danger of attack from North or South Korea. (1%)

·········· There is a danger of counterattack from the communist bloc as long as American bases exist in Japan. (33%)

— — — — The danger of aggression or attack is inconceivable. (10%)

——··— The U.S. should be considered to have already launched a sort of aggression against Japan. (8%)

——·— I do not know and other answers. (37%)

Age

A. 20 to 29
B. 30 to 39
C. 40 to 49
D. 50 to 59
E. 60 and over

Figure 7. Cross tabulation of item 20 from the questionnaire with respondents' ages

As Figure 7 shows, not all age groups are equally concerned about aggression. For example, only 37 percent of the respondents in their 40's and as low as 19 percent in their 60's and over felt any danger of communist counterattack due to American bases. The finding that respondents in their 40's have the highest rate (37 percent), followed by those in their 30's (36 percent), and in their 20's (35 percent), may reveal the keen sensitivity toward war of the people in their 40's, who spent their youth during World War II.

The people on Okinawa Island differ from those on the Japanese mainland with regard to the issue of national defense and the perception of imaginary enemies. First, the proponents of maintaining or strengthening the security treaty, as Table 1 indicates, were consider-

Table 1. Results of poll on preferred national security system, Japan and Okinawa (in percentage)

Respond-ents	Strength-ened security treaty	Continu-ation of security treaty	U.S. forces in Japan only in case of emer-gency	Creation of Japanese forces and neu-trality	Unarmed neu-trality	Coopera-tion with the com-munist bloc	Other an-swers	Do not know
Mainland Japan	2	22	9	11	20	1	3	31
Okinawa	1	13	9	11	18	2	1	43

ably lower in Okinawa than in Japan. The Okinawans, living under the administration of the American armed forces, probably were reacting against life under the American security system. (See the appendix to this selection giving the results of a poll on Okinawa in 1970.) Second, with regard to the perception of imaginary enemies, the Okinawans did not fear aggression from the communist bloc as much as the Japanese on the mainland, but the former more strongly expressed danger from communist counterattack than the latter (see Table 2). It may very well be that the Okinawans have become very sensitive to American bases that have been used for bombing against North Vietnam. It is highly probable that more Japanese on the mainland

Table 2. Results of poll on perception of imaginary enemies, Japan and Okinawa
(in percentage)

Re-spond-ents	Com-munist China	U.S.S.R.	North Korea	South Korea	Counter-attack from com-munist countries	No danger	Aggres-sion by the U.S.A.	Other an-swers	Do not know
Mainland Japan	4	6	1	1	33	10	8	3	35
Okinawa	3	4	0	0	38	13	8	1	33

would fear Communist counterattack if the U.S. bases in Japan (at Itazuke [Kyushu], Tachikawa [Tokyo], and Chitose [Hokkaido]) were used for bombing against North Vietnam.*

The Okinawa Problem†

The return of Okinawa to Japan began to be seriously considered both in and out of the government at the time of the 1966 poll. Around the fall of 1967, major presses like *Asahi* and *Mainichi* began large-scale public-opinion polls on the issue, probably in the hope that their findings would influence the proposed visit of Premier Satō to the United States in November 1967 as well as the proposal on Okinawa to be presented by the premier's advisory council. Our 1966

* In this respect it is interesting to note the responses to the *Asahi* poll's question: "In view of the present U.S.–Japan Security Treaty which obliges the U.S. government to secure a prior agreement from the Japanese government whenever the U.S. forces stationed in Japan engage in a direct military operation for the security of the Far East, do you think the Japanese government should or should not consent to such a direct military operation from American bases in Japan?" Of the respondents, 54 percent answered that the Japanese government should not and 14 percent thought that it should, while another 65 percent felt that it should depend on the circumstances each time. *Asahi,* June 23, 1970.

† On June 17, 1971, the U.S. and Japan signed a treaty which would restore Okinawa and other Ryukyu Islands to Japanese sovereignty during 1972. The treaty enables the U.S., however, to retain military installations on Okinawa. But the U.S. no longer will be able to launch air or ground military operations, including B-52 bombing missions to Indochina, from the huge Kadena Air Base in Okinawa without Japanese government approval. The treaty also obliquely prohibits the U.S. from storing nuclear weapons on the island, a sensitive issue in Japan where the memories of the atomic bombings in 1945 are still strong. This treaty was ratified by the Japanese Diet and by a two-thirds vote in the U.S. Senate.

poll, preceding these others, might have been premature and lacking in conciseness, but it did spur on other pollsters to similar undertakings.

Only a very few Okinawans preferred independence, United Nations' trusteeship, or incorporation of the island into American territory, whereas as many as 78 percent chose to merge with Japan, thereby manifesting their strong historical and ethnic ties with the Japanese on the mainland. In fact, both Japanese leaders and American administrators of the island had to shelve any methods of settling the issue other than returning the island to Japan and were obliged to focus their attention on the specific questions of when and under what conditions the return should be effected. It was not known whether or not the 44 percent who favored the immediate return of the island wished it to be on equal footing with the mainland or with nuclear weapons remaining on the island. It was not clear, either, as to why 34 percent of the respondents preferred a gradual return of the island beginning whenever possible.

Japanese national security and the Okinawa problem are both affected by the people's sensitivity to American bases and the peace and security treaties between the United States and Japan. It should be noted that Article 3 of the United States–Japan Peace Treaty recognized the transitionary administrative power of the United States over the island until such a time when Okinawa would be transferred to the United Nations' trusteeship with the U.S. as the sole administrator. According to Figure 8, the immediate return of the island was favored by 65 percent of the proponents of armed preparedness and neutrality, followed by 61 percent of the advocates of cooperation with the communist bloc and an equal percentage of those desiring nonarmament and neutrality, as well as 43 percent of the supporters of a strengthened security treaty. A gradual return of the island was highly favored by advocates of the continuation of the Security Treaty (48 percent), followed by a much lower rate (33 percent) of the proponents of nonarmament and neutrality. Thus, the case for the immediate return of Okinawa seemed to have become a united effort, transcending political ideology, party affiliation, as well as age, occupation, and educational background. The strong reaction by the Okinawans against life under the administration of the American armed forces may partly account for the finding that the advocates of cooperation with the communist bloc had the lowest rate of all

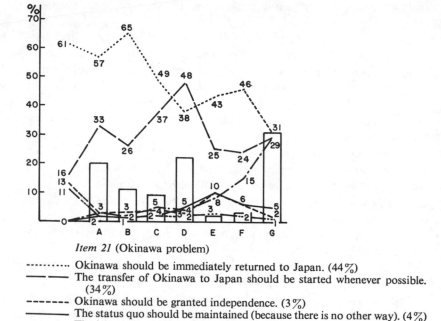

Item 21 (Okinawa problem)

---------- Okinawa should be immediately returned to Japan. (44%)
———— The transfer of Okinawa to Japan should be started whenever possible.
     (34%)
------- Okinawa should be granted independence. (3%)
———— The status quo should be maintained (because there is no other way). (4%)
—····— The island should be transferred to the U.N. trusteeship. (2%)
—·—· I do not know. (12%)
     Okinawa should be incorporated into the U.S. (omitted in the figure due
     to a very small percentage).

Item 19 (security system)

A. We should shift our cooperation away from the United States to the communist
   bloc.
B. The ideal of unarmed neutrality should be maintained, and nonaggression
   treaties should be concluded with both the East and West.
C. The treaty with the U.S. should be discontinued and replaced by our own military
   forces. We should also maintain neutrality.
D. The U.S. bases should be removed, and the American forces should be allowed
   to station in Japan only in case of an emergency.
E. Japan should gradually strengthen her own defense system, while maintaining
   the Security Treaty.
F. The U.S.–Japan Security Treaty should be strengthened (and nuclear weapons
   should be introduced into Japan).
G. I do not know and other reasons.

Figure 8. Cross tabulation of items 19 and 21 from the questionnaire

groups (16 percent) who favored the gradual return of the island, while having higher rates of respondents who supported the independence of the island (13 percent) or the UN supervision thereof (11 percent).

Conclusions

First, as was anticipated, the trend for the SDF to become a *fait accompli* was more conspicuous in 1966 than 1965. Even in 1965 it was warned that "the case for the SDF and the rationalization thereof would increase a great deal," and that the "provision of Article 9 would be bound to undergo changes, if not formal amendment." The persistent attempts by the conservative party to amend Article 9 or to construe the provision in such a manner as to justify the SDF have undoubtedly become a "fixed" practice.

Second, ironic as it may sound, the SDF has not necessarily been moving quickly in the direction of perfecting "the duty of the SDF" in Article 3 of the Self-Defense Force Law. In this sense, the people's strong desire to maintain the constitutional principle of peace has not been lost, and conversely, public opinion in favor of the positive expansion of armament or the amending of the Constitution to rearm Japan on a full scale still remains low. The real intention of the respondents who approved of the SDF as an established fact seems to lie in their image of the SDF as actively serving the public, particularly in case of disasters—the image that Article 3 of the SDF Law does not purport to project. This finding might be useful in dealing with the question of reorganizing the SDF in the future.

Third, a further detailed analysis should be made in connection with the security-treaty system. Item 20 dealing with imaginary enemies, which is designed to supplement item 19, reconfirms how subtle and serious are the problems caused by the presence of American bases in Japan. Particularly our finding that an unexpectedly small number of respondents feared unilateral aggression whereas a large number expressed a concern about communist counterattack due to the American bases indicates not only the serious problems involved in the existing security treaty but also the absence of a national consensus, which the government claims to exist in favor of extending and strengthening the present treaty. Furthermore, the existence of so many proponents of neutrality should probably be accounted for by their sense of nationalism, their reactions against Japanese dependency upon the American military system, and their adherence to the constitutional principle of peace.

Fourth, since the issues of Article 9 of the Constitution are highly political in nature, involving the government's diplomatic discretion, it would be expected that many people would have no opinion on the issue. Nevertheless, it is regrettable that an extremely large proportion of the respondents had no knowledge of the Mitsuya Study in the 1965 poll or the Eniwa trial in 1966. Mass communication media are to blame to a certain degree, but the issues surrounding Article 9 are mostly remote from the average Japanese living in the mass society, where a peaceful mood prevails. This situation gives both the ruling and opposition parties a great deal of opportunity to draw many of the uninformed to their sides. It also places a big responsibility upon teachers to educate the people about the Constitution.

Notes to Selection 9

1. The "nuclear umbrella" refers to a situation in which Japan would be protected by American nuclear weapons.

2. See Naoki Kobayashi, ed. *Nihonjin no kempō ishiki* [Constitutional consciousness of the Japanese] (Tokyo, 1968), p. 166.

3. Ibid., p. 167.

4. According to the government poll in February 1962, 35 percent of the respondents chose the answer that the "Constitution does not forbid armed forces for the national defense" and that "it is even better to have one" while 20 percent of them answered the opposite. It is not clear whether the 35 percent of the above-mentioned respondents expressed their approval of the existing Self-Defense Force or any armed forces for self-defense after amending the Constitution accordingly. This is an example of ambiguous and misleading phrasing in poll questionnaires.

5. Hideo Wada, "Kokkakan'nen to kokkaruikei" [Notion of state and types of state], *Gendaihō to kokka* [Modern law and state] (Tokyo, 1965), p. 22.

Appendix to Selection 9

The *Yomiuri* Press poll, given in August 1970 to 1,200 Okinawa residents, included the following questions and responses (published in the *Yomiuri*, September 6, 1970):

Question: Do you think each of the following items to be desirable for Japan?*

Defense method	Very much	Somewhat	Cannot say one way or the other	Not much	Not at all	Do not know or would not answer
Strengthened self-defense force with conventional weapons	7.6	16.8	12.6	21.4	19.3	22.3
Acquisition of nuclear weapons	2.3	5.8	6.3	16.6	51.5	17.7
Armed neutrality	8.6	17.8	11.5	15.0	15.5	31.6
Unarmed neutrality	18.7	13.9	12.9	10.3	9.8	34.3

Question: How do you think the American bases in Okinawa should be disposed of, after Okinawa has been returned to Japan?

Immediate and complete removal from Okinawa	26.4
Gradual but complete withdrawal	34.0
Number, size, and function of the bases should be reduced to those of the American bases in Japan proper	17.5
Maintain status quo	7.0
Other answers	0.3
Do not know or would not answer	14.8

Question: After the turning over of Okinawa to Japan, the United States–Japan Security Treaty would oblige the U.S. government to get the prior approval of the Japanese government whenever the U.S. bases in Okinawa are directly used for military operation against Vietnam, Korea, or Taiwan. Should the Japanese government refuse to comply with such a U.S. request?

It should refuse	54.4
It should not refuse	4.7
It depends each time	16.9
Other answers	0.1
Do not know or would not answer	23.9

* All responses are given in percentages.

Question: Do you feel uneasy about your livelihood when you think of transferring Okinawa to Japan?

Response	Average	Unemployed	Housewife	Worker at U.S. base	Field worker	Worker in agriculture or fishery	Self-employed in commerce or industry	Clerical workers at U.S. base	Clerical workers off base	Managerial workers
Very much	24.5	26.9	22.8	29.4	20.3	20.2	37.2	43.5	24.0	16.7
A little	36.2	19.4	40.8	36.5	35.9	35.0	32.7	47.8	37.3	20.0
Not much	20.9	25.4	18.3	20.0	21.4	22.1	19.5	4.3	22.7	46.7
Not at all	9.1	7.5	8.0	4.7	13.5	8.6	6.2	0	12.7	13.3
Do not know or would not answer	9.3	20.9	10.1	9.4	8.9	14.1	4.4	4.3	3.3	3.3

Question: Is the existence of the American bases helpful to your livelihood?

Very much	18.8
A little	23.6
Not much	15.1
Not at all	34.1
Do not know or would not answer	8.4

Notes on Authors

Naoki Kobayashi (Selections 2 and 3) and Nobuyoshi Ashibe (Selection 6) both hold Doctor of Law degrees and specialize in the Japanese Constitution in the Faculty of Law of Tokyo University. Kobayashi is the author of numerous books, including *Nihon niokeru kempōdōtai no bunseki* [Analysis of constitutional trends in Japan] (Tokyo: Iwanami, 1963), and Ashibe edited *Gendai no rippō* [Modern legislation] (Tokyo: Iwanami, 1965).

Hideo Wada (Selection 9) also holds a Doctor of Law degree and specializes in the Constitution and administrative law in Japan at Meiji University, where he is Dean of the Graduate School. He has authored numerous books including *Kempōseijl no dōtai* [The dynamics of constitutional politics] (Tokyo: Nihon hyōronsha, 1969) and *Gendai chihojichiron: hōsei to jittai* [On contemporary local autonomy: legal system and reality] (Tokyo: Hyōronsha, 1965).

Shigeo Misawa (Selection 1) is professor of political theory and government at Saitama University and edited *Sengo nihon shiryō* [Collection of materials on postwar Japan, 1945–1965] (Tokyo: Nihon hyōronsha, 1966).

Jōji Watanuki (Selection 5) of Sophia University and Ritsuo Akimoto (Selection 7) of Waseda University are political sociologists, well versed in behavioral methods and research techniques. Watanuki is interested in the voting behavior of various social groups and organizational theory, and his works include *Nihon no seijishakai* [Political society in Japan] (Tokyo: Tokyo University Press, 1967) and "International Attitudes and Party Support of the Japanese People" in *Peace Research in Japan, 1968* (Tokyo: The Japan Peace Research Group, 1968). Akimoto has been active in the study of community power structure and authored a number of works on the subject.

Hiroshi Suzuki (Selection 4) is a political sociologist at Kanazawa University and has done several studies on voting behavior.

Saburō Matsumoto (Selection 8) teaches Asian politics at Keiō University and has been interested in the voting behavior of various countries at the United Nations' General Assembly, as exemplified by his recent article, "Kokusairengō to chūshōkokka: Hattentojyōkoku no kokuren niokeru danketsu shuchō to kōdō" [The United Nations and the small and medium states: unity, assertions, and behavior of developing countries in the UN], *Kokusai Mondai,* no. 131 (February 1971).

Bibliography

Allen, G. C. *Japan's Economic Expansion*. London and New York: Oxford University Press, 1965.

Bakke, E. Wight. *Revolutionary Democracy: Challenge and Testing in Japan*. Hamden, Conn.: Archon, 1968.

Beardsley, Richard K. *Studies in Japanese History and Politics*. Ann Arbor, Mich.: University of Michigan Press, 1967.

———, John W. Hall, and Robert E. Ward. *Village Japan*. Chicago: University of Chicago Press, 1959.

Beasley, William G. *The Modern History of Japan*. New York: Praeger, 1963.

Becker, Theodore L. *Comparative Judicial Politics: The Political Functionings of Courts*. Chicago: Rand McNally, 1970.

Burch, Betty B., and Allan B. Cole, eds. *Asian Political Systems: Readings on China, Japan, India, Pakistan*. Princeton, N.J.: Van Nostrand, 1968.

Colbert, Evelyn. *The Left Wing in Japanese Politics*. New York: International Secretariat, Institute of Pacific Relations, 1952.

Dator, James Allen. *Sōka Gakkai, Builders of the Third Civilization: American and Japanese Members*. Seattle: University of Washington Press, 1969.

Dore, Ronald P. *City Life in Japan: A Study of a Tokyo Ward*. Berkeley and Los Angeles: University of California Press, 1958.

———. *Land Reform in Japan*. London and New York: Oxford University Press, 1959.

Fukui, Haruhiro. *Party in Power: The Japanese Liberal-Democrats and Policy-Making*. Berkeley: University of California Press, 1970.

Halloran, Richard. *Japan: Images and Realities*. New York: Knopf, 1969.

Hellmann, Donald C. *Japanese Foreign Policy and Domestic Politics: The Peace Agreement with the Soviet Union*. Berkeley: University of California Press, 1969.

Henderson, Dan F., ed. *The Constitution of Japan: Its First Twenty Years, 1947–67*. Seattle: University of Washington Press, 1969.

Ike, Nobutaka. *Japanese Politics: An Introductory Survey.* New York: Knopf, 1957.

Jan, George P., ed. *International Politics of Asia: Readings.* Belmont, Calif.: Wadsworth, 1969.

Jansen, Marius B., ed. *Changing Japanese Attitudes toward Modernization.* Princeton, N.J.: Princeton University Press, 1965.

Kajima, Morinosuke. *A Brief Diplomatic History of Modern Japan.* Rutland, Vt.: Tuttle, 1965.

Kawai, Kazuo. *Japan's American Interlude.* Chicago: University of Chicago Press, 1960.

Kubota, Akira. *Higher Civil Servants in Postwar Japan: Their Social Origins, Educational Backgrounds, and Career Patterns.* Princeton, N.J.: Princeton University Press, 1969.

Kurzman, Dan. *Kishi and Japan: The Search for the Sun.* New York: Obolensky, 1960.

Langdon, Frank. *Politics in Japan.* Boston: Little, Brown, 1967.

Levine, Solomon B. *Industrial Relations in Postwar Japan.* Urbana: University of Illinois Press, 1958.

Lockwood, William W., ed. *The State and Economic Enterprise in Japan: Essays in the Political Economy of Growth.* Princeton, N.J.: Princeton University Press, 1965.

McNelly, Theodore. *Contemporary Government of Japan.* Boston: Houghton, Mifflin, 1963.

———, ed. *Sources in Modern East Asian History and Politics.* New York: Appleton-Century-Crofts, 1967.

Maki, John M. *Government and Politics in Japan: The Road to Democracy.* New York: Praeger, 1962.

———, ed. *Court and Constitution in Japan: Selected Supreme Court Decisions, 1948–60.* Seattle: University of Washington Press, 1964.

Maruyama, Masao. *Thought and Behaviour in Modern Japanese Politics.* Expanded edition. Edited by Ivan Morris. London and New York: Oxford University Press, 1969.

Mendel, Douglas H. *The Japanese People and Foreign Policy: A Study of Public Opinion in Post-Treaty Japan.* Berkeley: University of California Press, 1961.

Morris, Ivan. *Nationalism and the Right Wing in Japan: A Study of Post-War Trends.* London and New York: Oxford University Press, 1960.

Osgood, Robert E. *Alliances and American Foreign Policy.* Baltimore: Johns Hopkins University Press, 1968.

Packard, George R. *Protest in Tokyo: The Security Treaty Crisis of 1960.* Princeton, N.J.: Princeton University Press, 1966.

Passin, Herbert. *Society and Education in Japan.* New York: Teachers College, Columbia University, 1965.

Pye, Lucian W., ed. *Cases in Comparative Politics: Asia.* Boston: Little, Brown, 1969.

——, and Sidney Verba, eds. *Political Culture and Political Development.* Princeton, N.J.: Princeton University Press, 1965.

Quigley, Harold S., and John E. Turner. *The New Japan: Government and Politics.* Minneapolis: University of Minnesota Press, 1956.

Reischauer, Edwin O. *The United States and Japan.* 3d ed. Cambridge, Mass.: Harvard University Press, 1965.

Scalapino, Robert A., and Junnosuke Masumi. *Parties and Politics in Contemporary Japan.* Berkeley: University of California Press, 1962.

Schubert, Glendon, and David Danelski, eds. *Comparative Judicial Behavior: Cross-Cultural Studies of Political Decision-Making in the East and West.* New York: Oxford University Press, 1969.

Steiner, Kurt. *Local Government in Japan.* Stanford, Calif.: Stanford University Press, 1965.

Stockwin, James A. A. *The Japanese Socialist Party and Neutralism: A Study of a Political Party and Its Foreign Policy.* New York: Cambridge University Press, 1968.

Thayer, Nathaniel B. *How the Conservatives Rule Japan.* Princeton, N.J.: Princeton University Press, 1969.

Tsuneishi, Warren M. *Japanese Political Style: An Introduction to the Government and Politics of Modern Japan.* New York: Harper and Row, 1966.

Von Mehren, Arthur T., ed. *Law in Japan: The Legal Order in a Changing Society.* Cambridge, Mass.: Harvard University Press, 1963.

Ward, Robert E. *Japan's Political System.* Englewood Cliffs, N.J.: Prentice-Hall, 1967.

——, ed. *Political Development in Modern Japan.* Princeton, N.J.: Princeton University Press, 1968.

——, and Dankwart A. Rustow, eds. *Political Modernization in Japan and Turkey.* Princeton, N.J.: Princeton University Press, 1964.

White, James Wilson. *The Sōkagakkai and Mass Society.* Stanford, Calif.: Stanford University Press, 1970.

Yamamura, Kōzō. *Economic Policy in Postwar Japan: Growth Versus Economic Democracy.* Berkeley: University of California Press, 1967.

Yanaga, Chitoshi. *Big Business in Japanese Politics.* New Haven, Conn.: Yale University Press, 1968.

INDEX

JAPANESE POLITICS
—AN INSIDE VIEW

Designed by R. E. Rosenbaum.
Composed by Colonial Press, Inc.,
in 10 point linotype Times Roman, 2 points leaded,
with display lines in Optima Semibold.
Printed offset by Colonial Press, Inc.
Bound by Colonial Press.

Library of Congress Cataloging in Publication Data
(For library cataloging purposes only)

Itoh, Hiroshi, comp.
  Japanese politics—an inside view.

  Bibliography: p.
  CONTENTS: Pt. 1. Policy-making at the national level: Misawa, S. An out-
line of the policy-making process in Japan. Kobayashi, N. The Small and
Medium-Sized Enterprises Organization Law. Kabayashi, N. Interest groups in
the legislative process.—Pt. 2. Public opinion and voting behavior: Suzuki, H.
Electoral behavior in a conservative stronghold. a case study of the Ishikawa
prefecture. Watanuki, J. The voting behavior and party preference of labor.
Ashibe, N. Consciousness of human rights and problems of equality. [etc.]
  1. Japan—Politics and government—1945–
— Addresses, essays, lectures. I. Title.
JQ1615 1973.I86   320.9'52'04   72–12407
ISBN 0–8014–9138–X